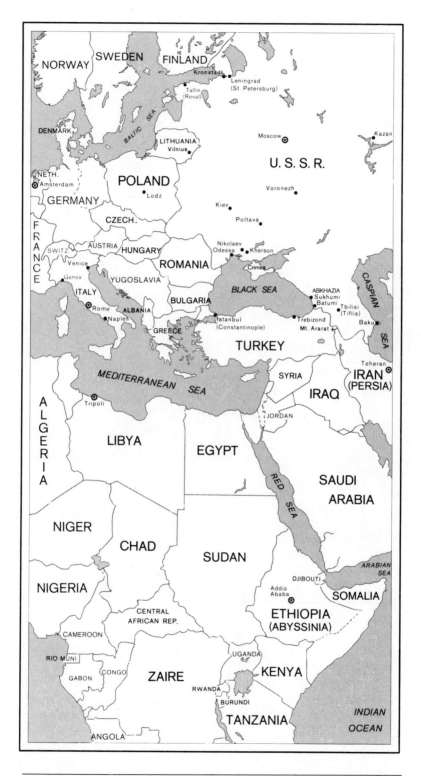

Proximity of Russia to black Africa. Prepared by Department of Geography Cartographic Services Laboratory, University of Maryland.

RUSSIA
AND THE
NEGRO

Arab, an alphabet card from nineteenth-century Russia. As in other European societies, early Russian conceptions of blacks often fused disparate racial and cultural types. (Courtesy James L. Rice)

ALLISON
BLAKELY

RUSSIA
AND THE
NEGRO

BLACKS
IN
RUSSIAN
HISTORY
AND
THOUGHT

HOWARD

HOWARD UNIVERSITY PRESS   WASHINGTON, D.C. 1986

Printed in the United States of America

Library of Congress Cataloging in Publication Data

Blakely, Allison, 1940–
  Russia and the Negro.
Bibliography: p.
Includes index.
1. Blacks—Soviet Union—History.　I. Title.
DK34.B53B55　1986　　947'.00496　　85-5251
ISBN 0-88258-146-5

TO MY MOTHER, ALICE

CONTENTS

LIST OF
ILLUSTRATIONS

FOREWORD

Here is a long-awaited book, a pioneer narrative of skill and substance, but above all a work showing profound feeling for the subject, backed by thorough, painstaking research in well-known but mostly obscure sources of both Russian and Western origin.

The wonder is that no one before Dr. Blakely has come forth gathering and telling this meaningful story. Since the early eighteenth century, the world's academics, and also some curious laymen, knew that there were Negroes in Russia, even if only a few. They knew that Alexander Pushkin, Slavdom's greatest poet, was a descendant of a dark Ethiopian lad brought to those snowy plains to become a favorite of Tsar Peter the Great; that this Abram Hannibal, as he was called by the sovereign, had a distinguished career and left many notable descendants to serve and glorify the Russian Empire. Among them was Pushkin, that celebrated Russian bard who, in the early nineteenth century, proudly spoke of himself as an *arap*—a Negro.

Later in the last century, word came from Russia's Caucasus mountains of a Negro settlement on the northeastern shores of the Black Sea. Its dwellers were quite likely descendants of black slaves who were bought by local Abkhazian princes in Turkey, once a major slave market where African captives were taken by Arab traders. Until 1861 and the liberation of Russia's serfs by Alexander II, the Romanov court and certain of its nobles sought to add blacks purchased in foreign lands to their human property as a kind of whimsical yet picturesque oddity. It was the era's chic for an artist to include in the royal portraits a black boy in Oriental attire, standing discreetly in the background near his exalted owner.

But increasingly, Negroes also came to tsarist Russia as free persons, of their own choice. These were primarily males from the United States and the West Indies, who were attracted by job opportunities in the aristocratic households or at large. Some were in restaurant or other catering services, sometimes becoming owners of such enterprises. Further, there were Negro jockeys and horse trainers; a few achieved nationwide (and even West European) renown. Among the musicians, singers, and actors who arrived, the most prominent was the celebrated Shakespearean tragedian Ira Aldridge.

The attraction was mutual; so was the accommodation. Russians viewed these black-skinned men and women as rare and exotic, yet useful as well as ornamental. In turn, blacks who went to Russia—especially those who made the journey of their own volition—regarded the land of the tsars (and later of the commissars) as a land of unique people and fascinating customs. Yet, from a more practical perspective, Russia offered them a chance to gain a good and prosperous life that was singularly devoid of discrimination and humiliation because of their color.

During the Soviet era, however, the image of social justice, of brotherhood, and complete equality with whites was the magnet. Dr. Blakely tells this part of his narrative with particularly keen understanding, without censure of the black pilgrims' naivete, and yet with no praise for their illusions. For example, the epic of Paul Robeson as a folk hero in the Soviet Union is presented with a fine balance. Dr. Blakely recounts Robeson's intense and unswerving loyalty to an ideal of racial equality that was not at all a reality in Robeson's native land.

Most enlightening are Dr. Blakely's chapters on Red Moscow's early involvement in the problems of the American Negro. His detailed and thoughtful treatment of the Kremlin's ignorance and ineptness at dealing with this critical and complex phenomenon fully deserves our admiration. Equally searching and dispassionate is Dr. Blakely's discussion of more sophisticated efforts by Soviet communists to right the wrongs toward—and to profit from the woes of—the African Negro.

This work fills a void and opens the field of Soviet scholarship to further investigations, fresh insights, and interpretations by those scholars who see the Negro's role in world affairs as a theme of unheralded significance. Dr. Blakely's classic study has given such researchers and writers a remarkable beginning.

Albert Parry
Colgate University

PREFACE

When Peter Chaadaev observed in his famous first "Philosophical Letter" in 1836 that Russia was "without a past or a future, in the midst of a flat calm," the authorities promptly declared him insane. By insisting that Russia was neither Asian nor European, and himself having been enamored of Roman Catholicism and Western civilization, Chaadaev had challenged the very essence of Russian autocracy and Orthodoxy. Still incensed by that portrayal, the government probably missed the full significance of Chaadaev's later "Apology of a Madman," in which he made one of the earliest and most perceptive statements of an idea that has been central to the Russian intellectual tradition from the pre-Revolution era to the present. Chaadaev said that owing to Russia's retarded acquisition of European civilization, she was "called upon to resolve most of the ideas which have come up in the old societies, and to decide most of the weighty questions concerning the human race." This concept of a unique, messianic role for Russian society can also be discerned in such diverse schools of thought as the Slavophile, Westernizer, populist, and Soviet communist. Even in the 1980s, the novelist Alexander Solzhenitsyn continues to argue the case for "Old Russia" in his controversial philosophical views.

A great deal of scholarly attention has been devoted to the significance of Russia's late start in economic, political, and intellectual development in comparison with Western states. Thus far, however, little has been done in the areas of Russian social and cultural history. As one of its main concerns, the present study poses the question of whether the Negro experience of Russian society can be instructive for a better understanding of the Negro experience within the major Western societies. At the same time, the Negro experience in Russia may be suggestive of broader comparisons which might be made with other societies regarding, for example, the experience of non-Europeans in Russian society, and Russian views of foreigners, of the Soviet treatment of minorities, and of Soviet racial attitudes. Specialists in Russian studies have devoted little attention to any groups or individuals who were neither of European nor of Asian origin. This study also, necessarily, delves into Russian foreign affairs, due to Russian interest in the African slave trade, the global strategic significance of black Africa, and tsarist and Soviet responses to colonialism involving Negro populations. Here, the question Chaadaev raised concerning Russia's unique mission becomes particularly imposing for world history. For the general subject of Negro history, the main contribution of the present study is that of offering additional knowledge about a peripheral area of what has been termed the "black diaspora."

As a study of the presence and role of the Negro in Russian history and thought, this is actually a study of two Russias: tsarist Russia and Soviet Russia. Some attention is also given to differences between regimes within the two, and to the distinction that should, at times, be made between the state and the people. Like "Russia," the term "Negro" also demands further definition. The choice of an appropriate term to denote people of black African descent is uniquely complicated in the Russian setting. Consider, for instance, the various meanings of the expressions "White Russian" and "Caucasian." The latter term is especially confusing in the present context because the largest part of the Negro population native to Russia lived for centuries in the Caucasus mountains and was, therefore, Caucasian. The problem goes even deeper for the student pursuing this subject in old Russian sources. There is a Russian term, *chernye liudi*, which means "black men," but designated not an ethnic group but a certain economic category in the lower classes. A similar term, "black plowmen," describes one category of the peasantry.

The term "Negro" as used here denotes only people of primarily black African descent. This is not the definition—peculiar to the United States—that would include Alexander Pushkin and also Alexandre Dumas père (who traveled extensively through Russia in 1858 and 1859 and left a detailed account). In terms of the definition used here, Pushkin's maternal great-grandfather and Dumas's paternal grandmother were Negroes; the two writers were not. Nevertheless, attitudes that Pushkin and other Russians have expressed concerning his African heritage do figure prominently in the present work.

Beyond its intrinsic interest, the Negro theme derives its greatest utility from what it provides for comparative study and from the fact that it cuts across geographical boundaries and academic disciplines. However, these characteristics of the subject also limit the depth of treatment possible by a single individual or in a single work. Another limitation is the difficulty of finding sources for Negro and Russian history. A fuller treatment should be possible if the current revival of Soviet interest in history results in more varied studies and greater exploitation of untapped Soviet archives.

This study was originally inspired by my students, whose curiosity prodded me into a serious examination of themes I had never broached on my own. Among my colleagues, I wish to thank Andrew Billingsley and Lorraine Williams for their timely encouragement at the beginning stages of the research. For aid in the identification of sources, I am especially indebted to Albert Parry, who placed his own sizeable collection of relevant materials at my disposal. Others who suggested important sources are Sergius Yakobson, Nicholas Riasanovsky, Harold Lewis, Simon Karlinsky, Michael Haltzel, John Brown, Hans Rogger, and Robert Allen. The research was supported in part by grants from the Howard University Research Program in the Humanities and Social Sciences and from the Department of History. My research was facilitated by excellent staff assistance at the Moorland-Spingarn Research Center of Howard University, the U.S. National Archives, and the Lenin Library in Moscow. I profited from comments on the manuscript from Albert Parry, John Fleming, Regina Avrashov, and Michael Winston. The manuscript gained further clarity through insightful criticisms from Janell Walden of Howard University Press. Finally, my wife, Shirley, provided constant moral support essential for the completion of the project.

PART ONE

IMPERIAL RUSSIA

Russia's Imperial Age is usually dated from the reign of Peter I (1682–1725), the great modernizer who won access for Russia to the open seas and built his new capital, St. Petersburg, as a "window into Europe." This period—which spurred so many important developments in Russian history—is also the most convenient starting point for a study of the Negro in Russian history and thought. As the first tsar to tour Western Europe, Peter initiated unprecedented contact between Russia and the outside world and was the first to perceive the significance of Africa for Russia's interests. As there were no Negro inhabitants of the original Russian lands, it was mainly through the subsequent expansion of contacts with the outside world that blacks came to be involved in the Russian experience.

Arriving late in traversing the open seas, and although gaining a large territory in North America, Russia did not achieve a large maritime empire like the western European powers and did not participate in the African slave trade. However, Russia did expand into a gigantic landed empire including numerous non-Slavic peoples. Among these are small populations of African descent. Moreover, as a recognized world leader, after helping defeat Napoleon in the early nineteenth century, Russia took an interest in all aspects of world affairs, including the African slave trade and European imperialism in

Africa. The government's increasing awareness of the strategic significance of black Africa gave further impetus to concern about the Negro
and fostered attempts to learn more about him. At the same time,
Negro slavery became one of the topics addressed by the emerging
Russian intelligentsia.

Peter I's conscious imitation of certain Western techniques and
styles included the importation of black servants for his court, a
practice continued by all his successors. This fad was followed by
some of the Russian nobility as well. In the late eighteenth and
nineteenth centuries, the Negro presence was increased slightly through
Russia's participation in world trade, as black seamen regularly visited
the empire and some even stayed. Other black immigrants and visitors
also came. Russian perception of blacks was, therefore, gradually
shaped by the combination of the limited presence of Negroes in
Russia and by Russia's growing exposure to developments and ideas
from abroad. This was to continue even after the 1917 Revolution
brought an end to Imperial Russia.

CHAPTER ONE

NEGROES
OF THE
BLACK SEA
REGION

The question of the earliest presence of Negroes in the geographical region which became the Russian empire centers on the origins of the small scattered settlements of Negroes which until recently were located along the western slope of the Caucasus mountains near the Black Sea. It might be noted, incidentally, that this general area is, perhaps, richer in mystery and fable than any other in the world: Close by is Mt. Ararat, reputedly the landing place of Noah's Ark and the setting for the legendary Greek hero Jason and his successful quest for the Golden Fleece. Moreover, it was in the Caucasus that Prometheus was said to have been chained for revealing the secret of fire to mankind. Such a treasure of epic tales surrounding this area is, to be sure, more of a hindrance to the historian seeking to trace some factual pattern amid a broad, colorful tapestry woven of real and imaginary strands. Like other fascinating historical phenomena, the Negro settlements in question have been "discovered" a number of times by the outside world, each time with amazement but often in ignorance of prior such "discoveries" that had been made. It will be useful here to begin by outlining the story of these discoveries.

When one considers the rugged terrain of this region, it is not surprising that these black Caucasians remained highly isolated for centuries and were generally unknown to the Russian public. The

Rosim Ababikov, a native of Abkhazia, where his family had lived for generations at the time of this 1913 photograph. Reprinted from V. P. Vradii, *Negry batumskoi oblasti* (Batumi, 1914), p. 13.

Negroes resided in what is now the small state of Abkhazia and in parts of what is now the Georgian Soviet Socialist Republic, an area which gradually became fully a part of the Russian Empire between the beginning of the nineteenth century and the 1870's.[1] Even after nominal rule had been established, the nature of the land made actual physical control very difficult for the tsarist authorities. Therefore, geographical and political circumstances largely account for the fact that it was not until early in the twentieth century that the Russian public was made aware of the existence of settlements of several hundred Negroes in the Black Sea region.

The news first surfaced in an article by Russian naturalist V. P. Vradii, which was published in March 1913 in *Kavkaz*, a newspaper in Tiflis (now Tbilisi), capital of Georgia. Based on Vradii's 1912 visit to Batumi, a seaport area in southwest Georgia, the article drew a number of responses that were published in subsequent issues of *Kavkaz*.[2] The letters revealed that there were also Negro settlements around the port city of Sukhumi in northwest Georgia and in other areas of the Caucasus. During the same period, a similar article by F. Elius appeared in *Argus* magazine presenting information which, when placed beside Vradii's, created confusion about the actual number of

Adzhi-Abdul-Ogly, a Negro Adzhar of Abkhazia, whose features show the racial mixture that had occurred over the centuries. Reprinted from Vradii, *Negry batumskoi oblasti*, p. 11.

Negro settlements and raised the question of which investigator had been the first to discover them.[3] Although Vradii presented the best argument for having made the initial discovery, given the conditions of the region already mentioned, there is no way to determine, for example, whether Vradii's estimate of twenty to thirty, or Elius's of two hundred more closely approximated the actual Negro population of Batumi province.

However, further public interest in this minor controversy was soon overshadowed in 1914 by the impact of World War I, which was, perhaps, a more absorbing event for Russia than for any of the other nations involved. It was not until 1923 that the Abkhazian Negroes were again "discovered." This time the explorer was a journalist, Zinaida Richter, who had visited an entire village of Negroes near Sukhumi and reported her findings in a series of articles in the Moscow *Izvestiia*. Discovery of the Caucasian Negroes was also noted abroad in the 1920s and 1930s, for example, in a 1925 article by Albert Parry appearing in *Opportunity* magazine, and in *Abbot's Monthly* in 1931. Also in 1931, a *New York Times* article described research in Abkhazia by a European anthropologist, Professor B. Adler. He reported finding small, isolated colonies of Negroes of relatively unmixed blood. The oldest Negro he found said he had been brought to Russia from Africa at the age of four with about three hundred other Africans.[4] After the 1930s, little notice was given to the Abkhazian Negroes until the late 1960s, when a number of studies, mainly by Soviet scholars and journalists, were devoted to the group's origins, ethnography, and anthropology.[5] Ironically, scholarly interest peaked at a time when the Negroes had apparently become largely assimilated and scattered throughout the Soviet Union.

One of the most interesting features of the accounts by visitors to Abkhazia is that their descriptions of the Negroes there have varied considerably. For example, when first informed of their existence, Vradii learned that they were at times referred to as Arabs, Lazs, or Adzhars by the local people around Batumi. The latter two peoples— indigenous to the area for many centuries—had experienced some intermarriage with the Negroes. Of those Vradii encountered, some were black with pronounced Negroid features, and others looked more like the lighter-complexioned Adzhars. The designation "Arab," how- ever, was apparently used to differentiate those Negroes whose physical features seemed totally foreign to the area. As far as Vradii could determine, most of the Negroes were Moslems and spoke only the Abkhazian language.

However, a traveller who had first visited the region in 1884, and again in 1887, responded to Vradii's article. During his second trip, the traveller had hired a Negro boy as a servant. He later found the boy was Roman Catholic. Nevertheless, most of the Negroes were farmers, who in some cases formed small communities of their own. Others resided in villages or communes with other peoples. All such accounts, at least up to the 1960s, agreed in depicting the region as an idyllic, tropical setting, with houses shaded by palms and magnolias, all framed by snow-capped mountains. It is the land that in ancient times was called *Apsni* (Soul's Land). One of the recent Soviet investigators concludes that the reception of the Africans in the region was so cordial that all of the new arrivals—although they too worked as plantation slaves, growing tea and citrus fruit— ". . . found themselves (unlike the American blacks) in a more favorable environment."[6] The Soviet journalist Slava Tynes contends that the Abkhazian Negroes' enslavement was somewhat improved because of the class solidarity instilled by their commonality of interests with the other enslaved peoples of the area, and, after emancipation, their commonality of interests with the poor in general. The Negroes of Abkhazia, along with the other subject peoples of Transcaucasia and Central Asia, were pressed into the tsar's "native division" during the final desperate phase of World War I.

As might be anticipated, the question which has generated the most diverse opinion is the origins of these Black Sea Negroes. From his interviews, Vradii determined only that several groups of Negroes had lived near Batumi since "time immemorial." An old man, who remembered the period of Turkish rule in the area, recalled that when the region became part of the Russian Empire, some Negro households had elected to move into Turkish territory. Consequently, there were also Negro families residing around Turkish Black Sea towns such as Trebizond.

The most prevalent explanation of how the Negroes came to the Black Sea area is that they were brought as slaves for Turkish and Abkhazian rulers between the sixteenth and nineteenth centuries. When the Turks withdrew they took their slaves with them, and those remaining gained their freedom sometime during the nineteenth century. This school of thought is best illustrated by the following excerpt from one of the letters to *Kavkaz*, from E. Markov:

> Passing for the first time through the Abkhazian community of Adzhiubzha (22 versts from Sukhumi) on the bank of the Kodor, I was struck by the purely tropical landscape: Against the background of a bright green primeval jungle there stood huts and sheds built of wood and covered with reeds; curly-headed Negro children played on the ground and a Negro woman passed by grandly carrying a bundle on her head. Black-skinned people wearing white clothes in the bright sun resembled a typical picture of some African scene. . . . These Negroes do not differ in any way from the Abkhazians among whom they have been living for so long; they speak only Abkhazian and profess the same faith. It seems to me that these Negroes and those at Batumi oblast are a chance phenomenon, and were brought here not earlier than the appearance of the Turks on the Black Sea coast of the Caucasus, for, as is known, they always had many African slaves whom they used to bring from their colonies in Africa. There is nothing surprising about the fact that some of these former slaves settled in some places along the coast and became assimilated with the local population in everything except the color of their skin, this owing to the rarity of mixed marriages.[7]

There is, however, another persistent line of thought which places the advent of Negroes in the area centuries earlier, perhaps even in antiquity. This point was first raised by E. Lavrov in a letter to *Kavkaz* in 1913. In an effort to remind the readers of the historical background of the area, Lavrov pointed out that this was the area the ancient Greeks called Colchis, mentioned in their poetry as early as the eighth century B.C. Moreover, Herodotus (484?–425? B.C.), the first Greek to write about the area from personal experience, described the Colchians as black-skinned with woolly hair. This led him to conclude that they were of Egyptian origin, and perhaps descended from remnants of the army of the legendary Egyptian Emperor Sesostris, who supposedly sometime before the second millennium had conquered parts of Asia.

Lavrov probably derived this information from an 1884 compilation of classical writings mentioning the Caucasus, which had grown out of an archaelogical congress held in Tiflis in 1881. That collection also mentions Pindar (522?–443? B.C.), the Greek poet who refers to the Argonauts going to the river Phasis, where Aieta attacked the dark-skinned Colchians. Lavrov observed as well that in the Bible, Moses describes the land settled by the House of Ham as a rich land far to the East and watered by a river Fisson. Furthermore, the compiler of these classical references concludes that the Laz people of Abkhazia had formerly been called Colchians. While admitting that there are gaps in the evidence, the compiler cites a number of Greek writers, including Procopius, to support this contention.[8]

Half a century later, this same line of investigation was pursued even more intensively in an article by Patrick English in the *Journal of Near Eastern Studies*. Also beginning with Herodotus and other classical writers, English marshals an impressive array of contemporary scholarly data to support the plausibility of the hypothesis that the Abkhazian Negroes' lineage may extend back to ancient times in the Black Sea region. He notes, for example, Herodotus's close attention to detail in distinguishing between Egyptians, Ethiopians, and Colchians, and in observing that the Colchians wove linen like the Egyptians and like no one else. As a major argument for rejecting the notion that the Negroes were brought to Abkhazia as slaves, English questions the likelihood that slaves would be imported to an area so famous for the export of slaves from its local population. He then presents linguistic and anthropological evidence supporting his theory, such as the dolichocephaly of the Abkhazians and their possible linguistic ties with the Bantu. To substantiate the historical continuity of a Negro presence in the area, English relies upon such sources as the *Iliad*, the Bible, and the writings of the Church Fathers. He also posits a possible link between the Abkhazian Negroes and the creation of the Khazar empire, which existed north of the Caucasus between the sixth and eleventh centuries A.D.[9]

Recent Soviet scholarship on this subject is no more conclusive than that already described. A booklet, *Africans in Russia*, by Lia Golden-Hanga, herself a Russian Negro, revived the issue in the Soviet Union in 1966 (although the work was apparently only for foreign dissemination). Based on the author's personal research in Abkhazia, the book's main purpose is to illustrate that Russians have had contacts with African peoples. In relating the story of the Abkhazian Negroes, she accepts the interpretation of Vradii and the other Russian scholars and adds that the presence of Africans there should not be surprising since, starting from ancient times, slave-trading colonies had been established on the Black Sea alternately by the Greeks, Romans, Arabs, Genoese, and Turks. She notes that the tsarist officials frequently listed the Negroes as Arabs and Jews.[10]

Slava Tynes, also of African descent, reported his findings on this topic through a series of newspaper articles published in the United States in 1973. The evidence he introduces gives further support for English's thesis. Tynes discusses the work of Dmitri Gulia, an Abkhazian linguist and ethnographer, who believed the Colchians had "Abyssino-Egyptian" origins. Through meticulous investigation Gulia showed the similarities between many Abkhazian and Egyptian geographical names, those of deities and families, and names of similar manners and customs. In studying the folklore, he also discovered references to Africans in Abkhazian epics. For instance, in one called the Nart Epic, which is believed to be thousands of years old, the heroes' search for adventure takes them to what must have been sub-Saharan Africa, where they became the guests of black-skinned people. Eventually, some of these people returned home with the Narts to the Caucasus to see how they lived. Some of the black people were said to have liked the country so well that they remained. Tynes also interviewed an Abkhazian scientist, Viano Pachulia, who had visited eleven villages in Abkhazia in which he had met many Negroes. All had said that their grandfathers and great-grandfathers were from Africa; but they did not know which part. They were also unanimous in the belief that their families had always been respected members of the communities in which they lived.[11]

Still other historical data might be cited augmenting those offered by Golden-Hanga, English, and Vradii, and attesting to a long presence of Negroes in the Black Sea area. For instance, the seventeenth century Arab traveller Ezliya Chlebi encountered black Crimean potters. When the Turks resettled the *Makhadzhary* (those relocated) between 1866 and 1877, in order to pacify the Turkish part of the Black Sea region, they might also have removed a sizeable number of Negroes. And the existence of small Negro communities in Yugoslavia and Iran raise still other questions.[12] Enumeration of such facts, while intriguing, will still not resolve this question of origins until more interdisciplinary research is done, involving scholars with expertise in the whole range of cultural and national elements included in the historical data.

For now, it seems valid to assert that both of the answers offered to this question may be correct. The presence of Negroes from ancient times would not preclude the more recent importation of others as slaves. With regard to English's point about the importation of slaves to a slave exporting region, it should be kept in mind that the Ottoman capture of the Byzantine Empire in the fifteenth century disrupted the Black Sea slave trade, which was one factor leading to the European shift to black Africa for their source of slaves.[13]

In any case, Negro slaves were prized by local magnates on the Black Sea coast as exotic status symbols. This is evident in the family history told in the early twentieth century of one Bashir Shambe. Shambe was born in Teheran, one of several children of a couple who had been purchased in a North African slave market by agents of the Persian nobility. Shambe was in turn purchased by a Georgian prince, Kimshiashvili, a tsarist army officer who happened to visit Shambe's master during one of the Russian incursions into Persia. Shambe accompanied the prince on military campaigns. He recalled that his master bought him a white donkey as a mount to heighten the comic effect. In general, Shambe was used mainly for his master's amusement.[14]

It may very well be that most of those Negroes of the Black Sea region who retained their distinctively African features into the twentieth century could trace their origins along a path similar to Shambe's. It is likely that those who descended from many centuries of assimilation were hardly identifiable as Negroes by Shambe's time. This is especially true for an area like Abkhazia, which to this day can boast of more than a hundred languages for its population of half a million.

Although the present status of the Abkhazian Negroes is a topic for the second part of this book, their position in Imperial Russia represents a good illustration of the great variety of peoples included within the Russian Empire. And, as Golden-Hanga pointed out, this group's presence does indicate a little-recognized tie between Russia and Africa.

CHAPTER TWO

NEGRO SERVANTS IN IMPERIAL RUSSIA

Very few of the Negroes native to the Black Sea area ever moved beyond the Caucasus during the tsarist period of Russian history. They may, therefore, be considered as a separate category from the rest of the Negro population. The remainder was comprised primarily of servants, who in some cases were originally purchased as slaves. Interchangeably, the Russians called them *arapy*, *efiopy*, or *negry* (blackamoors, Ethiopians, or Negroes). It should be pointed out here that there was no significant practice of Negro slavery in Russia. In fact, all authorities agree that by the late eighteenth century chattel slavery, which had been widespread in earlier centuries, no longer existed, at least in the Russian parts of the empire. Some of the reasons for the virtual absence of Negro slavery, and the Russian attitude toward the massive African slave trade, will be dealt with in Chapter Three: Russia and Black Africa.

As with many developments in the history of modern Russia, the time from which the arrival of Negroes in Russia can be most clearly traced is the reign of Peter the Great. Moreover, it was this innovative tsar-reformer who was most instrumental in bringing about their presence in Russia. He was personally responsible for bringing some as slaves or servants and at least a few others as immigrants. The Russian Ministry of Foreign Affairs records show that while on a visit to Holland in 1697, Peter hired at least one black servant, one sailor, and an artist among the several hundred foreign workers he took back to Russia.[1] All are described as *arapy*. The servant, Heinrich Sirin, was apparently a gift from the East-India Company. The sailor's name was Thomas Petersen, which obviously provides no clue in determining his origins. The painter's name was Jan Tiutekurin; he will be given further comment in Chapter Five: The Negro in Russian Art.[2]

It would have been consistent with Peter's general practice to deliberately seek out Negroes for his service. It is known that he later acquired a number of Negroes to embellish his court, in the manner that was fashionable in the rest of Europe at the time. A portrait of Peter, by the Dutchman Adriaan Schoonebeeck, executed during the period 1700–1705, shows a Negro boy behind the tsar and looking over his shoulder.[3] During this period, according to some accounts, it was in one such group of prospective court servants that Abram

Left: Engraving of Peter the Great by Adriaan Schoonebeeck, executed at the start of the eighteenth century. A Negro servant boy stands at the tsar's shoulder. Reprinted from D. A. Rovinskii, *Podrobnyi slovar' russkikh gravirovannykh portretov*, vol. 3 (St. Petersburg, 1886–89), col. 1560. *Right:* From the eighteenth century forward many wealthy Russian noble families retained a black servant or two. Princess Ekaterina Dolgorukaia is shown with a Negro servant in this engraving. Reprinted from Rovinskii, *Podrobni slovar'*, vol. 1, col. 710.

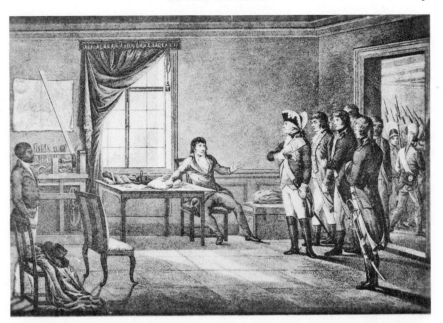

This engraving of tsar Paul's 1801 visit to the rebellious General Kosciuszko shows that the general was provided a black servant during his imprisonment. Reprinted from Rovinskii, *Podrobnyi slovar'*, vol. 3, col. 1473.

Hannibal, the maternal great-grandfather of Alexander Pushkin, was brought to the tsar from Amsterdam. The tsar's example was followed by many of the wealthy nobility; in fact, some of them probably had Negro servants before he did. Unavailability of Russian archival sources, such as estate records and those of various ministries, precludes any meaningful estimate of the number of Negro servants brought to Russia. However, judging from various contemporary writings and works of art, a few Negro servants in the wealthy households was commonplace. This practice continued through the eighteenth and nineteenth centuries.

There is a considerable amount of material available on the small, permanent staff of these servants, or "blackamoors," maintained by the tsars. This data probably provides a good indication of the general experience of Negro servants. Until the nineteenth century, these servants were normally acquired as slaves, principally by way of Constantinople, Tripoli, or Amsterdam. Upon arrival in Russia, they would be given their personal freedom in exchange for a lifetime service obligation. The staff at the tsar's court numbered less than ten in the eighteenth century and around twenty in the nineteenth century.

It was deliberately kept small; but when one left or died a replacement would be found.[4]

What is particularly interesting about the composition of the staff in the nineteenth century is its origins. A close look reveals that in addition to those from Africa, some even came from the Americas. The American minister to Russia in 1894, Andrew Dickson White, was surprised to discover that one of these Negroes, all of whom he had been told were Nubians, was from Tennessee.[5] Much earlier, a Negro named Nelson had accompanied the John Quincy Adams family to Russia in 1809 when Adams became minister to Russia. Adams allowed Nelson to join the tsar's service, and he also helped a black ship's cook named Alexander Gabriel, who had deserted an American vessel and joined the tsar's staff in 1810. The ship's captain had dolefully written to his home office concerning the incident, detailing how the ship's departure was being delayed because the cook had been made a special guest of the tsar after the tsar spotted the Negro in the crowd during a visit to Kronstadt.[6]

An occurrence in the United States during this same period may further explain how word spread of the tsar's black servant corps. In Boston, in 1808, Nero Prince was elected as the second grand master of the African Grand Lodge of the Masons, thereafter called the Prince Hall Grand Lodge in honor of the first grand master, who had died in December 1807. Prince had been one of the organizers and first officers of the African Lodge when it was founded in 1791. By one account, Nero Prince was said to be a native of Russia, a Jew who identified with colored people. As the story goes, he was summoned home to Moscow in 1811 when war with France was rumored and was among those who set fires in Moscow to help starve Napoleon's army. For this and other services he was made a bodyguard to the tsar. This version of Nero Prince's connection with Russia is highly implausible. A recent study of Prince Hall by Charles Wesley contains a more convincing explanation. Wesley reports that Prince was a skilled black cook who sailed to Russia in 1810 and remained as a butler for a noble family.[7] In any case, however, as a leading mason, Prince was certainly a possible link between the tsar's court and certain Negro circles in America.

Prince's experience and the incident involving the Adams family provide a clue to a main channel of access into Russia that Negroes could use once they learned of the opportunities there. A survey of United States Customs Bureau shipping records for the ports of Baltimore, Boston, New York, and Philadelphia shows that out of 132 ships bound for Russia from 1798 to 1880, there was rarely a ship which did not have at least one Negro crewman. For example, the ship *Margarett* of Philadelphia went to St. Petersburg in 1815 with five of its twenty crewmen described as having black or mulatto complexions and black hair. The bark Chasca of Boston sailed to Kronstadt in 1869, with nine of its twelve crewmen having black or mulatto complexions and woolly hair.[8]

The records examined show Negro seamen sailing to Archangel in the north and Nikolaev in the south of Russia, in addition to Kronstadt and St. Petersburg. Many others sailed to ports close to Russia, such as Constantinople. Some of these seamen made more than one trip to Russia. Also, after the advent of steamships in the second half of the nineteenth century, with crews numbering over two hundred men, the captains of those ships omitted the time-consuming task of providing physical descriptions while filling out their crew lists. When considering that black seamen sailed to Russia from other American ports and from many foreign countries, it is clear that Negroes were not an uncommon sight in at least the major port cities. One contemporary American observer in the mid-nineteenth century remarked that many Russians believed that the Negroes they saw were typical Americans; they thought all the English-speaking white men were British.[9]

It is difficult to determine how many black seamen actually remained in Russia for an extended period. Records from American foreign service posts in nineteenth century Russia show that it was not unusual for seamen, such as with Alexander Gabriel, to jump ship. Regrettably, records concerning the disposition of American citizens in Russia do not include physical descriptions. In any case, many of these seamen must have spent at least a winter in Russia because ships often arrived too late to leave before winter. One black seaman who later recounted such a layover was Matthew Henson, later famous as the first black man to reach the North Pole in Robert Peary's 1909 expedition. Henson made two voyages to Russia as a cabin boy in the 1880s. He later recalled that it was during one of those visits that he had his initiation to strong alcoholic drink. The occasion was one of the many celebrations the sailors and local peasants would hold after wolf hunts. The young Henson had gladly drunk many glasses of a clear liquid which seemed very effective in thawing him out from his long ride in an open sleigh. He discovered too late the inevitable effect of such a large quantity of vodka.[10]

The most revealing account available of these servants' life in Russia was left by Nero Prince's second wife, Nancy, who eventually joined him there. Her diary discusses in some detail nine years at court from 1824 to 1833. Her husband, Mr. Prince as she called him, was from Massachusetts. His first wife, Nabby Bradish, had come with him to Russia in 1810. Nancy Prince's account fails, however, to mention this. She also neglected to mention that Prince had been a founder of

the Prince Hall Lodge. According to her recollection, he had remained
in St. Petersburg to work for a noble family at the imperial court, and
subsequently for the tsar, after a voyage in 1812. When he returned to
Russia in 1824 with his new bride, she was presented at court to
Alexander I and the tsarina and was given a gold watch as a wedding
gift. Upon their arrival in St. Petersburg, the Princes first lodged with
a Mrs. Robinson (formerly Patience Mott of Providence, Rhode Island),
who had travelled to Russia in 1813 with the family of Alexander
Gabriel. Like some of the other black servants, the Prince family lived
outside the palace and had a house servant of their own. Nancy Prince
established a sewing shop, employing a journeyman and apprentices,
and she was active in the interdenominational Russian Bible Society,
which distributed thousands of Bibles in St. Petersburg. Although the
activities of the Bible Society were suppressed in 1826 and some of
its supporters punished, Nancy Prince was not affected. She also helped
establish an orphanage in St. Petersburg.[11]

Nancy Prince left descriptions of a number of the important events
of Russian history occurring during her years there, including the St.
Petersburg flood of 1824, which was enduringly storied by Pushkin in
his "Bronze Horseman." Her vivid, firsthand account is, in fact,
strikingly reminiscent of the product of Pushkin's artistic imagination.
She wrote:

> St. Petersburg was inundated October 9, 1824. The water rose sixteen
> feet in most parts of the city; many of the inhabitants were drowned.
> An island between the city and Cronstadt, containing five hundred
> inhabitants was inundated, and all were drowned, and great damage was
> done at Cronstadt. . . . I heard a cry, and to my astonishment, when I
> looked out to see what was the matter, the waters covered the earth.
> . . . The waters were then within two inches of my window, when they
> ebbed and went out as fast as they had come in, leaving to our view a
> dreadful sight. . . . My situation was the more painful, being alone, and
> not being able to speak [Russian]. . . . I made my way through a long
> yard, over the bodies of men and beasts, and when opposite [a neighbor's]
> gate I sunk; I made one grasp, and the earth gave away; I grasped again
> and fortunately got hold of the leg of a horse, that had been drowned. I
> drew myself up covered with mire, and made my way a little further,
> when I was knocked down by striking against a boat, that had been
> washed up and left by the retiring waters; and as I had lost my lantern,
> I was obliged to grope my way as I could, and feeling along the walk, I
> at last found the door that I aimed at.[12]

Mrs. Prince also looked on while the exciting climax of the
Decembrist Rebellion transpired in St. Petersburg in 1825. Her graphic
description is very detailed, although at variance with standard historical accounts:

> The day appointed the people were ordered to assemble as usual, at the
> ringing of the bells: they rejected Nicholas; a sign was given by the

leaders that was well understood, and the people, great and small, rushed to the square and cried with one voice for Constantine. The emperor [Nicholas I], with his prime minister and city governor, rode into the midst of them, entreating them to retire, without avail; they were obliged to order the cannons fired upon the mob; it was not known when they discharged them, that the emperor and his ministers were in the crowd. He was wonderfully preserved, while both his friends and their horses were killed. There was a general seizing of all classes, who were taken into custody. The scene cannot be described; the bodies of the killed and mangled were cast into the river, and the snow and ice were stained with the blood of human victims; as they were obliged to drive the cannon to and fro in the midst of the crowd, the bones of those wounded, who might have been cured, were crushed. . . . The prison-houses were filled, and thirty of the leading men were put in solitary confinement, and twenty-six of the number died, four were burned. A stage was erected and faggots were placed underneath; . . . A priest was in attendance to cheer their last dying moments, then fire was set to the faggots, and those brave men were consumed.[13]

The Princes also witnessed the great cholera epidemic of 1831. Nancy Prince left Russia in late 1833 because of ill health. Nero Prince planned to stay and work for two more years in order to increase their savings, but he died before that period elapsed.

The tsars' blackamoors continued to be noted with much interest by visitors throughout the nineteenth century. It is reported that as late as 1916 they were present at the imperial field headquarters at Mogilev. A black aristocrat prominent at the end of the imperial regime, Major General Egypteos, whose origins are unknown, was thought to be a son of one of the court servants. He was a member of the Naval Engineers and was credited with building several steamers and destroyers in the St. Petersburg shipyards.[14]

THE HANNIBAL FAMILY

Apart from the special staff of black servants, the tsars at times had special Negro favorites. Peter III, for instance, is said to have had one named Narcissus. Among Peter's pleas to his wife Catherine after she deposed him, and soon before his murder, was a request to have with him his physician, his dog, his mistress, his Negro servant, and his violin. Catherine later related that she granted him all he asked except his freedom.[15] But the most famous of all the royal favorites was Abram Hannibal. Furthermore, Hannibal and his family were the only Negroes to have lasting significance in tsarist Russian history. For that reason—and for what this family history can reveal about the nature of Russian society—it is necessary here to devote special attention to the Hannibals. Most of the story concerns the life of Abram Hannibal, the details of which are still hazy, despite the confident versions some authorities have published. Many of those facts about Hannibal's life which are substantiated by clear evidence are so colorful and improbable that it is extremely difficult to decide what of the remaining, apocryphal material to dismiss.

The major questions under dispute concern Hannibal's specific African origins and his emigration to Russia. There are, in addition, uncertainties about dates and other features of his life in Russia. All accounts agree that the African boy who much later assumed the name Hannibal arrived in Russia around 1700 in a small group of *arapy* obtained for the tsar. A recently discovered archival document pertaining to another *arap* named Alexei, but mentioning his brother Abram, strongly suggests 1696 as Hannibal's arrival date.[16] Some versions say the Negroes were stolen from the sultan's court by Russian emissaries in Constantinople, while another says Peter brought Abram from Holland as his cabin boy. Most of the evidence places his origins in Ethiopia, in the area of present-day Eritrea. By Hannibal's own account, he was the son of a prince of that region and was taken prisoner and enslaved as a result of war with the Turks.[17] That he was made a slave by the Turks is highly plausible; however, his later claim to noble birth need not be accepted out of hand. As corollaries to this assertion, various other accounts tell of a sister who drowned after throwing herself into the sea and swimming after the ship that took him away and of a brother who later came to St. Petersburg to ransom him back. Pushkin perpetuated these accounts in his notes.

The outline of Hannibal's biography becomes more definite through his listings in official Russian documents, some of which are extant.[18] These show that he entered the tsar's service in 1705. In 1707 he was baptized into the Russian Orthodox Church at Vilnius. Peter the Great was his godfather and Christina, the wife of the Polish king, Augustus II, was his godmother. One recent investigator of Hannibal's career suggests that this was only a mock ceremony, for Peter was notorious for staging these. However, regardless of his intent, the event was important. From that time on, Abram was treated as the tsar's godson. Although he chose to keep the name Abram, which he had taken sometime earlier, he now used the tsar's name (Petrovich) for his patronymic. Documents subsequently called him Abram Petrov. He became Peter's valet both at home and on his numerous military campaigns of the period, including the battle at Poltava.[19] Meanwhile, Peter had Abram educated, especially in mathematics.

In 1716 Abram was sent to Paris for higher education, along with a number of other students designated by the tsar. He remained abroad for seven years. It was with this part of Hannibal's life that Pushkin began his romantic *Negro of Peter the Great*. The truth concerning what Abram experienced in Paris probably lies somewhere between

Pushkin's depiction of him as a lion of the salon circuit and Abram's own letters home in which he constantly appealed for more money and complained of being destitute and helpless.[20] In 1718 Abram joined the French Army in order to obtain access to the best education in military engineering, which was the field Peter had selected for him. While fighting in the French war against Spain that year, Hannibal received a head wound during a sapper operation at Fontarabie and was captured by the Spanish.

After securing his release upon the war's conclusion, Abram was promoted to the rank of lieutenant and in 1722 enrolled in a new artillery school at Metz, France. He was ordered home to Russia in 1723 where he was assigned first as an engineer at Kronstadt and later as a mathematics teacher in one of Peter's personal guard units, the Preobrazhensky regiment. At this point Abram was one of the most highly educated people in Russia. He brought a library of some four hundred volumes from France, including philosophical as well as technical works; among the authors were Euclid, Machiavelli, Racine, and Corneille.[21] Whether viewed as simply one of Peter's social experiments or as an innovator of Russia's technical advancement, Abram's career was all that could have been hoped for. However, with the death of Peter the Great in 1725, the fortunes of his former servant suffered a considerable eclipse.

Peter was succeeded by his wife Catherine. The most powerful figure in Russia, however, was Prince Menshikov, her leading adviser and another who, like Hannibal, had been raised from common status solely through the tsar's favor. Abram was not on good terms with Prince Menshikov and in 1727 was assigned to Siberia. It would seem that he was quite accurate in his perception, expressed in his personal correspondence, that this was a form of exile. Abram had been involved with court intrigues through a circle led by Princess A. P. Volkonskaia, which was hostile to Menshikov's power. It is also possible that Abram, who had tutored Peter's grandson—the future Peter II—in mathematics, might have been considered a rival by Menshikov. In any case, just before the succession of Peter II to the throne, Abram was sent to inspect fortifications in Kazan, and the Volkonskaia circle's other members were dispersed from the capital in a similar fashion.

After twenty-five days at Kazan, Abram was ordered on to Tobolsk to build a fort; but upon arrival there he was directed to the Chinese border to await further orders. There is also a dubious story related by Pushkin that Hannibal was ordered to measure the Great Wall of China, which was obviously some distance away. While still enroute to his assignments, Abram wrote frantic letters to friends requesting intercession on his behalf. He wrote at least one such letter to Menshikov himself, begging Menshikov not to destory him: ". . . have mercy, intercessor and father protector of widows and orphans. . . .[22] Abram did not learn until much later about Menshikov's own fall from power and exile at the end of 1727, after the death of Catherine and the accession of Peter II. However, the power clique at court which succeeded Menshikov's, the Dolgorukys, were equally suspicious of Abram and his friends. Consequently, Abram spent three years in Siberia, mainly in Selinginsk, where he helped design and build a fortress. After his earlier years in Paris and the Russian capital he found this relocation to be severe punishment. In 1729 Abram apparently decided it was safe to return to the capital; but in December 1729 his arrest was ordered, and he was held at Tomsk in western Siberia for a short time. This might be related to the fact that the Dolgorukys had by then gained power to the degree that Tsar Peter II was preparing to marry one of them.

When Anna took the throne in 1730 upon the sudden death of Peter II, Abram was finally released from his Siberian isolation. He was promoted to major of the Tobolsk garrison in February 1730, and then to the rank of captain and assigned to the Baltic fortress of Pernau. In 1733, with the help of Field Marshall Burkhard Münnich, who headed the army, he was allowed to retire from the military and civil service due to an eye ailment and weak health. Pushkin's notes indicate that Abram was a personal enemy of Ernst Biron, Anna's favorite, who was responsible for a decade of terror involving the execution of several thousand people and the exile to Siberia of thousands more. It was Abram's protector Münnich who finally overthrew Biron in 1740.

Sometime during the 1730s, Abram adopted the surname Hannibal. The reason for this choice is uncertain; but it could be that he took a family name in anticipation of his first marriage, which he entered soon after returning from Siberia. His bride, Eudoxia Dioper, the daughter of a Greek sea captain, was apparently unwilling and reportedly balked at the idea of marrying a Negro. Although she acquiesced to her father's wishes and married Hannibal, she maintained a liaison with a preferred lover. According to Pushkin, she gave birth to a white daughter. Thereupon Hannibal initiated a divorce proceeding in 1732, which would take over twenty years to become final. Meanwhile, in the mid-1730's Hannibal illegally married Christina Regina von Shoberg, the daughter of a Baltic German army officer. Christina bore him eleven children and was his companion for life. The unfortunate Eudoxia was, at one point, imprisoned for five years for her infidelity after Hannibal accused her before the authorities and obtained her confession, some say through torture. After the divorce became final in 1753, Eudoxia was sent to a convent for the remainder of her life.

Notwithstanding these personal difficulties, Hannibal's professional achievements reached new heights during these years. Empress Elizabeth, one of Peter the Great's daughters, who came to the throne in

General Abram Hannibal. Raised as a favorite servant of Peter the Great, he was a great-grandfather of the writer Alexander Pushkin. Reprinted from L. Polivanov, ed., *Al'bom Moskovskoi Pushkinskoi Vystavki 1880* (Moscow, 1897), p. 294.

1741, was especially kind to her father's favorite. In 1741 she made him lieutenant colonel of artillery, assigned to the Reval Garrison. In 1742 he was given the rank of major general and served as commandant of the city of Reval from 1743 to 1751.[23] In 1746 the empress granted him a number of estates in Pskov and Petersburg provinces and thousands of serfs. Hannibal became major general of fortifications in 1752. In 1755 he was apparently appointed for two days as lieutenant general and governor of Vyborg; a second set of orders placed him again in the corps of engineers, where in 1756 he attained the rank of major general. In 1759 he became the main director of the Ladoga Canal, Kronstadt, and Rogervik construction projects. Hannibal retired to one of his estates, Suida, near St. Petersburg, in 1762. There he spent the rest of his life with so little public notice that the exact year of his death is unknown.

On one occasion in 1765, the Empress Catherine II, the Great, requested of him the plans for a canal between Moscow and St. Petersburg, which Peter the Great had projected. He responded with a letter; but it is unclear what became of this idea.[24] Hannibal died around 1781 in his early nineties. Family lore held that he had kept a diary in French but burned all his notes in one of the fits of morbid fear he was subject to during his final years. Judging from the pattern of Hannibal's career, it seems reasonable to suspect that his timing for retirement was related to the advent of a new ruler. Retiring while holding so many key posts made sense only if he lacked confidence in his position under Peter III, whose Germanophile inclinations might have revived fears of a return to rule of "the German party" which was so strong at court under Biron. Hannibal retired just before Catherine the Great's coup. Perhaps he would not have retired if she had struck more swiftly.

In the most extensive English language treatment of Hannibal's life, Vladimir Nabokov concludes after fifty pages of analysis:

> [A]lthough Abram Hannibal used to refer to himself, in humble letters to grandees, as 'a poor Negro,' and although Pushkin saw him as a Negro with 'African passions' and an independent brilliant personality, actually Pyotr Petrovich Petrov, alias Abram Hannibal, was a sour, groveling, crotchety, timid, ambitious, and cruel person; a good military engineer, perhaps, but humanistically a nonentity; differing in nothing from a typical career-minded, superficially educated, coarse, wife-flogging Russian of his day, in a brutal and dull world of political intrigue, favoritism, Germanic regimentation, old-fashioned Russian misery, and fat-breasted empresses on despicable thrones.[25]

This seems a rather harsh judgment, an overreaction to Pushkin's glamourous characterization of his forebear. But even Nabokov admits that Hannibal's professional achievements were important ones for which he received the highest awards. A fair appraisal should stress that side of his character. After all, the image of Pushkin would also suffer if the rest of his personality were given more scrutiny than his artistic genius. Hannibal appears to have been the first outstanding modern engineer in Russian history. He is credited with the building of a number of important fortresses, and his knowledge of canal construction surely made him a leading pioneer in an enterprise which had proven to be of utmost importance for Russia. As for Hannibal's personality, it is difficult to see how he could have won such loyalty from his friends, allowing him not only to survive but to prosper during the turbulent politics of his era, if it had been devoid of positive traits.

Few details are known about the lives of Hannibal's children. However, his son Ivan (173?–1801) had an illustrious military career rivaling his father's. By the 1760s he had attained the rank of lieutenant colonel in the field artillery. In 1770 Ivan Hannibal was made section master of naval artillery. In the fleet under Admiral G. A. Spiridov, he participated in the taking of Koron and Navarino and in the battle at Chesma. It is said that the officer in charge of the Russian forces at Navarino, who happened to be none other than one of the Princes Dolgoruky, decided the fortress could not be taken. The assignment was then given by Spiridov to Hannibal, who planned and carried out a successful fifteen-day seige from land and sea. In 1772 he was promoted to major general of brigadiers, and in 1776, to general of naval artillery. He was appointed a member of the Admiralty College in 1777. In 1778 he was sent to construct the fortress of Kherson on the Dnieper, and he is considered the founder of the city of that name. Hannibal rose to lieutenant general in 1779. He retired from the service in 1784 due to illness and died in 1801 in St. Petersburg. According to Pushkin, Hannibal's resignation came after a quarrel with Catherine the Great's favorite, Potemkin, although Catherine supposedly supported Hannibal in the dispute. Among Ivan Hannibal's friends and admirers was the great General Alexander Suvorov.

Two of Abram Hannibal's other sons, Peter (1742–1822) and Osip (1744–1806), also had respectable, although undistinguished careers in the military and civil service. Osip's daughter Nadezhda, however, gave birth to Alexander Pushkin in 1799. Her marriage into the old nobility of the Pushkin family is illustrative of the pattern that the Hannibal family followed throughout its history. It became completely assimilated into Russian high society.[26]

CHAPTER THREE

RUSSIA
AND
BLACK AFRICA

EARLY CONTACTS

Since the present study is concerned with Russian thought about the Negro, as well as his actual presence in Russia, it is imperative that special attention be given to the history of contacts and interactions between Russia and sub-Saharan Africa. In this regard, for Imperial Russia the main relevant area was Abyssinia (or Ethiopia). Mention of this land in Russian historical sources dates back to the *Primary Chronicle* in the eleventh century. Actual contacts, however, were much more recent. From the eighteenth century to the end of the Russian Empire, the Russian government found that there were religious, diplomatic, and economic reasons to court this small African empire. In the process, at least part of the Russian public became more knowledgeable about Africa and about Negroes.

The idea of the ties between Russia and Ethiopia was first raised at the end of the seventeenth century by the German Dukedom of Saxe-Gotha, which proposed creation of an anti-Turkish league to include Russia, the western European states, and Abyssinia.[1] Interestingly, this plan also suggested a rationale for Russian participation, which eventually became the basis of Russia's attitude toward Ethiopia. In its basic outlines the plan noted the similarity of their Orthodox religions, the military-strategic value of Ethiopian friendship, and the possible economic advantages. In this instance the military strategy was aimed at the Turks (later it would be directed toward the British). The hope for economic advantage was inspired by legends Europeans perpetuated about wealthy African kingdoms.

The Russian ruler at the time, Alexis, did not respond to this proposal. However, it was not forgotten in court circles. The historic visit of Alexis's son, Peter the Great, to Western Europe in 1696 was part of an unsuccessful Russian mission to enlist members in an anti-Turkish league. Peter was also interested in the fabled wealth of distant lands. He attempted to send two vessels to Madagascar to invite the king there to visit him to discuss trade relations. The expedition, however, had to turn back due to mechanical problems with one of the ships.[2] In additions, the fact that there was no such king of Madagascar is indicative of the state of Russian knowledge about Africa and its environs at the time. The tsar further hoped to use the island off the southeastern coast of Africa as a stopover point for journeys to India, where he believed the greatest treasure existed. Toward the end of his reign Peter also explored the possibility of reaching India by way of Egypt, Ethiopia, and Persia.

In the mid-eighteenth century, the Ethiopian ruler proposed an anti-Turkish alliance with Russia; but no action was taken. Russian acquaintance with at least North Africa improved in the late eighteenth century, for example, through Catherine the Great's activities on behalf of Egypt. However, it was not until the nineteenth century that ideas promoting concrete ties between Russia and Ethiopia bore fruit. In 1855, the proposal for an anti-Turkish alliance between Russia and Ethiopia was revived, this time by the Ethiopian Emperor Theodore II. This also did not materialize; but in the next decade, influential figures in the Russian Church advanced schemes which brought the Russian and Ethiopian Churches into formal relations with one another.[3] It should be kept in mind here that after the reforms of Peter the Great, the Russian Church was formally reduced to being an arm of the official state bureaucracy. For this reason alone, religious and political policies may be viewed as very closely joined. Besides, there is evidence that the chief proponent of a Russian-Ethiopian Church alliance, a monk named Porfirii Uspensky (1804–1885), who published an article with the broad title "Russia's Role in the Destiny of Ethiopia," was as much a political agent as a religious leader.

On the one hand, Uspensky's goal was to strengthen Ethiopia as a base from which to lead Africa to Orthodox Christianity. This was in opposition to similar efforts mounted by the Roman Catholic Church. At the same time, the impending construction of the Suez Canal raised to a new level the strategic significance of Ethiopia's location. One recent study argues convincingly that the opening of the canal in 1869 was, in fact, the main factor prompting Russia to seek close relations with Ethiopia at the end of the century.[4] However, there were several groups of Russian scientists and officials who visited black Africa much earlier. Among Russians who explored Africa and published accounts of their visits were A. S. Norov, who travelled in Egypt and Nubia in 1834–1835, and the physician A. A. Rafalovich, who visited the Nile Delta in 1846–1848. Colonel Egor Kovalevsky conducted expeditions into the southern Nile region, during the same period, in response to the Egyptian ruler Muhammad Ali's request to the Russian government for assistance. Kovalevsky did not find gold, as he hoped, but he did bring back a wealth of geographical information.[5] In some cases the Russians brought Africans home with them; in others, Africans were invited in groups of their own. Ethiopia remained the main African country involved in these exchanges. Although no significant move toward combining the Russian and Ethiopian Churches came about, formal diplomatic ties were eventually established in 1898.

Much like the earlier religious overtures, later scientific expeditions—such as those sponsored by the Imperial Geographic Society—may correctly be viewed as veiled political enterprises. However, the resulting cultural exchanges were no less real. Not only was information about Ethiopia disseminated through the writings of Russian scholars, but, foreshadowing certain Soviet policies, some Ethiopians were also brought to study in Russia. There were, as well, a number of instances whereby Russian technical assistance was rendered to Ethiopia.[6]

ATTITUDES TOWARD NEGRO SLAVERY

Before continuing to trace Russia's activities in Africa during the late nineteenth century, it is now appropriate to discuss Russia's relationship to the most important development concerning Africa and the European powers at the beginning of the century: the African slave trade. Among the European states, Russia was highly conspicuous for her lack of involvement in the slave trade. A number of reasons for this are readily apparent. First, in looking at other European societies, it is clear that none used slaves on a large scale at home. The slave trade served principally the colonies in the Americas. Although Russia had enormous holdings in America, they were mainly in the far north, did not lend themselves to a plantation economy, and were largely unexplored and undeveloped. Russia's vast, contiguous empire did include some cultures in which slavery was an integral part; but there was no demand for an outside supply of labor.

As for the Slavic nationalities, specifically in the Russian part of the empire, it is worth noting that as late as the seventeenth century slaves may have constituted the second largest segment of the population.[7] This is a rare but major occurrence in modern times of a people enslaving their own. However, Peter the Great's reforms finally abolished slavery by removing the legal distinctions between it and certain types of serfdom, which differed little from slavery except for the legal technicality. Consequently, despite Russia's overwhelmingly agricultural economy, which had some attributes in common with plantation systems in the New World, there was no need to import large numbers of slaves from abroad. Against this background, it can be seen that the relatively small number of Negroes brought to Russia were mainly decoration for wealthy households.

The African slave trade was, therefore, not of vital concern to Russia. Nevertheless, the Russian government chose to assume a very outspoken, progressive position on the issue. Representatives of the tsar at the Aix-la-Chapelle Congress of 1818 not only argued for the abolition of the slave trade, but they proposed the formation of an international court and naval force to enforce the ban.[8] The Congress decided against this proposal; but it is important as a reflection of what was apparently, at least in part, a humanitarian concern over the plight of the Negro. A cynic might conclude that this position was possible only because Russia had no vital stake in the African slave commerce. However, one should note Russia's general record of supporting enlightened principles regarding international law.

The Russian public, as well as the government, voiced opinions about Negro slavery. As early as 1790 Alexander Radishchev wrote, in his *Journey from St. Petersburg to Moscow* that:

> The Europeans, having laid waste to America, having watered her cornfields with the blood of her native inhabitants . . . these malicious preachers of meekness and love of mankind, added to their cold-blooded murder the purchase of slaves. These unfortunate victims from the sweltering banks of the Niger and Senegal, deprived of their homes and families, moved to lands unfamiliar to them to till the fields of America under a heavy iron yoke. . . . And should we call this despoiled land blessed just because her fields are not overgrown with thorns . . . where a hundred proud citizens roll in luxury, while thousands lack secure substance . . . ?

Radishchev held that the new American republic, whose ideals and promise he so greatly admired, had advanced beyond the barbarity of this stage of conquest. But, alluding to the Russian serf-owning nobility, he cautioned:

Tremble, my beloved ones; lest it be said of you: "change the name, and the tale speaks of you."[9]

His publication of this book led to its seizure by the government and to Radishchev's exile to Siberia until 1797.

In the early nineteenth century, quite predictably, Alexander Pushkin was among those who condemned Negro slavery. In a letter to a friend in 1824 he said, regarding the current Greek independence struggle: "It is permissible to judge the Greek question like that of my Negro brethren, desiring for both deliverance from an intolerable slavery." In 1836 he wrote:

> For some time now the United States of America has drawn the attention of Europe's foremost thinkers. It is not due to political events: America has been quietly fulfilling her destiny, up to now safe and flourishing, strong with a peace fortified by her geographical situation, proud of her institutions. But recently several thoughtful minds have investigated the morals and decrees of the Americans, and their observations have awakened anew questions which were assumed to be already decided long ago. Their respect for this new nation and its code, the fruit of the most advanced enlightenment, wavered sharply. They were amazed to see in democracy her disgusting cynicism, her cruel prejudices, her intolerable tyranny. All that is noble, unselfish, everything elevating the human spirit is suppressed by implacable egotism and the striving for satisfaction (comfort); the majority, an outrageously repressed society; Negro slavery amidst culture and freedom; genealogical persecutions in a nation without a nobility; . . .[10]

Such condemnation of Negro slavery, however, was not restricted to the most patently liberal circles. One of the Slavophiles of the 1840s, while staunchly defending Russian serfdom, averred that: "There is no economic slavery in Russia. Russian serfdom and Negro slavery are two entirely different things."[11] Without explaining how he reached that conclusion, he cited slavery among the attributes making America a philistine, materialistic society. Thus, the monarchist conservative Slavophile and the republican liberal Radishchev (with Pushkin wavering between the two), while holding differing views about America, were in total agreement on the issue of slavery.

Russian thinkers generally distinguished between Negro slavery and serfdom, as did the Slavophile, but they did not defend the one and decry the other. As the century wore on, the two institutions were compared ever more frequently as equally abominable. Since opposition to serfdom by Russians was more easily raised outside of Russia than within, it is not surprising that one of the most pointed of the early critiques by a Russian was that of an expatriate living in Western Europe: the escaped Decembrist political thinker Nicholas

Turgenev. Scoffing at Alexander I's strong stand against slavery at the Congress of Aix-la-Chapelle, he wrote:

> How can we understand the great men of the world? A Russian autocrat plays the role of advocate of some thousands of Negro slaves before an all-European Congress, while he could by his sovereign word alone decide the same cause in favor of many millions of his own subjects![12]

Turgenev's views are further elaborated in letters he published in the American abolitionist annual review *Liberty Bell*. A large part of one of these letters is instructive:

> When I come to speak of my work for Russia, particularly about the difficulties that the discussion of slavery and emancipation meets at every step because of the regime of this country, I cannot help casting an envious glance at the United States, where there is freedom of word and press and where in the South slavery is in full sway, while human liberty finds its advocates in the North. Legal crime triumphs in one part of the country, but in the rest of it eloquent voices, like that of Channing, are loud to brand this crime. Finally, sanctimonious missionaries too are found—real Christians, are they not?—who preach moderation to the masters and patience to the unfortunate slaves.
>
> The reading of your journals, Madame, has compelled me to think over the usual justification of slavery by quotations from the Bible. With regard to the honor of the human race, if not for the sake of the success of the holy cause of emancipation, one wonders whether the silence imposed on Russia is not preferable to the horrible blasphemies mouthed by those men who, protected by the principle of free discussion, dare to make God himself an accomplice of the abominable crime of slavery.
>
> But no, freedom of discussion can never harm a just and holy cause.
>
> There is no reason to doubt the benefits of free discussion at this time, when we witness the appearance of masterpieces in art, spirit, sentiment and eloquence, that do honor to your country and your sex, Madame. I mean the admirable volume *Uncle Tom's Cabin* which I read shedding tears not all of which were out of grief and sorrow. . . .
>
> Well! Americans might have sufficiently just reasons to be proud of themselves if, —along with their *admirable political organization, which surpasses all mankind could have had and even dreamed of since the creation of the world*, —they were not overshadowed by a very dark shadow, which—alas! must necessarily diminish, nay, lower its pride. . . .
>
> It is completely useless and superfluous to enter into endless discussions about the difference in the situation of the Russian slave and the American. . . . The Russian nobleman and the planter of the South can cordially shake hands, the one holding his whip and the other his knout.[13]

In a later letter Turgenev added:

> Exile and proscription have compelled me to live far from my own land, and to plead the cause of human rights in a language which is neither theirs (the Russian serfs') nor mine. I am thoroughly persuaded that all success obtained in America in the cause of the coloured race

will be eminently serviceable to my poor countrymen in Russia. It is, then, first as a man, and secondly as a Russian, that I hail the efforts of Mr. Garrison and his fellow laborers for the deliverance of their country from the hideous plague-spot of slavery.[14]

In the 1850s, Alexander Herzen, a better-known exile (initially self-imposed), most pointedly continued the abolitionist argument against both the American and Russian institutions:

> At the moment when all England was displaying profound active sympathy for the slaves in the Southern states of North America, incited thereto by the great work of Mrs. Beecher Stowe, no one seemed to remember that nearer to England, across the Baltic, is an entire population not of 3,000,000 but of 20,000,000! A friend of mine proposed to publish a pamphlet to remind English charity of this fact. But his pamphlet was never published. I have taken it up and added a few general considerations which, however insufficient in themselves, may, I trust, contribute to throw some light on the melancholy subject.[15]

In the early 1860s Nicholas Chernyshevsky, the radical publicist who helped ignite the late nineteenth century revolutionary movement, used the issue of Negro slavery to make indirect statements about serfdom that the tsarist censor would have considered far too radical in any other context. For example, he published in *Sovremennik* (The Contemporary) in November 1859 the following document of John Brown's military society:

> Whereas, Slavery, throughout its entire existence in the United States is none other than a most barbarous, unprovoked, and unjustifiable War of one portion of its citizens upon another portion, the only conditions of which are perpetual imprisonment, and hopeless servitude or absolute extermination in utter disregard and violation of those eternal and self-evident truths set forth in our Declaration of Independence: Therefore, we *citizens* of the *United States*, and the *Oppressed People*, who, by a recent decision of the Supreme Court are declared to have no rights which the White Man is bound to respect; together with all other people degraded by the laws thereof, do, for the time being, ordain and establish for ourselves the following Provisional Constitution and Ordinances, the better to protect our persons, property, lives and liberties: and to Govern our Actions.[16]

The constitution referred to was also published. Similarly, in 1858 *Sovremennik* had included sections of *Uncle Tom's Cabin* as free appendices to two of its issues.[17] The radical implications of placing these examples before the Russian public at that time is obvious. Chernyshevsky was probably able to present these documents with impunity because the tsar was himself at the time promoting an end to serfdom.

Chernyshevsky's position on the American Civil War is especially interesting for this study. In his view, the all-important objective of the war—notwithstanding Abraham Lincoln's assertion that it was for national unity—was the emancipation of the slaves. For Chernyshevsky, the freeing of the Negro slaves was a universal symbolic blow against Russian feudal reaction.

> In general, we did not understand the necessity for the restoration of the Union before reading Lincoln's message, and we do not understand it now. In our opinion it is all the same whether the Union is restored or not, as long as the main problem of slavery is solved.[18]

In the same vein, he later attacked Andrew Johnson for failing to act in accordance with these assumptions:

> A consequence of Johnson's inexcusable weakness and lack of political sense is that the situation of Negroes in the former slave-owning states is now no better, and perhaps even worse, then before the Civil War.[19]

This presentation of the views held by Chernyshevsky and others is not meant to imply that they were representative of the opinions of the general Russian public. The fact is that they inspired lively debate in Russian periodicals of the day, such as *Russkii Vestnik* (Russian Messenger) and *Vestnik Evropy* (Messenger of Europe). Even those conservatives or moderates who rejected the conclusions Chernyshevsky drew for Russia tended to accept the denunciation of slavery. In any case, the main significance of the excerpts quoted in the present context is that they were indicative of a continuing Russian interest in the plight of the Negro slave. Indeed, there was also cognizance of the situation of the free Negro, as witness these comments from the magazine *Illiustratsiia* (Illustration):

> There is news of a marriage in Brooklyn between a Negro "of the blackest color" and a young Irish girl. It is remarkable that in such marriages the family enjoys perfect agreement and peace. This proves that having the same color is not imperative for marital happiness.[20]

The Russian public also had more comprehensive accounts of American society detailing the role of blacks. Especially noteworthy are the writings of Eduard Tsimmerman, a famous traveller who toured the United States in 1857–58 and again in 1869–70; that is, before and after the American Civil War and the emancipation of the slaves. Tsimmerman initially published his observations serially, in *Russkii Vestnik* and *Russkaia Letopis'* (Russian Chronicle), then later in book form.[21] In the late nineteenth century Russian scholars also showed a special interest in the American black population. Around the turn of the century the sociologist Pavel Mezhuev wrote at great length about what he called "the Black question."[22] Highly sympathetic toward the former slaves, he pointed out the parallels between American slavery and Russian serfdom.

LATE NINETEENTH CENTURY RELATIONS WITH AFRICA

Although Russia did not manifest the kind of spectacular physical presence in Africa that was characteristic of the other great powers in the late nineteenth century, she was no less intensely interested in African developments. While it is true that in the age of the so-called "new imperialism" Russia chose to concentrate her efforts in adjacent Central Asia and the Far East, she was determined to minimize the relative economic and strategic advantage the other powers might gain on the great, "dark" continent.

In appraising the Russian attitudes toward the Negro, it is important to note that the question of racial equality, alluded to in the lines quoted from *Illustratsiia*, was quite separate from that of the abolition of slavery. Even among the radical intelligentsia one can find total opposition to slavery accompanied by a general acceptance of racist theories denigrating blacks. Consider the following segment from an 1868 article by Nicholas Dobroliubov, Chernyshevsky's young collaborator:

> We do not think it necessary to deal with the differences between the skulls of Negroes and of other lower races of man and the skulls of people among civilized nations. Who is not aware of the strange development of the upper part of the skull among these [lower] races . . .?[23]

Emanating from the Russian Westernizer tradition and swept along by the reigning penchant for science among Western intellectuals, the Russian radicals of the 1860s seemingly could not resist the prevalent racist theories, garbed as they were in the robes of scientific discourse. In this the radicals were in illustrious company. After all, most of the revered *philosophes* of the previous century had also opposed slavery while taking it for granted that the slaves were of an inferior race.[24] To the Russians' credit, unlike their Western counterparts, they had not yet experienced extensive contacts with black Africans that could have provided the basis for correcting a distorted image. As has been shown, such contacts would increase toward the end of the nineteenth century as Russia made more direct contact with parts of Africa.

The interest of the Russian public in the slavery issue naturally climaxed in the decade that saw emancipation of the Russian serf and the American slave. However, interest in the Negro was to continue because of contacts with Africa and the growing volume of economic treatises which accompanied the development of the populist and Marxist revolutionary movements in the late nineteenth century. There was even one attempt, albeit half-hearted, to establish a Russian colony in what is now Djibouti, then part of Ethiopia. This affair was bizarre from its origins to the culminating events of January-February 1889. In mid-January, some 150 Cossacks, including women and children, occupied an abandoned fortress at a place called Sagallo on Tajura Bay. Their leader, a Terek Cossack named Nicholas Ashinov, proclaimed two objectives: to found a colony, which he called New Moscow, and to set up formal ties between the Russian Holy Synod and the Ethiopian Church. There was also a corollary proposition espoused by N. M. Baranov, Governor General of Nizhni Novgorod and a supporter in court circles of Ashinov's project. Baranov urged the tsar to back Ashinov's colony and use it as a base to launch a "Russian Africa Company," modeled after the trading companies of the other great powers.[25]

The court maintained a strictly noncommittal attitude toward both these schemes. Although the tsar apparently decided not to prevent Ashinov's expedition, he also decided not to actually support it until the reaction of the other powers could be weighed. Meanwhile, the Foreign Ministry flatly opposed the venture because of problems it would raise in foreign relations, especially with France, an important ally at the time. It is, therefore, not surprising that the Russian government acquiesced when the French forcibly evicted the Russian settlers after they refused to recognize French sovereignty over Sagallo. On February 17, a French gunboat bombarded the fortress, killing or wounding several Russians. The Russian government then apologized to the French for the incident and denounced Ashinov, although he had enjoyed at least the tacit support of the tsar for his experiment.[26]

Although neither of Ashinov's objectives were realized, his effort demonstrated the persistence of these two aims in Russian policy toward Africa. Regarding the relations between the two Churches, it should also be noted that after an initial visit to Ethiopia in 1888 Ashinov escorted two Ethiopian priests to Russia to join the celebration of the nine hundredth anniversary of Russian Christianity. They also had an audience with the tsar. This visit did not lead to any closer connection between the two Churches, but the issue certainly remained alive. As late as 1902 the Abuna Matheos, head of the Egyptian Church, was received by the tsar. Another visit was scheduled to take place in 1914 to discuss the subject of union.

In assessing Russia's attitude toward Ethiopia, it is interesting to compare Russia's conduct to that of the other European powers active in Africa. Whatever her reasons, Russia seemed to show more respect for Ethiopia's integrity as a political entity and display a more genuine aim to be a friend and protector rather than a colonial master. It is significant that when Ethiopia was divided into spheres of influence by Britain, France, and Italy, Russia did not press for a share although her objectives in the area had not changed since her earlier efforts to gain a base there. Part of the explanation must be attributed to Russia's preoccupation elsewhere, particularly after the debacle of the war with Japan. However, throughout the history of Russia's relationship with Ethiopia, there is ample evidence of genuine respect for this African empire which had demonstrated such longevity and which the Russians valued as a stable base from which to exploit the vast riches of the rest of black Africa. The empire was also a vital link in the plan to secure Russian access to open seas. Therefore, a divided Ethiopia was not desirable.

This is not to say that there were no compelling arguments advanced for actual Russian domination in Ethiopia. The minister of war in 1889, General Peter Vannovskii, pressed for establishing a strong Russian presence there as a means of countering the British. Toward this end, he dispatched to Ethiopia Lt. V. Mashkov on a "scientific" mission to appraise the viability of such a plan. Mashkov was the author of a book which spelled out the advantages for Russia of economic, military, and religious control of Ethiopia. The ultimate concrete objective would be Russian possession of a port on the Red Sea. Although this domination never came about, Mashkov's two visits to the court of Menelik II in 1889 and 1891 set the stage for closer, formal ties between the two states. Mashkov was also important as a major propagator of knowledge about Ethiopia in Russia. Sensitive to the clash of cultures involved in the intrusion of European civilization into Ethiopia, in his writings and lectures on his experiences there, Mashkov increased Russian understanding of the Ethiopian people, as well as political and other questions involving the two empires.

Ethiopia was not a passive pawn amidst all these overtures from her great northern neighbor. As indicated earlier, Ethiopian rulers had their own designs in the arena of international politics, economics, and religion. Thus, it was not without premeditation that Menelik chose the occasion of another Russian "scientific" mission in 1895 to send his own mission to Russia. As another study has pointed out, it was more than coincidence that this first mission was sent when Ethiopia was on the verge of war with Italy and desirous of advanced weapons and technical expertise. While in Russia, the Ethiopian group witnessed military maneuvers and weapons demonstrations, and visited arms factories. The gifts they carried back to their emperor from the tsar included a collection of modern weapons and a large sum of money.[27]

Russian aid was not on a scale to have a decisive impact in Ethiopia's crushing defeat of Italy at Adowa in 1896. However, Menelik had at least one Russian officer among his military advisers. And Russian advisers were to play a conspicuous role in a number of subsequent actions as Ethiopia undertook to define her sphere of power as the European states continued their competition for control of Africa. The largest Russian presence in Ethiopia also came about in the wake of Adowa when the Russian Red Cross sent a medical team of about fifty people to Ethiopia in June 1896. Some of the doctors decided to remain, and in 1898 a Russian hospital was established in the capital city of Addis Ababa which continued for a number of years. Also, when the original Russian team returned home in 1897, it was accompanied by a number of Ethiopian students who were to study medicine in Russia. At about the same time, the Russian government instituted in Addis Ababa the full-fledged Russian diplomatic mission which functioned until the end of Imperial Russia.

By the end of the nineteenth century, Russia had clearly entered into Ethiopian history just as Ethiopia had entered into Russia's. It is not possible here to even begin to explain why Russia failed in her objectives in Ethiopia. Such a discussion would have to include such enormous topics as Russia's total foreign policy; the activities of other European powers in Northeast Africa; and the impact of such major events as the Russo-Japanese and First World Wars. Moreover, this issue was never put completely to rest.

It has been noted that tsarist Russian involvement in black Africa beyond Ethiopia was negligible. There was, however, one episode related to the Boer War in South Africa, which deserves mention here because it suggests one further way Russian leaders contemplated using the African Negro to their advantage. The Boer War had already been decided in favor of the British when a former Boer general, Pinaar-Joubert, sent a proposal to the Russian government outlining a plot to oust the British and place the new Boer South African state under Russia as a protectorate. The plan hinged on deliberately fomenting disturbances among Negroes in British African territories. British preoccupation with these would allow the Boers eventually to mount force sufficient to drive the British out. The tsar would then proclaim himself ruler of South and Central Africa.[28] Russian leaders discarded this proposal only after giving it thorough consideration, despite all the strain Russia was already experiencing at home and abroad from war and revolution. Russia's objectives in this area would have been roughly the same as in Ethiopia: strategic location along vital sea routes; access to the riches of interior Africa; and a check on the world's greatest imperial power, Great Britain. This elaborate scheme, although inconsequential, shows that even though the Russian Empire never annexed a large Negro population, it was willing to consider the idea. On the other hand, notably absent in the entire history of Russia's relationship with Black Africa was any type of racist ideology such as developed in the other major European states as partial justification for enslavement and colonial subjugation of the African Negro.

CHAPTER FOUR

NEGRO IMMIGRANTS AND VISITORS AND THE RUSSIAN RESPONSE

NEGRO IMMIGRANTS IN IMPERIAL RUSSIA

The practice of importing Negroes into Russia to work as domestic servants appears to have waned as the nineteenth century progressed. This was surely influenced in part by Russia's early opposition to the African slave trade and later changes in attitude accompanying the emancipation of the serfs in the 1860s. Another probable factor was the growing impoverishment of the Russian nobility. Nevertheless, some Negroes still came to Russia after the middle of the nineteenth century seeking to improve their lot. In some cases they made their start in the familiar role of servant, so that in this sense they do not form a completely separate category from that group. There were a few instances in which Russian travelers to Africa brought back young Africans whom they later adopted. There is little information available on Negro immigrants.[1] What data there are show that most of the Negro immigrants were from the Americas. More specificity on this question is hampered by the difficulty of acquiring data on West Indian emigration. Also, with regard to the United States, the information is sketchy, but it does include a few detailed accounts. Unclear bits of data exist, such as the following quote from an 1877 black newspaper, which indicates that there is more to this story of immigration if it could only be discovered:

> The Russian fleet are shipping Negroes; applications for passports have been made for about twenty.[2]

There was, however, a basic pattern of experiences which was probably common to all Negro immigrants. A striking example is the career of George Thomas, an American Negro who moved to St. Petersburg in 1890. Later, Thomas adopted the Russian name, Fyodor. Initially having found employment as a valet, he eventually managed to amass a small fortune by engaging in various amusement enterprises throughout Russia. By the time of the First World War, he owned a large amusement complex in Moscow called the Aquarium. A visitor described it as follows:

> The entertainment he provided consisted of a perfectly respectable operette theatre, an equally respectable open-air music hall, a definitely less respectable verandah cafe-chantant, and the inevitable chain of private "kabinets" for gypsy-singing and private carouses.[3]

When the Bolsheviks seized power in 1917, Thomas fled to Constantinople because his wealth caused him to be considered an enemy of the new regime. There he established a successful Russian cabaret called "Stella," in which he provided employment for other Russian emigrés, and free meals and drinks for those who asked. He went bankrupt in the late 1920s and later died in debtor's prison.[4]

As Thomas's success demonstrates, the entertainment area held much opportunity for foreigners in Russia; and it was in this general area that most Negro immigrants found a place for themselves. Among the most successful were professional athletes like the famous jockey Jimmy Winkfield. He had won two Kentucky Derbys before moving to Russia to ride for wealthy noblemen. He married a Russian noblewoman and they had one son. At the height of his career in 1916, he reportedly earned $100,000 a year. When he fled the Russian Civil War in 1919, after fifteen years of residence in Russia, he is said to have lost $50,000 and four thousand shares of Russian railroad stock.[5] Other Negroes became well known as circus performers and as singers. It should also be noted that they did not work only in the capital cities; for many years, around the turn of the century, the resident singer in hotels in Irkutsk and Vladivostok was a Negro named Johnson. Another famous entertainer of this type was Pearl Hobson, a favorite in Odessa in the decade before World War I.[6]

The American tragedian Ira Aldridge was decorated by the Imperial
Academy of Fine Arts for his triumphant Russian tours between 1858
and 1866. (Courtesy Moorland-Spingarn Research Center, Howard University)

NOTABLE VISITORS

In studying the history of Russian attitudes about Negroes, and,
conversely, the image of Russia among Negroes, the experiences of
certain perceptive Negro visitors to Russia can be equally as instructive
as those of Negro residents. Perhaps the best illustration of this was
the experience of Ira Aldridge, the great Shakespearean actor who had
been forced by racism to leave his native America and make his
reputation in Europe. He assumed British citizenship in 1863. Aldridge
first visited Russia in 1858 at the height of his career and won wide
acclaim from the Russian critical press. He was made an honorary
member of the Imperial Academy of Fine Arts, and he became a friend
of the Ukrainian poet Taras Shevchenko. At the time, the educated
Russian public was debating the merits of the emancipation of the

serfs, the terms of which were being worked out by special committees upon the tsar's orders. Aldridge was cited by some as an example of the level of achievement which the enslaved masses might attain if liberated. Aldridge returned to England in 1859; but two years later he returned to Russia and from 1861 to 1866 made several tours through the European provinces, often introducing Russian audiences to Shakespeare's tragedies for the first time.

Aldridge was only the most conspicuous of the performers who visited nineteenth century Russia. There were many others who came for brief engagements. The Russian public became accustomed to Negro talent, and was introduced to some of the very latest art forms created by Negroes. For example, the Fisk Jubilee Singers visited Russia toward the end of the century, and in 1902 Olga Burgoyne performed the cakewalk there. She then remained to study dramatic acting in St. Petersburg.[7]

It was just as Ira Aldridge was winding up his extended stay in Russia that another notable American set out to visit the tsar. His name was T. Morris Chester. His mission: to tour Europe in order to raise funds for the Garnet League, a freedmen's aid society in which he was a leader. (Incidentally, there is some indication that Aldridge sent donations to similar organizations in the United States.) From 1866 to 1868, Chester would visit England, Russia, France, Holland, Belgium, some of the German states, Denmark, and Sweden. He would be well received in all these countries and be granted an audience with a number of rulers. He would also happen to meet Aldridge in Western Europe.

Among the rulers who showed Chester special hospitality was Tsar Alexander II. The American minister to Russia, the colorful and controversial former abolitionist Cassius Clay, expressed great pleasure in his diplomatic correspondence as he described how Chester was not only presented to the tsar but accompanied him on horseback for a grand review of forty thousand troops as well. Chester spent the winter in Russia before travelling on.[8]

Chester initially approached Russian society through a public lecture, which he delivered soon after his arrival in St. Petersburg was announced in the press in early December 1866. In February 1867, he published an appeal for donations in the liberal daily newspaper *Golos* (The Voice), which circulated in several major cities. The editor prefaced his presentation of Chester's appeal with a brief background discussion of the plight of the American former slaves. He also explained the character of the Garnet League, stating that its main objectives were the education and moral uplift of the freedmen by providing them with trained Negro teachers. Chester's assignment was to bring home funds for the Negro colleges that were being founded. Having appealed earlier in the column to his audience's sense of Christian duty, Chester concluded with this exhortation:

> I respectfully appeal to the charitable, generous Russian public with a fervent request that it assist in the moral revival of these millions of people yearning for education. In the name of humanity, in the name of world brotherhood, in the name of the warm friendship which is developing between the Russian and American peoples—I entrust the cause of the freed slaves to your enlightened generosity![9]

The response was quite gratifying, as the following remarkable letter shows:

> To the Honorable American Citizen, Capt. T. Morris Chester: Having read in No. 35 of the "Goldoss" (Sic) your appeal, I have a profound respect for the man who has taken on himself so toilsome, and, at the same time, so beautiful a mission as that of assisting in the intellectual renovation of millions of human beings. Belonging, in my own great country—Russia—to the number of twenty three millions of former slaves set free by the kindness of our great Alexander II, I consider the new citizens of America as brothers, not merely on account of the principle that all men are brethren, but by the force of those feelings which must unite the freedmen of one land to those of another. The name of the benefactor of humanity, Lincoln, will descend to our posterity together with the name of our own emancipator Alexander. Receive the six roubles here inclosed, as a small contribution towards the great and noble object of the "Garnet League." Allow me, the obscure citizen of a Great Empire, to press the hand of a citizen of a Great Republic, who has served his country well. God grant there may be many such friends of humanity—men not of words, but of deeds.
>
> "Teodor Tak Seminoff,
"Peasant Landholder.
"St. Petersburg, 5th February, 1867.[10]

It is significant that Chester was well received despite the increasingly conservative Russian mood that was evident at the time. Chester's visit is important also because Negroes in the United States shaped their conception of Russia through accounts by prominent individuals such as Chester. While Nancy Prince, for example, spent a longer time in Russia than Chester did, she was an unknown in the United States and had to publish her diary herself. Chester, on the other hand, had already published as a war correspondent for the *Philadelphia Press* and had worked with Frederick Douglass and other prominent black Americans. When he finally returned to the United States, after four years in Europe, he was an experienced lawyer, having gained admittance to the bar and having practiced law in London. Again in the United States, he gained high state and federal political appointments and was a frequent public speaker. Invariably, his introduction would include mention of his sojourn to Russia. It was in such contexts that the notion of Russia as a place of equal opportunity was circulated, particularly through the black press, in the American black community.

This is how prospective emigrants such as George Thomas and Jimmy Winkfield could come to consider Russia as a destination. Others like them, however, visited for shorter periods of time. For example, the boxing champion Jack Johnson came to Russia in 1914 to stage exhibitions and to tour the empire. He and Thomas became fast friends. However, their plans were cancelled upon the sudden outbreak of World War I. Johnson later recalled his amazement in discovering at this time that Thomas was a close confidant of Tsar Nicholas. Both Thomas and Johnson became privy to high military councils during Russia's hurried mobilization, as military officers set up temporary headquarters at Thomas's Aquarium complex. At first glance, Johnson's recollections seem exaggerated. However, it should be remembered that during this same crisis the tsar placed even greater trust and authority in the hands of the infamous Gregory Rasputin, whose credentials for statesmanship were even more suspect than were Thomas's and Johnson's.[11]

The visitor who left the most detailed analysis of conditions in Russia was another American Negro intellectual: Richard T. Greener, who served as the American commercial agent at Vladivostok from 1898 to 1905. A graduate of Harvard College, a lawyer and Republican politician, Greener sent many valuable reports to Washington regarding the economic potential of Siberia, as well as observations about various aspects of Russian society. His official dispatches bear the tone of an explorer who was in the process of making exciting new discoveries and could not understand the apparent lack of interest expressed by his audiences.[12] Seeing himself as the principal agent for the expansion of American business into Siberia, he quickly toured most of Vladivostok immediately after his arrival, to acquire a sense of its dimensions and gauge the trend of its growth. He discovered that five other commercial agencies, representing Belgium, China, France, Germany, and Japan, had preceded the United States in surveying Siberia's potential.

Greener was struck by the great diversity of Russian society, reflected in Vladivostok by thousands of Chinese, Japanese, and Korean coolies, along with the natives of the area and a few Europeans and Americans. Among these Greener noted one other Negro, who worked as a handyman. He was impressed by the amount of construction in progress and watched with interest the completion of the Trans-Siberian Railroad and the growing migration from European Russia. His immediate recognition of Siberia as a wide open frontier region with tremendous potential for economic exploitation led him to press the

Richard T. Greener served as the United States Commercial Agent at Vladivostok from 1898 to 1905. Reprinted from *The Crisis*, February 1917; reproduced with permission of The Crisis Publishing Company, Inc.

State Department to establish a consulate-general in Siberia. However, the Russian government at the time would not even accept foreign representatives at the rank of consul, which Greener had initially held. Vladivostok remained a free port until 1901; a customs house first opened there in 1900. Greener had become anxious for American interests to take full advantage of the relative freedom then existing. Early in 1900, consistent with some of Greener's earlier forecasts, the city council announced a proposed electrical tramway, which was to include electric lighting. This project was to be followed by a waterworks project and American bidders were invited to participate. Greener made inquiries with a view toward protecting the prospective American interests.

His perceptions about the rapid growth in importance of Vladivostok, and of Siberia in general, were even more accurate than Greener knew. He was aware of the anticipated completion of the Trans-Siberian Railroad, construction of which had begun at Vladivostok in 1891. And soon after his arrival there, he learned that, contrary to what was generally believed in the United States, the port of Vladivostok was

not completely closed during the winter. But, like most other west-
erners, he did not know the magnitude of the great migration then in
progress from European Russia to Siberia. He had gained only a
fragmentary knowledge of it from the Siberian newspapers; but he,
like most Russians, was not aware of its scope.[13] During the first two
years of his stay in Vladivostok, there was a new high in Russian
eastward migration, with well over two hundred thousand migrants
annually from 1898 through 1901. Although settlement took place
primarily in the western part of Siberia, this tremendous growth of
what was almost entirely a rural peasant population (in conjunction
with the completion of the railroad), presented a rich potential market
for more industrial economies.

Although he tried to broaden the scope of his office, Greener did
not neglect other tasks, such as formulating specific proposals for
American enterprise and transmitting special reports on the natural
resources and development of Siberia. For example, he suggested
establishment of a regular American steamship line between the
Pacific coast and Vladivostok; a department store featuring American
goods; an American mineral water industry involving a Russian
partner; and the introduction of California fruit products into Siberia.
More than once the State Department complained that his reports
were too long; but they were, nevertheless, well written and to the
point.

At the same time, Greener in 1904 sent a very critical report to
Washington about the imperial decree of 1903 concerning the "He-
brews." The decree severely restricted the rights of Jews in property
ownership and limited them to occupations such as small traders and
artisans. However, Greener remarked later in a letter to Booker T.
Washington that, in contrast to the situation of the Negro in the
United States, at least if a Jew accepted the precepts of the Russian
Orthodox religion and government he would no longer be treated as a
pariah.[14]

Not only did the State Department receive literature from the
American agent, but the Primorsky (Maritime Province) governor-
general did as well. One of Greener's main functions was to establish
and maintain favorable ties with the Russian authorities. He found
that his knowledge of French and his rank of commerical agent enabled
him to be treated like any other member of the upper class in his
dealings with the Russian officials. In fact, the Russian governor
sponsored Greener's election to the Statistical Society of Amur and
Primorsky provinces, whose membership consisted only of leading
officials and a few members of the highest merchant class. Greener
had sent the governor a regular flow of circulars, catalogs, and extracts
from American newspapers concerning public improvements, and the
governor rewarded him for this service.

Judging from his success in a number of difficult matters in which he dealt with local officials, Greener must have achieved a fairly high stature in their eyes. In one instance he found himself acting as a lawyer for a brief period when called to the aid of three Americans and two Japanese who were arrested for seal poaching. They were tried, convicted, and sentenced to sixteen months' imprisonment. Greener and the Japanese agent appealed the sentence, and Greener, who had brought his law diploma to Russia with him, spoke in defense of the Japanese when their lawyer was not available. The sentence was reduced to six months' imprisonment. An account of his role in the affair appeared in *Vostochnyi Vestnik* (The Eastern Herald), one of the local newspapers.

However, international competition during this period did not confine itself to diplomatic and commercial activities. Greener's stay in Vladivostok was twice punctuated by war, and even more often by the threat of war. During such hostilities, he had to expand his duties even beyond those he had previously sought. In a telegram dated July 1, 1900, he warned the State Department of great mobilization activity in the Amur and Transbaikal regions and in Primorsky province. He told of four thousand Russian troops at Port Arthur and four thousand more coming through Siberia. He also heard official rumors that a thousand Americans had crossed from Nome. He suggested that the State Department alert Alaskan miners regarding this situation. Later, he learned that these activities were part of the prologue to the Boxer Rebellion. The only direct effect of this upheaval on Vladivostok was that local Chinese fled the city and martial law was put into effect. However, Greener became involved when he agreed to act as secretary in a drive to raise funds for victims of the war in China's Shansi province, at the request of the Chinese commercial agent. In appreciation, the Chinese government awarded Greener a service decoration.

The Russo-Japanese War, however, touched Vladivostok much more directly and placed Greener in a very delicate political situation. When the Japanese were evacuated from the city, Greener was instructed by his government to look after the Japanese interests in Siberia. One of his first tasks in this was to aid in the evacuation of the Japanese on Sakhalin Island. Due to friction between Russia and Britain (which had a pact with Japan), the British agent also eventually withdrew and Greener was ordered to look after British interests as well. In this instance he asked not to be required to represent the British government, although he was willing to aid British subjects. Presumably his reservations grew out of a long-standing antipathy he held for England as an imperialist power. The State Department, however, overruled his objection and instructed him that he was to act on behalf of both government and private British interests, although not as their official representative.

The Japanese inflicted little physical damage on Vladivostok; the only attack was a bombardment by the Japanese fleet in March 1904. There was only slight damage and the shore batteries did not reply. However, tension within the city and suspicion of all foreigners grew apace with the war. As a result, under circumstances not clear from available materials, Greener was forced to leave the city in May 1905. There is no record of where he went; but he returned to the city in late October from Khabarovsk. His term in Vladivostok ended soon thereafter.[15] While Greener's residence had made no lasting impact in eastern Siberia, he had raised American awareness of this area. Besides the State Department, his activities had been followed closely by the black press; and he also received praise in some of the white press.[16] A prolific journalist and public speaker, Greener would for years draw upon his experience in Russia for his political, social, and economic analyses.

State Department records indicate that still another Negro, Ivan Smit, was the Ameerican agent in the Baltic port city of Libau for a short time in 1908. No further information is available on Smit. However, it is worth noting that Libau is one of the cities in which a number of Negroes were noticed among emigrés fleeing Russia after the Revolution. According to one source:

> Among them appeared several Negroes who were Russian subjects yet descendants of American Negroes, and with odd names such as Misha Smith, Tania Johnston, and Sasha Bruce.[17]

Not all of the Negro visitors to Russia were Americans. Many Africans also travelled there in connection with cultural and economic ties between Russia and certain African countries. However, the most accessible account of such a visit is that of Salim bin Abakari, who travelled as a servant accompanying his German employer. A native of Zanzibar, Abakari later recorded in Swahili the story of their trip taken in 1896, which took them from Berlin through St. Petersburg and Moscow, the middle Volga region, through Siberia (as far as the Altai mountains and the border with Mongolia), and then back through Central Asia and the northern Caucasus. Himself a Moslem, Abakari was particularly impressed by the number of Moslems they met in the main cities, as well as in Central Asia. He also noted the varied reactions to his color. For instance:

> When we reached Samara the people were quite startled to see a black man. They said that I was the only black person they had ever seen. When I went for a stroll in the roadway, they ran away from me, they thought that Satan had come down to their place. Both the old people and the children would run away on seeing me.

But on other occasions his appearance was viewed as a positive mark of distinction:

> The trouble about a horse-carriage is that it hurts one's sides, because of the way they climb up the stony hills. You have to sit on cushions, putting them all around your side in the carriage. And as we travelled through the country districts by carriage, with my master going on in front, the country people when they saw him greeted him, but not more so than they did me; me they greeted profusely as though I were a King, because they saw my master (to be) white like themselves, but I was black, and they had not yet seen a black man, so they thought that this was surely *my* safari.[18]

Abakari's travel account is a clear example of how African impressions of Russia were relayed back to the African continent.

CHAPTER FIVE

THE NEGRO IN RUSSIAN ART

IN LITERATURE

Modern Russian literature, like a number of other important intellectual developments there, most clearly dates from the middle of the eighteenth century and the contributions of the truly seminal thinker Michael Lomonosòv. It was, however, only in the nineteenth century that the literary language fully developed and literature reached full bloom. The most singular figure in this process was Alexander Pushkin. Among the numerous themes he introduced into Russian literature was that of the Negro. There is, of course, in addition, the circumstance that he was of Negro descent. Since Pushkin was very proud and conscious of his African heritage, it is appropriate to consider what possible impact his attitude had on his artistry. Although he was not a Negro in the sense of the definition used in this study, his career represents the one instance in Russian literature where there may have been a direct influence related to Negroes.

Throughout his life, Pushkin made references to his African ancestry, both privately and publicly. This indicates that it must have played a considerable role in shaping his world view. That is not to say that he placed more importance on his maternal lineage than that of his father. He was even more proud of being a descendant on his father's

The writer Alexander Pushkin included his own African heritage among his literary subjects. Portrait by Orest Kiprenskii reprinted from Polivanov, ed., *Al'bom Moskovskoi Pushkinskoi Vystavki 1880*, after p. 294.

side of one of the oldest Russian noble families. However, his African descent was something special: first, because Hannibal, in addition to achieving an illustrious career, was a favorite of Peter the Great, whom Pushkin greatly admired; and second, because this kind of personal distinction was especially appealing to the poet in Pushkin. Consider these lines from "Iur'evu" (To Iurev), written in 1820:

> And you are happy with your fate.
> But I, an eternally-idle rake,
> An ugly offspring of Negroes,
> Not knowing the sufferings of love,
> I please youthful beauties
> With the shameless rage of my desire;[1]

Again, in *Eugene Onegin*, begun in 1823:

Will (it) come the hour of my freedom?
Time, time!–I call to it;
I roam above the sea, I wait for the (right) weather,
I beckon to the sails of ships.
Under the cope of storms, with waves disputing,
on the free crossway of the sea
when shall I start (on my) free course?
Time to leave the dull shore
of a to me inimical element,
and 'mid the meridian swell,
beneath the sky of my Africa,
to sigh for somber Russia,
where I suffered, where I loved,
where (my) heart I buried.[2]

In the 1820s, Pushkin became increasingly enchanted by his African ancestry. Even in his boyhood he had spent days visiting the households of his Hannibal cousins. But his mature interest in the subject dates from his exile in 1824 to Mikhailovskoe, one of the estates that had been awarded originally to Abram Hannibal. Since then, rather than just allude to his Negro forebears, he began to weave into some of his writings biographical fragments from the lives of Abram and Ivan Hannibal. In the poem "K Iazykovu" (To Iazykov), he related:

In the countryside, where Peter's foster-child,
Favorite slave of tsars and tsarinas
And their forgotten housemate,
My Negro great-grandfather hid,
Where, having forgotten Elizabeth
And the court and magnificent promise,
Under the canopy of lime-blossom lanes
He thought in cool summers
About his distant Africa,
I wait for you . . .[3]

His letters from the period reveal the intensity of his interest. In a letter to his brother Lev, at the beginning of 1825, he instructed him to advise Conrad Ryleev, "to put our grandfather in Peter I's suite, in his new poem. His ugly blackamoor *phiz* would produce a strange effect on the whole picture of the Battle of Poltava." Surprisingly, Pushkin omitted Hannibal in his magnificent "Poltava," which he composed in 1828. He pursued the topic further in a letter of August 1825 to Praskovia Osipova: "I am counting on seeing my old Negro Great-Uncle, who is, I suppose, going to die one of these fine days, and I must have some memoirs from him concerning my great-grandfather."

A verse of uncertain date commenting on Hannibal's marital predicament, was very likely written during this period:

When the tsar's Negro decided to marry,
The Negro strolled amongst the boyarynias,*
The Negro looked at the boyaryshnias.**
The Negro chose himself a lady,
Like a black raven choosing a white swan,
And how black the Negro was . . .
And how white she was, the sweet soul.[4]

Pushkin continued the same theme when he began his uncompleted novel, "The Negro of Peter the Great," a fictionalized biography of Hannibal. The completed portions, which do not reflect Pushkin's best work, covered only Hannibal's stay in France and the initial period following his return to Russia. Nevertheless, this is an important work for primarily two reasons. First, its scope clearly suggested a work of major proportions. However, none of the parts completed were published during his lifetime. It is also significant that Pushkin selected this biographical theme for his first attempt at prose fiction. Second, the work represented one of the earliest characterizations of the Negro as hero in world literature. Moreover, regardless of the story's shortcomings, it was a strikingly bold characterization for its time. In two completed segments of the work, Hannibal comes through as a strong positive figure—perhaps, as Vladimir Nabokov concluded, too positive. For example, while in Paris, the hero has an affair with a French countess resulting in the birth of a child whose existence has to be cleverly concealed from the count. The story surrounding Hannibal's first marriage to a Russian woman of noble birth is central to the remainder of the completed fragment. That this Negro character even existed in 1827 is remarkable; that he fares well at all, even more so. Alexandre Dumas père had more Negro blood than Pushkin and wrote more prose, but gave no Negro character comparable stature.

The following passages convey some idea of Pushkin's sensitivity. The first is taken from Hannibal's farewell letter to his lover before leaving Paris to return to Russia:

> Think: ought I to expose you any longer to such agitations and dangers? Why should I endeavor to unite the fate of such a tender, beautiful creature to the miserable fate of a Negro, of a pitiable creature, scarce worthy of the name of man?[5]

Later, contemplating his marriage, which the tsar had arranged, he confided:

> I am not going to marry for love, I am going to make a marriage of convenience, and then only if she has no decided aversion to me . . .[6]

---

* Married ladies
** Maiden ladies

In depicting a character who often engages in self-denigration, Pushkin apparently tries to capture the prevailing attitude of the social milieu toward Negroes. At the same time, however, he shows Hannibal as accomplished and generally likeable, so there is no hint of real inferiority.

Any assessment of the literary quality of Pushkin's fictional account of Hannibal should recognize that Pushkin was experimenting with forms of literary expression totally new to Russian literature, and that he was expanding the literary language to new dimensions. Furthermore, both he and a number of his contemporaries were quite aware of his pioneering role. Just as Abram Hannibal, in life and in fiction, resembled Othello, Pushkin was truly the Russian counterpart to Shakespeare. That Pushkin was inspired to draw upon the Negro element in his family history for his first prose effort is strong evidence that he gave much thought to this subject. Among his notes is a lengthy passage written in 1830, "The Beginnings of an Autobiography." It summarizes all he had learned of his genealogy on both sides of his family; two-thirds of it deal with the Hannibals.

Also that year, Pushkin found a practical use for the genealogical data compiled from his search for his African roots. One of his enemies, critic Faddey Bulgarin, anonymously published the following satirical piece in his magazine *Severnaia pchela* (*The Northern Bee*) in August 1830:

> Byron's lordship (lordstvo) and aristocratic capers, combined with God knows what way of thinking, have driven to frenzy a multitude of poets and rhymesters in various countries; all of them have started talking about their six-hundred-year-old nobility! . . . It is openly related that some poet or other in Spanish America, likewise an imitator of Byron, being of mulatto descent on his father's or (I do not quite remember) mother's side, began to affirm that one of his ancestors was a Negro prince. A search in the town hall's archives disclosed that in the past there had been a lawsuit between a skipper and his mate on account of that Negro, and that the skipper maintained he had acquired the Negro for a bottle of rum.[7]

Pushkin responded with "My Geneology," a poem he decided not to publish upon the advice of friends. However, as with many Pushkin writings, several copies were circulated unofficially. The following verses directly show Pushkin's defense of his Negro ancestry:

Postcriptum.

Figliarin, snug at home, decided
That my black grandsire, Hannibal,
Was for a bottle of rum acquired
And fell into a skipper's hands.
This skipper was the glorious skipper

Through whom our country was advanced
Who to our native vessel's helm
Gave mightily a sovereign course.
This skipper was accessible
To my grandsire: the blackamoor,
Bought at a bargain, grew up stanch and loyal
The emperor's bosom friend, not slave.[8]

The term "Figliarin" (which translates approximately into "buffoon") is a mocking reference to Bulgarin. Pushkin later found it politic to explain these verses to the authorities, who kept him under constant surveillance throughout his career because of the radical tone of some of his works and his close association with some of the Decembrist rebels. In late 1831 he wrote to Alexander Benkendorf, head of the Third Section, secret police:

> About a year ago in one of our journals was printed a satirical article in which a certain man of letters was spoken of, who manifested pretensions of having a noble origin, whereas he was only a bourgeois-gentleman. It was added that his mother had a mulatto whose father, a poor pickaninny, had been bought by a sailor for a bottle of rum. Although Peter the Great little resembled a drunken sailor, I was the one referred to clearly enough, since no Russian man of letters besides me may number a Negro among his ancestors. Since the article in question was printed in an official gazette, since indecency had been pushed to the point of speaking of my mother in a *feuilleton* which ought to be only literary, and since our gazeteers do not fight in duels, I believed it my duty to answer the *anonymous* satirist, which I did in verse, and very sharply. I sent my answer to the late Delvig, asking him to insert it in his journal. Delvig advised me to suppress it, calling to my attention that it would be ridiculous to defend oneself, with pen in hand, against attacks of this nature and to flaunt aristocratic feelings, when everything considered, one is only a gentleman-bourgeois, if not a bourgeois-gentleman. I yielded to his opinion, and the affair rested there; however, several copies of this response circulated, at which I am not displeased, considering that nothing is in it which I wished to disavow. I confess that I pride myself on what are called prejudices: I pride myself on being as good a gentleman as anybody whatever, though it profits me little: lastly, I greatly pride myself on my ancestors' name, since it is the only heritage which they have left me.[9]

This letter and poem show that Pushkin would have been forced to recognize his African heritage even if he had not wanted to do so himself. Bulgarin was not the only critic to direct jibes at Pushkin about his African origins. His critics' main objection to his work was his penchant for realism, which was not yet accepted as a legitimate literary technique. Some in Russia conjectured that his realism stemmed from his "common" origins and vices. In retrospect, it appears that they may have been right. It would seem that Pushkin's perspective on life and art were conditioned significantly by his general attitude toward his African origins. Here was a nobleman who had good reason to identify with the Negro slaves: He was a highly cultured man with an inherent appreciation of variant forms of culture and civilization. It is within this context that Pushkin's African heritage can be shown to have had a profound impact on the nature of his art.

As the letter to Benkendorf suggests, Pushkin's emphasis on his African forebears in his work also affected his personal life. During the last few years of his life, he was assigned to a nominal position at court, apparently to enable the authorities more easily to monitor his activities and to ensure the presence of Pushkin's attractive wife at court balls. Pushkin's official title was "Gentleman of the Chamber." He was insulted because it was a role usually reserved for eighteen-year-old aristocratic youths, and it entailed wearing a uniform featuring a short tunic, patent-leather boots, and a plumed tricorne. One wonders if Pushkin's position was not made even more humiliating by the presence of the tsar's blackamoors wearing costumes of red balloon trousers, saffron leather shoes, and fez. It was during this period of complex emotional strain that the chain of events leading to Pushkin's fatal duel took place. The obvious subject of the duel was his flirtatious wife; however, the underlying cause was a long period of what Pushkin perceived as accumulated insults. When he took the field on the fateful day in January 1837, he was defending the honor of the Hannibals as well as the Pushkins.

No other writer in Imperial Russia besides Pushkin gave significant treatment to Negro characters. However, a number featured them. In *Woe From Wit*, Alexander Griboedov features a characterization which stands in stark contrast to Pushkin's. A noblewoman visiting a lady friend offers:

> Out of boredom I took with me
> A Negro girl and a doggie;
> Order them to be fed, my dear,
> Give them something leftover from supper.
>
> . . . Oh Sophie, my friend,
> What a Negress I have for a servant,
> Woolly-haired! Hump-backed!
> Angry! Cat-like in all her ways!
> And how black! And how frightful!
> How could God have created such a race?
> She is a real devil . . .[10]

A more neutral image is provided by Leo Tolstoy in *War and Peace*:

> "And do you remember," Natasha asked with a pensive smile, "how once, long, long ago, when we were quite little Uncle called us into the study—that was in the old house—and it was dark. We went in and all at once there stood . . ."

"A Negro," Nikolai finished for her with a smile of delight. "Of course I remember! To this day I don't know whether there really was a Negro, or if we only dreamt it, or were told about him."

"He had grey hair, remember and white teeth, and he stood and stared at us. . . ."[11]

These references, while relatively insignificant in the respective works, further illustrate how Negroes were perceived in Imperial Russia. They also show how prevalent was the practice of maintaining Negro servants, at least in the eighteenth century.

The fascination with the African continent itself also manifested itself in Russian literature, most strikingly in poetry. Fyodor Tiutchev in his 1848 work *Russkaia geografiia* (Russian geography), went so far as to include the Nile among the Russian rivers.[12] In the last decades of tsarist Russia, poet Nicholas Gumilyov displayed a passionate attachment to equatorial Africa. In "Vstuplen'e" (Introduction), a part of his collection of verses entitled *Shatyor* (The tent), he wrote:

Deafened by the roar and clatter,
Invested in flame and smoke,
About you, my Africa, in a whisper
The seraphims speak in heaven.[13]
. . . .

Another poem, "Niger," is even more ecstatic:

And the cities around, like a handful of grapes,
Such as Bussa and Gomba and tsar Timbuktu,
The very sounds of these words are to me like the sun, delightful,
Like the beat of drums, it arouses a dream.
But I don't trust myself, I will check it in the book,
Really, there must be some end to stupidity!
Yes, it is written the Niger . . . oh, regal Niger,
This is how people have dared to insult you!
You flow as a great sea across the Sudan,
You battle with predatory shoals of sand
And where you approach the ocean,
The banks cannot be seen from your middle.[14]

Shatyor was written shortly before Gumilyov's arrest and execution by the Cheka (political police) in 1921, allegedly for his participation in an anti-Bolshevik conspiracy.

THE PLASTIC AND GRAPHIC ARTS

Perhaps the earliest Negro artist noted in Russian sources was painter Jan Tiutekurin, listed among the three *arapy* Peter the Great enlisted for his services in 1697. Tiutekurin was initially employed by Peter

Countess Samoilova and Her Foster Daughter, c. 1832, by Karl Briullov, one of the important Russian artists of the early nineteenth century. (Courtesy Hillwood Museum, Washington, D.C.)

in Amsterdam as an artist in his Armory. Upon arrival in Russia Tiutekurin was transferred to the Vladimir marine department. He was given his first assignments (to create an ornate table and an icon depicting Christ being removed from the cross) while still in Amsterdam. The table is said to have been done in an East Indian style. This, coupled with the description of Tiutekurin in one early twentieth century Russian source as an Arab (arab rather than arap), clouds the question of whether he was a Negro.[15] However, Foreign Ministry documents describe all three of Peter's colored recruits with the term arap. The question of their racial identities must ultimately be resolved by Soviet scholars with full access to relevant materials. From what is known about him, if Tiutekurin was a Negro, he would be an interesting footnote in Negro history. However, he would be significant for Russian art only if he had achieved some influence on iconography or some other Russian craft, and it is uncertain whether any of Tiutekurin's work has survived.

In general, the only indication of African or Negro influence in Russian art is the inclusion of Negroes among the subjects treated in paintings, engravings, sculptures, and figurines. Examples of this sort include the engraving of Peter the Great by Schoonebeeck; a statue from the 1730s of Empress Anna by K. Kastrelli; a 1756 portrait of Catherine the Great by R. Lisievska; paintings by Karl Briullov and Konstantin Makovskii; and a statuette by the court jeweler Carl Faberge from the nineteenth century.[16] As is suggested by the nationalities reflected in some of these names, much of the art of this type was by foreign artists working in Russia. Some have speculated that the Negro boy in the Schoonebeeck engraving is Abram Hannibal. However, Peter obtained a number of Negro boys during this period, and Hannibal's biographical data make it unlikely that he modeled for the engraving.

In all of these works and others like them, Negroes are portrayed as subservient. Much like the Negro characters described in Tolstoy's and Griboedov's writings, such art gives further evidence of the fad for Negro servants. It is also interesting to note that Russian archives include a few portraits of Negro noblemen. They are believed to be portraits of the Hannibals, especially since they are attired in Russian military dress. On the other hand, Vladimir Nabokov's study of Abram Hannibal contends that the portrait generally accepted as Hannibal is not. Of course, this raises an intriguing question: What is the true identity of the gentleman portrayed? In the extreme case that the painting is a product of an anonymous artist's imagination, it is worth noting that some eighteenth century Russian painters conceived of Negroes in roles other than that of house servant.

An additional source of images of blacks for Russian art were the visits of Russians to America, which became more frequent during the second half of the nineteenth century. A good example of this reflection in Russian art is in the work of Vasili Vereshchagin, a painter who deliberately used his art for social commentary. During

This detail from *The Sisters A. A. and O. A. Shishmareva* by Karl Briullov (1839) shows a black servant holding the horses. Reprinted from *Russkie khudozhniki* (Moscow, 1964).

two short visits while an exhibition of his works toured major American cities between 1889 and 1891, he executed a number of drawings featuring black subjects.[17]

Bathsheba, one of the best known works by Karl Briullov, 1832. Reprinted from *Russkie khudozhniki.*

Negro Boy by Konstantin Makovskii, one of the prominent Russian artists of the late nineteenth century. Reprinted from *Russkoe iskusstvo*, vol. 5 (Moscow, 1962), p. 175.

THE IMPACT OF IRA ALDRIDGE

The one realm of Russian art in which a Negro actually made a deep impression was drama. Before the nineteenth century, the only instance of a Negro presence in Russian drama was in Iakov Kniazhnin's eighteenth century tragedy "Didona," in which Tsar Iarb was traditionally played in blackface.[18] It was Ira Aldridge, however, in the middle of the nineteenth century, who first brought about a real Negro contribution.

Aldridge probably decided to accept his invitation to Russia in 1858—instead of exploiting his first opportunity to return to the American stage since departing in his youth around 1824—because of the enthusiastic reception and royal treatment he had already received in several European countries. Subsequently, he enjoyed comparable success during the years he toured in Russia. Since the impression he made had artistic as well as political and social implications, it will be useful to consider all of these aspects in evaluating his contribution.

As had Abram Hannibal before him, Aldridge also claimed to be of royal African origins. (Incidentally, this was not their only similarity, when one considers the Othello-like character of certain aspects of Hannibal's career.) With respect to Aldridge's claim to have descended from African royalty, however, all the evidence seems to show that he was born in New York in 1807, regardless of the social status of his ancestors.[19] The legend of his African birth appears to have been a romantic fiction he supported only for its publicity value.

There is considerable validity to the interpretation, advanced in the leading biographies of Aldridge, that shows a direct correlation between the nature of his reception in Russia and the prevailing social and political climate there. Aldridge's initial arrival in 1858 coincided with a period of unusually liberal official encouragement of free expression of ideas. At that time, Alexander II attempted to elicit public support for his proposed emancipation of the serfs and other reforms. However, when the initial reforms provoked increasingly more radical demands from part of the intelligentsia, the reactionary forces acquired sufficient support to again tighten censorship. This reaction is reflected in the fate of the journal *Sovremennik*, one of the periodicals that found Aldridge's visit to be of utilitarian value for the contemporary debates. This journal, by the way, was originated by Alexander Pushkin in 1836. In 1862, after the mysterious distribution of certain outright revolutionary proclamations, the radical press was temporarily muzzled; and Chernyshevsky, the main editor of *Sovremennik*, was sentenced to fourteen years hard labor on the strength of dubious evidence. In 1866, *Sovremennik* was banned forever by order of the tsar.

During this time, the Russian reaction to Aldridge changed from an unqualified enthusiasm to one of guarded suspicion, although the evaluations of his work, with a few exceptions, remained consistently high. By 1862 theatrical productions of *Macbeth* and *King Lear* were forbidden, apparently because they offended the tsarist regime. By 1864 Aldridge remarked in personal correspondence that he was no longer allowed in St. Petersburg.[20] His continued work in Moscow became particularly difficult because of the general official attitude such reactions reflected. This may be the main reason why he spent much of the period from 1862 to 1866 on long tours in the provinces, where his art could receive greater public consideration.

What was probably the most common reaction to Aldridge's first appearances in St. Petersburg is expressed in a reminiscence of the famous historian Michael Pogodin:

> General opinion puts the Negro at the lowest level among the members of the human family. He is forced to accept the mental and moral superiority of his white brothers, as if they were of nobler blood. Look at Aldridge, then; here he is—an African, with a swarthy face, dark skin, kinky hair, dilated nostrils, guttural speech. He does not attract us with an exquisite form, such as we are accustomed to; external beauty does not help him to create a favorable impression in the beginning to gain him friendship. Moreover, he speaks a foreign tongue, but such is the power of his soul, such is the majesty of his art that you yield to him from the first moment, you understand everything he says, you divine all that he feels, you seem to hear the beating of his heart, you are following a magician through all the gamut of human passions, you experience all possible degrees of fire, and reach, at last, the point where the very breath is caught, where mercury freezes. . . . Love, hatred, humility, rage, goodness, fury, meekness, jealousy, malice, wrath, are revealed by this Negro with the same amazing force. He presents to you with astonishing clarity the minutest and finest nuances of the human emotions which the greatest master and clairvoyant Shakespeare portrays.[21]

It should be noted here that Pogodin was a prominent right-wing intellectual. Indeed, Aldridge's popularity with the more liberal public must have been overwhelming.

Given the nature of Aldridge's roles, it was inevitable that they would evoke some racist comment. The most full-blown expression of such sentiment appeared in the newspaper *Syn Otechestva* (Son of the Fatherland), and in such periodicals as *Den'* (The Day), edited by the pan-Slavist Ivan Aksakov, and *Nashe Vremia* (Our Time). A letter to the editor of *Den'* by a minor writer, N. S. Sokhanskaia, and submitted under the pseudonym N. Kokhanovskaia, read:

> A full-blooded Negro, incarnating the profoundest creations of Shakespearean art, giving *flesh and blood* for the aesthetic judgment of educated European society and our Russians as well—the Venetian Moor is not only in the role, but in a black skin. . . . How much nearer can one get to truth, to the very source of the highest aesthetic satisfaction: But *what is truth*—at the least, that which we call artistic, i.e. the highest enjoyment and expression of the human spirit? As the spirit is not the body, so the truth of art is not this profoundly raw flesh which we can take hold of, and call by name and, if you please, feel, pinch with our unbelieving, all feeling hand . . . and lo, from beyond the sea

they take, transport to us, and handing over, let us look and see, so to speak, the apotheosis of Shakespearean creation; not an imaginary, but a genuine savage, black, natural-born Othello. And we saw . . . what did we see? Savage, wild flesh in earrings and shining armour, shaming the spirit of contemporary art. And that genuine shame is ours, the shame of our aesthetic feeling which thinks, from the skin-surface blackness of Aldridge, to make a deeper and fuller penetration into the spirit of Shakespearean poetry—which thinks that thick blue lips, because they are thick and blue, express more truthfully the cry of the human spirit, the cry of a spirit expressing the world spirit of the poet! And what emerged? Emerged that which must necessarily have emerged from the immutable action of flesh, impinging on spirit. The cries emerged terribly, naturally savage; the howls and moans of a beast, feeling that he is wounded like a man, were genuine, leonine, animal cries. . . . Not the Moscow Maly Theatre, but the African jungle should have been filled and resounded with voices at the cries of this black, powerful, howling flesh. But by the very fact that flesh is so powerful—that it is genuinely black, so naturally *un-white* does it howl—that savage flesh did its fleshly work. It murdered and crushed the spirit. Our aesthetic feelings made a mistake in its expectations. . . . This blatant flesh introduced into art, this *natural* black Othello, pardon me, causes only . . . revulsion.[22]

Aldridge's style in *Othello* tended to feed the false rumor that he was so uncontrollably violent that he injured his leading ladies. So catching was this story that it inspired cartoons in some of the periodicals. An interpretation that sharply contrasts with such racist reactions is given in a highly credible review by the famous French writer and drama critic, Theophile Gautier, who happened to be touring in Russia when Aldridge opened in St. Petersburg:

He was the lion of St. Petersburg, and it was necessary to go some days beforehand to obtain a good seat at one of his performances. He played Othello first, and his origin exempted him from all need of artificial coloring,–liquorice-juice, or coffee-grounds, or sleeves of chocolate-colored net. . . . Consequently, his appearance on the scene was magnificent; it was Othello himself as Shakespeare has created him,–his eyes half-shut, as if dazzed by an African sun, his nonchalant oriental bearing, and that easy negro gait which no European can imitate. . . . I was anticipating a manner like that of Kean, energetic, violent, stormy,–a little savage, perhaps; but the great negro tragedian, doubtless wishing to appear as civilized as a white man, had a rational, moderate, classic, majestic style, much resembling Macready's.

Gautier marvelled even more at Aldridge's self-control as King Lear:

A flesh-colored skull-cap, whence hung some few locks of silvery hair, covered his wooly curls and came down to his eyebrows; a wax addition was made to his own flat nose, and a thick coat of paint covered his cheeks. For the rest, a great white beard concealed the lower part of his face, and fell upon his breast: the transformation was complete. Cordelia never could have suspected that her father was a black man! . . . The

King Lear was a better performance than the Othello, in my judgment.
In the former he acted his part, in the latter he was simply himself. He
had superb outbursts of indignation and fury, accompanied by attacks
of weakness and senile tremblings, and a sort of somnolent babbling, as
one would expect in an old man, almost a centenarian, passing from
idiocy to madness, under the weight of intolerable woes. One thing in
the performance was remarkable, showing how perfect was the actor's
mastery over himself; although a man of robust strength and in the
flower of his age, Ira Aldridge never, through all the evening, allowed
one youthful motion to escape him; voice, step, and gesture, all were
those of extreme old age.[23]

Judging from the literature of the period, Aldridge's supporters far
outnumbered his attackers. One such commentator was A. Urusov, a
lawyer who was soon to be exiled in connection with the Sergei
Nechaev affair, a scandal concerning the revolutionary movement. He
pointed out that many resented Aldridge's mastery and, in looking for
some weak point on which to attack him, finally resorted to slander
and racial demagoguery because they could find none. However, one
of Aldridge's defenders, the critic S. Almazov, unintentionally revealed
that even their impressions were not entirely free of racial overtones:

> There are people to be found who attribute certain shortcomings to
> Aldridge because of his Negro descent. They consider that he plays with
> unnecessary naturalness, breaking and insulting the laws of fine art;
> that he is like an animal and that his acting is a matter of flesh and not
> spirit. But these gentlemen it seems do not take into consideration that
> Aldridge is not a savage Negro, captured only yesterday, but a Negro
> who has received in Europe an aesthetic education. Truly, in parts of
> the play, where it is necessary, he very vividly represents the movements
> of a man in whom is suddenly awakened the feelings of a savage, but
> he does this deliberately and these are not his personal feelings, but the
> result of his observations of the nature of Negroes, which he has had
> the opportunity of studying most closely.[24]

Although Aldridge's advocates and detractors would be vulnerable
to criticism by today's standards, it must be concluded that Aldridge
was treated very well by the Russian press. The overt racism was only
a small part of the voluminous discussion he generated. And what is
most significant for present purposes is the existence of the discussion
itself. For it went beyond art to politics and social criticism, just as
those aspects of life were implied in some of Aldridge's performances.
One of his favorite presentations was to follow Othello with the ballad
opera The Padlock by Isaac Bickerstaff, in which Aldridge played a
somewhat rebellious Negro slave. In some performances he inserted
Russian folk songs, which he sang as the slave Mungo. This type of
art was as direct a questioning of certain policies of tsarist Russia as
were the banned productions of King Lear and Macbeth.

Ira Aldridge as the slave Mungo in Isaac Bickerstaff's opera *The Padlock*.
(Courtesy Folger Shakespeare Library, Washington, D.C.)

Considering the strong elements of protest in his art, Aldridge's ability to continue performing in Russia for nearly a decade is in itself remarkable. Part of the explanation for his survival is that he confined his protest to his art. He did not, for example, maintain contacts with those among the radicals who voiced special interest in his work. The one exception was his friendship with Taras Shevchenko, the Ukrainian poet who had just been released from a sentence of lifetime military service for writing satirical verses offensive to the censors.[25] However, that acquaintanceship was brought about by the influential Count Fyodor Tolstoy, then vice-president of the Imperial Academy of Arts. Ultimately, Aldridge's best protection was his own artistic genius. The prevalent opinion of the critics is that, without exaggeration, Aldridge ranks among the best Shakespearean actors to have ever played the bard's classic roles. This factor did not escape an appreciative Russian audience.

Aldridge's main impact in Russia emerged during his first season there, when he gave thirty-one performances in the Imperial Theatre. Twenty-one of those were as Othello. The Russian public had already been exposed to performances of most of Shakespeare's tragedies; the only major ones they had not seen were *Macbeth* and *Richard III*. However, they had never seen interpretations such as Aldridge's and were stunned by the power of his performances. It was especially the realism of his style that they found so startling:

> In so far as the performance of the African tragedian is concerned, we are puzzled by it. It contains so much of the unusual, peculiar and untamed—elements unknown to us until now. If we look upon this interpretation from the point of view of our scenic art, it appears to us somewhat strange and at times inexplicable, but the talent of the actor is so tremendous that it obliterates those conventional impressions and transports us into a different, to us unknown world, into that world of uncontrolled, primitive passions as portrayed by the one and only Shakespeare. As Othello Aldridge was magnificent. . . .[26]

And as *King Lear* and *The Merchant of Venice*:

> Aldridge is the true Lear. . . . His acting enchants, arouses pity, horrifies and touches. This is Lear. This is the idea we get when we think of Lear!

And from the same critic:

> In Shylock he [Aldridge] does not see just a Jew but a man persecuted by age-old hatred and he expresses his feelings with wonderful force and truthfulness.[27]

That "the African Roscius," as he was often called by the European press, was able to achieve such brilliant effect is all the more extraordinary when one takes into account that Aldridge played that first season with a German troupe. He spoke only English, except for some cue lines. The same was true when he played opposite Russian actors. There was some advantage in this for him, since the Russians considered a native speaker of English a more authoritative interpreter of Shakespeare. The clearest tribute to his success and his profound influence on Russian drama is the fact that the Russian dramatists themselves eagerly attended most of his performances. Gautier recalled:

> The successes of this black tragedian piqued to emulation the great Russian actor, Samoiloff; he also performed Lear and Othello. . . . An artist to the fingertips, he designs his own costumes, and draws caricatures that are as clever in the execution as they are in the idea. His performances were well attended, though not so successful as those of Ira Aldridge. But Samoiloff could not make himself a negro![28]

In his biography of Aldridge, Herbert Marshall shows convincingly that Aldridge directly influenced the art of a number of Russian actors, especially during the period between 1861 and 1866, when he played in Moscow and toured the provinces.[29]

While in Moscow for the first time in 1862, Aldridge became an instant sensation. He initially performed in the Maly Theatre, which had its own company. The interest in his performances was so great that subsequent shows were given in the Bolshoi Theatre, a site usually reserved for ballet and opera. His immense popularity was also due in part to the fact that there was no other Shakespearean actor working in Moscow at the time. He, therefore, became the standard for this dramatic art form, especially for those newly initiated to Shakespeare's works. As in St. Petersburg, the critical press again showered him with plaudits:

> Our audience, usually so apathetic, knew no limits to its applause and calls during the progress of the play and its close were incessant. What we have hitherto read of M. Aldridge was not exaggerated; he is certainly a very great artist, and everyone who wishes to see Shakespeare represented to the life must go and see Ira Aldridge, who develops and explains all the grandeur of the great Poet.[30]

Since an artistic conquest such as Aldridge's could not transpire without arousing resentment and jealousies in some local quarters, negative reactions with racial overtones were not surprising. Despite such obstacles, his Russian tours must be assessed as a tremendous triumph. In his several tours, encompassing much of European Russia, Aldridge presented Shakespeare's plays to more Russian towns than had any actor before him. That he continued on this circuit for so many years proves that the venture must also have been financially

The Ukrainian poet Taras Shevchenko made this drawing of Ira Aldridge.
(Courtesy: Collection of Mary O'H. Williamson, Moorland-Spingarn
Research Center, Howard University)

and artistically satisfying. The major drawback, however, was that so
much travel apparently weakened his health, and perhaps contributed
to his death in 1867.

In that year, Aldridge once again made preparations to return to his
native land for a tour. The conclusion of the Civil War and the
emancipation of the slaves had created a much more favorable climate
in America than ever before for a Negro Shakespearean actor. Aldridge
had returned to England for his wife and was bringing her back to
Russia with him for a few final performances prior to the expected
American tour when he became gravely ill in Lódz, Poland. He died
there of a lung ailment on August 7, 1867. Thus, he came to be buried
in the soil of the Russian Empire, where he had practiced his art for
nearly a decade amid great acclaim.

PART TWO

SOVIET RUSSIA

Soviet Russia is one of the most colossal and fascinating experiments in world history. As an arrogant attempt to create a society with a structure and with values radically different not only from Imperial Russia's, but also from any nation yet known, it has, from its beginning in 1917, evoked hatred and fear as well as hope and praise from the rest of the world. Although for quite different motivations than those driving Imperial Russia, Soviet Russia from the start exhibited a compulsion toward accelerated development to catch up with the leading world powers. That the new state virtually accomplished this within two decades is truly remarkable given the tremendous material and psychological traumas Russia suffered during the first half of this century. During its early decades, successive shock waves were delivered Russia by World War I, the Russian Revolution and Civil War, the Five-Year Plans, Stalin's purges, and World War II. The Marxist ideology guiding the leaders of Soviet Russia has caused them to show an even greater interest in the world at large than their tsarist forebears. More specifically, as the self-proclaimed champion of the oppressed and the archenemy of capitalism and imperialism around the world, the Soviet Union has forcefully courted the allegiance of all the world's peoples against the prevailing economic, political, and social systems. Among these peoples are the large black populations of Africa and the Americas.

Thus, the general subject of the Negro has been raised to a new level of importance in Soviet Russia. Concurrently, the high level of prestige the Soviet ideology ascribes to the existing lower classes, in general, and to popular culture, in particular, has attracted a greater number of blacks than ever to visit Russia. Initially the Soviet interest in what was called "the Negro Question" was primarily political, as was expressed through the Communist International (Comintern), the Russian-dominated alliance of world communist parties, which from 1919 to 1943 attempted to incite the worldwide revolution promised in Marxist doctrine. Comintern included selected blacks from the Americas and Africa, who were among those brought to its schools in Russia. It also appointed some of them to official positions. However, the needs of the Soviet economy for foreign technicians in its rapid mobilization of agriculture and industry also resulted in the arrival of some black workers and scientists among the thousands who came from abroad. The Negro question became even more prominent in Soviet strategy with the growth of the civil rights movement in the United States and with the evolution of independence movements and, later, independent states in black Africa. Racial equality became one of the axioms for Soviet society, which was made literate on an unprecedented scale and imbued with uniform principles.

Since World War II, the international ideological rivalries and competition for strategic bases and natural resources have made black Africa more important than ever on the global scene. Russia, hoping to gain more favor than the Western capitalist countries, has vied with them in extending unprecedented amounts of material aid to Africa and has educated thousands of African students at her own expense and on her own territory. As was the case in Imperial Russia, this broadening of Soviet interest in the black world, and the greater awareness of it within Russia, has expressed itself not only in the political arena, but also in the arts and in intellectual circles generally.

CHAPTER SIX

BLACK SEA NEGROES IN SOVIET SOCIETY

In Soviet society, as in tsarist Russia, the largest native Russian Negro population are the Negroes who have for centuries resided in the Black Sea area. In Soviet Russia, they have become dispersed over a broader area of the Soviet Union and have become more completely assimilated into the general population. However, due to the conflicting nature of available relevant information, the situation of this twentieth century black population is almost as much a mystery as is the origin of its ancestors.

Preoccupied with the First World War and the Russian Revolution and Civil War, the Russian public understandably forgot about this newly discovered Negro population until relatively stable living conditions were reestablished in the early 1920s. Recent investigations reveal, however, that some of these Negroes became involved in Soviet affairs as early as the Civil War. The careers of the brothers Shaaban and Shirin Abash of the Abkhazian village of Adzhiubzha are excellent illustrations.

Shaaban was the son of an African woman named Sophia who reportedly was 112 when she died in 1952. According to family tradition, their forefathers had been taken from Africa to Turkey, and from there brought to work on the estate of a Prince Abashidze in Abkhazia. After emancipation, the descendants had shortened their name to Abash in a deliberate break with the slave heritage. When drafted into military service during World War I, Shaaban became exposed to revolutionary propaganda. After the October Revolution in 1917, he joined the forces supporting the Bolsheviks. For his services in the Abkhazian Red Mounted Regiment, he was awarded a special certificate from the Revolutionary War Council of the Caucasian Workers' and Peasants' Army. The citation was signed by the future prominent leader Gregory Ordzhonikidze. As a further reward, Shaaban was elected to the Central Executive Committee of the Abkhazian Soviet—the highest local executive authority. Shirin Abash, along with his brother Shaaban, worked as a shepherd on the Abashidze estate before the Revolution and also readily supported the Bolsheviks. A leader in the organization of collective farms in the area, Shirin was elected the first chairman of the collective farm board in Adzhiubzha.[1]

The Abash family remains prominent to this day. In 1963, Nutsa, a daughter of Shirin, published a short article in *Pravda*, which is worth presenting here in its entirety for several reasons. It summarized the history and present status of the Abkhazian Negroes from the official Soviet point of view; it is a rare personal statement by one of the Black Sea Negroes; and it shows the international significance the Soviet Union perceives for the welfare of this group in Soviet society. The article was entitled "In Defense of My Sisters."

> Reading the lines of news reports about the outrages perpetrated by racists in the U.S.A. is enough to make rage boil up in your breast. It is impossible to reconcile oneself to the thought that in the 20th century a racist plague is raging in a country which prides itself in its degree of civilization. People without conscience or honor, if not to say degenerates, cruelly trample on the fundamental rights of the multi-million Negro population of the U.S.A.
>
> It hurts me to think about the fate of Negroes in America. Not only because I have been brought up in the spirit of humanism and proletarian internationalism, but also because my skin is the same color as my sisters' in America.
>
> In the last century, at the whim of the Georgian Prince Abashidze a group of Negroes was brought to Abkhazia from Africa. For many years they were deprived of all rights and bore the yoke of slavery. But then the October Revolution arrived in Abkhazia. And today the descendants of the Negroes delivered here from Africa live freely and happily among Abkhazians, Georgians and Russians.
>
> I was born during the Soviet era. And neither I nor any of my relatives have ever in our lives encountered even a hint of what might be called discrimination. I, like everyone in our country, received a free higher education. Recently I was appointed the head doctor of a district hospital.
>
> To us, full citizens of the land of the Soviets engaged in building communism, racial prejudices are unknown. The facts of everyday life in the U.S.A., where cruelties are committed against Negroes with impunity, seem simply preposterous. I add my voice to the demand of

all the peoples of the world: down with racial discrimination in the U.S.A., freedom for American Negroes![2]

A cousin of Nutsa Abash, Shamil Chamba, when interviewed on another occasion, gave similar testimony regarding life as a Negro in Abkhazia. Chamba, a bus driver, was married to a Russian, as was his cousin. The trend in these families seems to be toward intermarriage and total assimilation. Both Chamba's and Nutsa Abash's mothers were Abkhazian.

Bashir Shambe, whose family history was described in Chapter One, had a comparable experience in Soviet society. When the Reds won the Civil War and Georgia became a Soviet Republic, he joined the Red Army. Through his service, he gained formal education and eventually became a fireman in the Tbilisi fire department. He joined Komsomol (the Communist Youth Organization) in 1923 and soon was elected to the Tbilisi Soviet. In 1928 he was admitted to the Communist Party. He became a delegate to the party's Tbilisi district committee. As a final honor, he was awarded the Order of the Red Banner of Labor decoration by the Georgian Soviet Republic. He married a Russian, by whom he had a son. Thus Shambe, both of whose parents were African, also followed the pattern of assimilation.[3] This depiction of the situation of the Black Sea Negroes in Soviet society is echoed by all the Soviet studies on the subject and by a number of foreign observers as well. In 1973 members of a delegation visiting the Abkhazian capital, Sukhumi, including several American Negroes, were briefly guests at a nearby collective farm that included some Negro families. One such family lived in the mountain region some distance away from the collective farm village, but was scheduled to be moved closer to the village within the year. Supposedly, their home was to be made into a museum commemorating the coming of Africans to Abkhazia. Only a few Negro families remain in the entire area surrounding Sukhumi.

An interesting report concerning the general situation of the Abkhazian and other Black Sea Negroes casts light on the question of their present-day location. Svetlana Allilueva, the expatriate daughter of Joseph Stalin, presents a picture of the Abkhazian Negroes' experience in Soviet society in one of her books published in the United States that constrasts decidedly with Nutsha Abash's testimony. Her information was admittedly secondhand, but seems quite plausible when analyzed with other available data. Her informant was a friend she called Bertha, a scholar in the African Institute of the Academy of Sciences who had included materials on the Abkhazian Negroes in a book she wrote on Negroes in Russia.

According to Allilueva, Bertha had confided to her that she had

been horrified at what she found upon visiting some of the Negro
villages: groups of Negro Moslems living in dire poverty and almost
totally illiterate. The other local peoples had allegedly refused to mix
with the Negroes and had driven them back into the mountains. Since
they spoke only Abkhazian, and Bertha did not, she could talk to them
only through official interpreters. Nevertheless, she somehow learned
they feared that her coming meant they would all be transported
elsewhere. Some of the women began wailing. Here Allilueva inter-
jected that such removal had been a common fate of Caucasian peoples,
for example, the Chechen-Ingush, the Kabardians, and the Balkars. A
few of the young men who knew some Russian were able to calm the
people after talking with Bertha. They also told her that they longed
for education and that their race was dying out. Allilueva contended
that Bertha could not include this information in her book, which was
published for foreign dissemination only.[4]

Allilueva's unpleasant account, if accurate, helps to dispel some of
the mystery surrounding the present situation of the Black Sea Negroes.
The book by L. Golden-Hanga, which is clearly the one Allilueva
alludes to, states that today African descendants live in Azerbaidjan
and the Crimea, and several hundred remain in Abkhazia. If this is
so, why is it that descriptions of their life in Soviet society have
centered on just a few families around Sukhumi? And why do the
state tourist agency and local scholars in Tbilisi and Sukhumi consistently insist that there are only a few Negroes remaining near these
cities? If Allilueva is correct, there has probably been a policy of
deliberate relocation of the Negroes. Such a process could, of course,
be voluntary. However, Allilueva's description of the reaction to
Bertha's arrival suggests that some of the Negroes had already been
moved away against their will. It is not likely that the villagers would
have been aware of any relocation by the authorities of Caucasian
peoples other than their own.

An important bit of evidence supporting this line of reasoning is
found in the 1931 report on the previously mentioned visit to the area
of the anthropologist Adler. He observed that the small colonies of
Negroes he found in Abkhazia were not intermarrying with other
peoples despite Soviet official encouragement to do so.[5] There were
also black Americans, who, in the early decades of the twentieth
century, recounted having visited distinct communities of Negroes in
the Caucasus region. Among these was the young communist Otto
Hall, who went to the Soviet Union in 1925 for political training.
Having learned from an Abkhazian woman in Moscow that there were
native Negroes in a village near Sukhumi, he took a trip there during
a vacation period. He spent several weeks among a community of

some eight hundred families. The village elder told him that he and others had been Numidian mercenaries from the Sudan serving in the Turkish army in the late nineteenth century. They had deserted and settled in Abkhazia after having launched raids into the area on a number of occasions. The elder had later served with the Caucasian Cossacks in the tsarist cavalry. This account is quite comparable to other explanations presented here of the Negro presence in the Caucasus region. Hall indicated that there was definite evidence of intermarriage between the blacks and the local populations. Nevertheless, there were some villagers who seemed fully African.[6]

Given the amount of attention the Soviet leadership was directing at the time to "the American Negro problem," it is understandable that the Soviets might have been sensitive to the potential embarrassment caused by an isolated Russian Negro population. While Allilueva's account speaks of hostility from local peoples as the reason for the isolation, it is just as likely that there was some reticence within the Negro communities themselves against marrying their lighter-skinned neighbors and assimilating the various cultural complexes to which these neighbors belonged. At the same time, the attitudes of Georgians and Abkhazians about intermarriage with Negroes are not uniformly positive. Therefore, if the Soviet government determined that total assimilation of the Negroes into the general population was desirable, the effect might have been developed more expeditiously by encouraging and helping the Negroes to relocate, individually or in small groups, to other areas throughout the Soviet Union.

This reconstruction of the history of the Black Sea Negroes in Soviet society is admittedly conjectural and is far from complete. However, until Soviet investigators present more of the details that only they can obtain, this reconstructed history is the best that the available data will allow. Assuming that the general pattern of what has been outlined above is true, the most important and puzzling question that remains concerns the present status of the relocation process and the assimilation of Negro populations in Russia. It is not absolutely certain, however, that no sizeable Negro communities still remain. In December 1975, an American tour group encountered a sizeable group of black people in a Moscow train station late one evening, whom they at first took to be Africans. However, when a Negro in the American group inquired about their origins, he was told they were from Georgia.[7]

Since there is no such nationality as "Negro" included in the census or other official Soviet records, it is not possible to determine the actual number of Soviet Negroes. The multinational character of the

Soviet population renders a count of those without pronounced Negro features all the more impossible. Thus, the most likely fate of the Black Sea Negro descendants is that they will eventually become totally assimilated. However, the devoutly Moslem families may be the last of the Negro population to become absorbed into the main-stream.

CHAPTER SEVEN

THE BLACK "PILGRIMS"

If some Negroes viewed Russia as a land of promise in the nineteenth century, in the 1920s and 1930s other Negroes, especially from the Americas, saw the Soviet Union, and its idea of the "new society," as "the promised land" itself. To see this in proper perspective, it should be kept in mind that there was a long-established tradition of migration and immigration schemes and experiments involving American Negroes, the most current being Marcus Garvey's "back to Africa" debacle. The bright humanitarian ideals of the Soviet Union represented one more alluring option to Negroes seeking a society where they would not be persecuted because of their color. Thus, the Soviet Union assumed the role of a kind of mecca of human rights for some and an escape from the Great Depression for others. One observer estimated that by the early 1930s several hundred Negroes had visited the Soviet Union.[1] At least a small segment of that number remained for several years or permanently; others followed them in subsequent decades—politicos, technicians, and artists. A picture of their experience in Russia, which can be gleaned from autobiographies and articles in the American and Soviet press, is one of the most insightful components of this study.

Judging from the poverty of information on this topic, it may well be necessary to reiterate that Negroes have been going to Russia since the very beginnings of the Soviet state. A July 1976 article in a Russian emigré newspaper, "Negroes in the Soviet Union," reported that Negroes in Russia were such a rare and exotic sight that before 1960, none were there besides the actor Wayland Rudd, who by chance happened to end up in Moscow.[2] However, there is much more Negro presence in Russian history than the article suggests. For example, there were, in addition to the Abkhazians, other Negroes who fought in the Red Army during the Russian Civil War. A memoirist recalled that a man named George fought on the Ural front in 1918 as a signal corpsman in an international communist detachment assigned to the division commanded by Vasili Chapaev. He was said to have shown outstanding bravery and skill. Another Negro, this one a cavalry officer, who died leading a charge near Voronezh, inspired Boris Kornilov's poem "Moia Afrika" (My Africa), published in 1935. In fact, the Soviets claimed to have won over an entire African regiment from the forces the French employed to aid the Whites during the Civil War.[3]

In the 1920s several Negroes were among the first foreigners invited to attend special schools established to train Communist Party leaders for various parts of the world. As part of Comintern's training program, in 1921 it founded the Communist University for the Toilers of the East (sometimes called the Far East University). It was attached to the Commissariat of Nationalities and intended primarily for students from the Soviet East and from colonial countries. However, it soon admitted four American Negroes and one African then residing in the United States. Later, in 1926, the more prestigious and advanced Lenin School opened in Moscow. It was to serve students from Western Europe and North America. Although there were also Negroes in its first American quota of seven students, the majority of the Negro students studying in the USSR continued to be enrolled in the Far East University.[4]

The communist students represent only a small minority of the Negroes who have been so fascinated by their impressions of Soviet society that they paid a visit. Most were neither pro- nor anti-communist; their only definite objective was to find a society where a person's worth was not defined by his skin color. The most interesting and well-documented visit of this type was that of the writer Claude McKay in 1922 to 1923. McKay (1889–1948) was of peasant origins in Jamaica. He left there in order to complete his education and to gain a wider audience, after having established a reputation as a poet. After a few years of college, odd jobs, and writing endeavors in the United States, by 1918 he began to achieve some success in publishing for periodicals there. He was originally invited to Russia in 1920 by John Reed, after Lenin had raised the issue of the Negro question at the Second Comintern Congress; but at the time McKay felt unqualified for the mission. Having missed that opportunity, in 1922 he raised

The Jamaican Claude McKay wrote articles about his visit to the Soviet Union in 1923–24 for the American press. (Courtesy: Rose McClendon Memorial Collection Photos by Carl Van Vechten, Moorland-Spingarn Research Center, Howard University)

the fare for what he called his "magic pilgrimage to Russia" by taking James Weldon Johnson's advice and selling copies of his works with autographed photos. He then signed on as a stoker on a freighter bound for Liverpool, England. From there, he went on to Moscow by way of London and Berlin. His one concrete objective was to write of his experiences for the black press. Although he was sympathetic toward the Russian Revolution, he was not a member of the American Communist Party.[5] Nevertheless, he was received warmly as a poet and representative of his oppressed race. His arrival in November 1922 was just in time for the Fourth Comintern Congress and the fifth anniversary of the Revolution.

Petrograd was magnificent in red flags and streamers. Red flags fluttered against the snow from all the great granite buildings. Railroad trains, street cars, factories, stores, hotels, schools—all wore decorations. It was a festive month of celebration in which I, as a member of the Negro race, was a very active participant. I was received as though the people had been apprised of, and were prepared for, my coming. When Max Eastman and I tried to bore our way through the dense crowds that jammed the Tverskaya Street in Moscow on the 7th of November, I was caught, tossed up into the air, and passed along by dozens of stalwart youths.[6]

Another American Negro, Otto Huiswood, had come to the Soviet Union as part of the American delegation to the Comintern Congress. However, it soon became obvious that the Soviet leaders preferred McKay as a representative Negro. The reason was the Huiswood was light-skinned whereas McKay was dark-skinned and therefore better fit the Russian preconception of a Negro. This was highly ironic considering Huiswood's credentials. A native of Dutch Guiana whose father had been born a slave, Huiswood would eventually become one of the most prominent Americans in the Comintern. As a delegate from New York, under the name J. Billings, he was the only Negro among the ninety-four founders of the American Communist Party. He became a member of its executive committee and its main organizer for the Caribbean area. McKay later claimed that the American delegation tried to have him deported because he had arrived with a British group and not with them. However, the prominent Japanese communist Sen Katayama interceded on McKay's behalf and he was allowed to stay. The Soviet leaders apparently had a specific objective in mind; for McKay soon found himself being photographed with Zinoviev, Bukharin, Radek, Katayama, and other Party luminaries. At the opening of the Congress, McKay, and not Huiswood, was seated on the platform as representing the symbolic presence of the black American worker.

On subsequent occasions, McKay assented to give brief remarks on the situation of the Negro in America. He noticed that his audiences were disappointed when he informed them that revolution in America was a long way off. Despite this, McKay was made a literary celebrity. His poems and articles appeared on the front pages of newspapers; and he was on occasion paid the equivalent of fifty dollars for an article. This was more than ten times what Russian journalists were paid. The State Publishing House commissioned him to write a book on the American Negro. This he did in the form of a series of articles. The collection was published in Russian in the Soviet Union during the second half of 1923, entitled *The Negroes in America*. The book's main thesis was that "the Negro question is one of the chief problems of the class struggle in America." It also stressed the affinity between black and white workers internationally and characterized women's liberation as inseparable from Negro liberation. The book was intended

Claude McKay was treated to a brief flight while visiting a Red Army unit in 1923. Reprinted from *The Crisis*, January 1924; reproduced with the permission of the Crisis Publishing Company, Inc.

to serve as a demonstration, consistent with Soviet realism, that only propagandistic literature is valuable.[7] In due course, McKay was introduced to a number of leading Soviet artists, including the poet Vladimir Mayakovsky.

Along with Huiswood, McKay was made an honorary member of the Moscow Soviet (city council). Among the other important people McKay met was Lenin's wife, Krupskaia. At the time, Lenin was too ill for an interview. (However, Huiswood was able to meet him.) McKay also met Trotsky, who impressed him as having a more realistic perspective about American Negroes than did the other Soviet leaders, and as being more predisposed to listen and learn. Trotsky described a proposal to McKay (later aired elsewhere) for training a group of Negroes as Red Army officers. The cadets and officers at a military school visited by McKay made the same suggestion.[8] McKay's exposure to such queries may have been related to an itinerary that included a series of inspection tours of units of the Red Army. The military equipment he saw ranged from submarines to airplanes. He even took a brief flight from Petrograd to Kronstadt.

However, McKay did not uncritically accept everything he witnessed. He deliberately sought out the haunts of non-partisan, and
even anti-Bolshevik groups. During those years, he found some latitude
for freedom of expression. He noted as well some signs of class
stratification and openly criticized what he viewed as discrimination
based on class. For example, he told one military commander that he
thought it unfair that officers from the old regime should be superseded
by proletarian cadets, and that the offspring of the former would be
considered inferior to those of the latter. Later, while in Paris, he
learned that an officer he had spoken to had been imprisoned for
"sabotage" in connection with McKay's complaint. This must have
diminished his estimation of freedom of expression in the Soviet
Union.

McKay's subsequent writings show that he actually had few illusions
about the Soviet Union as it was at the time. Rather, he dreamed of
its great potential as an alternative to existing social systems. As a
writer, he articulated better and more fully than anyone the attitudes
toward the Soviet Union held by black "pilgrims" of the period. A
closer look at some of his impressions may, therefore, explain the
attitudes of other black sojourners whose experiences will soon be
described. McKay began one article with the following:

> The label of propaganda will be affixed to what I say here. I shall not
> mind; propaganda has now come into its respectable rights and I am
> proud of being a propagandist. The difference between propaganda and
> art was impressed on my boyhood mind by a literary mentor, Milton's
> poetry and his political prose set side by side as the supreme examples.
> . . . But inevitably as I grew older I had perforce to revise and change my
> mind about propaganda. I lighted on one of Milton's greatest sonnets
> that was pure propaganda and a widening horizon revealed that some of
> the finest spirits of modern literature—Voltaire, Hugo, Heine, Swift,
> Shelley, Byron, Tolstoy, Ibsen—had carried the taint of propaganda.

He then explains why the Soviet Union poses a special hope for the
Negro:

> Besides brandishing the Rooseveltian stick in the face of the lesser new
> world natives, America holds an economic club over the heads of all the
> great European nations, excepting Russia, and so those bold individuals
> in Western Europe who formerly sneered at dollar culture may yet find
> it necessary and worthwhile to be discreetly silent. As American in-
> fluence increases in the world, and especially in Europe, through the
> extension of American capital, the more necessary it becomes for all
> struggling minorities of the United States to organize extensively for
> the worldwide propagation of their grievances. . . . And the Negro, as
> the most suppressed and persecuted minority, should use this period of
> ferment in international affairs to lift his cause out of his national
> obscurity and force it forward as a prime international issue.

Though Western Europe can be reported as being quite ignorant and apathetic of the Negro in world affairs, there is one great nation with an arm in Europe that is thinking intelligently on the Negro as it does about all international problems. . . . Russia is prepared and waiting to receive couriers and heralds of good will and interracial understanding from the Negro race. Her demonstration of friendliness and equality for Negroes may not conduce to promote healthy relations between Soviet Russia and democratic America, the anthropologists of 100 percent pure white Americanism may soon invoke Science to prove that the Russians are not at all God's white people.[9]

These observations reveal both the conclusions McKay drew from his visits and the assumptions on which he based them. His sharing of these views served to awaken the interest of other Negroes regarding the Soviet Union. McKay continued to regard the Soviet Union more highly than he did the other major powers even after he gradually came to renounce Marxism. In his later years, he concluded that the Negro's dilemma would not be alleviated by his inclusion in a universal proletariat responding to Soviet direction. Finally, two decades later, McKay converted to Catholicism and became anti-Soviet; but by then he had little audience.[10]

The period between McKay's visit in 1923 and the end of the 1920s was one of great turmoil among the Soviet leadership, owing to the power struggle which followed Lenin's death in 1924. The potentates with whom McKay could boast of having met were gradually demoted, en route to eventual oblivion. However, despite these internal developments, Negro visitors continued to be welcomed and given special attention. This was an especially active period for Negroes who were affiliated with the Communist Party in a leadership capacity. Two such persons, whose experiences with the Soviet Union have been detailed at some length, are William L. Patterson (1891?–1980) and George Padmore (1903–1959).

Patterson was born in San Francisco. His mother had been born a slave and he described his father as a West Indian monarchist. His schooling included a number of years at the University of California at Berkeley and at the Hastings Law College. It was during these years, he recounted, that he gradually moved from race-consciousness to class-consciousness. In 1919 he undertook his first "pilgrimage" to escape racism; he left California as a cook aboard a freighter bound for Liberia by way of England. That it was a "pilgrimage" is indeed evident in that upon arrival in Mexico he kissed the ground, symbolizing his being in a land where he could breathe as a free person. However, when he arrived in England he decided to return to the United States and fight the system he detested rather than leave it altogether. He moved into New York's Harlem, which was at the time just being taken over by upper-class blacks. He eventually started a

successful law practice there and became involved with the Communist
Party. Among his close friends during this period was Paul Robeson,
who, at the time, was a law student at Columbia University. Other
associates included Negro communists such as Richard B.
Moore, Cyril Briggs, and Lovett Fort-Whiteman. Patterson also actively supported the defense in the celebrated Sacco and Vanzetti case.

In 1927, Patterson was sent to the Soviet Union by the Communist
Party Worker's School he had been attending. The purpose of the trip
was to allow him to study the nature and cure of racism by visiting a
country where the working class had come to power. In Moscow he
enrolled in Far East University and found that the students were not
exclusively communists. Other American Negroes whom he met there
were the brothers Haywood Hall (Harry Haywood) and Otto Hall,
James Ford, Maude White, and a man called Denmark Vesey. He also
met a son of Chiang Kai-shek and a niece of Pundit Nehru. The Negro
students apparently had some policy-making influence on Comintern
during this period. Not satisfied with Bukharin's initial statement on
the role of the American blacks in the anti-colonial struggle at the
Sixth Comintern Congress in 1928, Patterson, Harry Haywood, and
James Ford convinced the leaders to place more stress on the role of
the Afro-Americans.

For his study of the cure for racism, Patterson travelled in Georgia,
Azerbaijan, Uzbekistan, and other Soviet republics. In 1929, he married
a Russian, Vera Gorokhovskaia, by whom he was to have two daughters
who both remained in the Soviet Union. He also took trips to Western
Europe from Russia. In 1930 he returned to the United States to
resume his Party work there. He later returned to the Soviet Union
on a number of occasions. Patterson believed that he had found in the
Soviet Union all that he had hoped for. With respect to the absence
of racial tension, he wrote:

> It is as if one had suffered with a painful affliction for many years and
> had suddenly awakened to discover that the pain had gone.[11]

Harry Haywood is another who was to come to view the Soviet
experiment as a panacea for racism. The younger brother of Otto Hall,
he assumed the name Harry Haywood when applying for an American
passport in 1925 to travel to the Soviet Union. The name was based
on the first names of his mother and father, Harriet and Haywood.
Haywood was also the first name of the Colonel Hall of Martin County,
Tennessee, who had once owned his father. His mother had also been
born a slave. Harry was born in Omaha, Nebraska, where his father's
family fled after Harry's grandfather killed a Ku Klux Klan night rider
while defending his family. Harry's father in turn moved his family
from Omaha to Minneapolis, Minnesota, following a racial attack by

a gang of whites. Haywood dropped out of school at age fifteen, having reached only the eighth grade, in part because of his reaction to the racist environment. After working at odd jobs, he moved to Chicago and became a dining car waiter on the railroad. When the United States entered World War I, he joined the 8th Illinois National Guard Regiment in the winter of 1917. His military experience only served to further impress upon him the depth of racial injustice in American society. When his unit went to France after being federalized, he discovered that black American troops were initially only being allowed combat assignments as part of the French Army. In the United States Army, they were not only placed in segregated units, but were relegated to quartermaster and stevedore duties.

Upon returning home from the war and mustering out of the service, Haywood witnessed the Chicago race riot of July 1919. This final blow brought him to the conclusion that he "had been fighting the wrong war."[12] Based upon ideas he gleaned from activists, including his brother Otto, and inspired by the ideals of the recent Russian Revolution, he decided to dedicate his life to fighting capitalism. While supporting himself mainly through resumption of his work for the railroad, Haywood pursued his political education through reading and participation in study groups. He also observed the evolution of current black nationalist movements such as Garveyism and the African Blood Brotherhood, as well as labor movements such as the moribund Industrial Workers of the World and the vigorous labor movement in the Chicago area.

Haywood first approached his brother Otto with the idea of joining the Communist Party in 1922. However, at that time, Otto was already a member, and he discouraged Haywood from joining the party because the black members in the Southside branch were protesting paternalism shown by the white leadership.[13] Nevertheless, Haywood joined the Communist Youth League in 1923 and finally the party in 1925, the same year that his brother went to the Soviet Union. Haywood followed him the next year, departing from Canada, after learning that the FBI was investigating him. He arrived in Leningrad in April 1926, by way of Hamburg and Berlin, Germany, and Stettin, Poland. In Moscow he joined Otto as a student at Far East University and immediately became a staunch supporter of the Stalinist regime, which was just then consolidating its power.

In his pursuit of a cure for racism, which had initially attracted him to communism, Haywood was particularly interested in Stalin's ideas on the nationalities question, the Soviet Union's counterpart to the civil rights issue in the United States. The Russians and other Slavic groups in the USSR accounted for around three-quarters of the population. However, there were over a hundred languages spoken in the

Soviet population as a whole; and the non-Slavic quarter of the population was a highly diverse mixture of peoples, some of whom had very distinctive and ancient cultures. The Soviet leaders were faced with the challenge of resolving the resultant tension between the nationalities' aspirations for independence and the highly centralized political regime which controlled them, without violating any of the lofty democratic socialist ideals. Stalin's approach, which he had articulated in writings even before the Revolution, was to reject cultural-national autonomy, but to avow regional autonomy and the equality of nationalities.[14]

Visits to the Crimea and the Caucasus regions in 1927 and 1928 convinced Haywood that the Soviet Union had succeeded in reconciling nationalist aspirations of its diverse cultures and proletarian solidarity. However, he based this on the somewhat dubious impression that the Soviet regime intended to preserve the native cultures, including the use of native languages in the schools. Probably more important for shaping Haywood's attitude was his own treatment in Soviet society. During his stay of over four years, he experienced only one incident of racial insult, and this was delivered by a drunk. Moreover, the man was arrested by other citizens and held for the authorities. This event had to make a deep impression on one whose entire family history had been torn by racial injustice. In 1927 Haywood also married a Russian. However, after his return to the United States, his subsequent efforts to arrange her emigration failed.

Haywood's journey to Russia had expanded his world in a number of ways. Most important among these was his meeting a number of other like-minded black students there, which gave him a greater sense of self-confidence in his own development. For example, there was John Golden, who during the next decade would bring a number of black American technicians to work in the Soviet economy. There was also an African named Bankole, who was an Ashanti from the Gold Coast (now Ghana). The son of a lawyer, Bankole had studied journalism in London and was a student at Carnegie Technical Institute in Pittsburgh, Pennsylvania, when recruited by the Communist Youth League. Another student, Harold Williams, was a West Indian and former British merchant marine recruited in Chicago. There was also a black American from Ohio named Mahoney.

In the autumn of 1927, Haywood transferred to the new Lenin School, where he was its first black student. Among those who would later enroll were Otto Huiswood, H. V. Phillips, Leonard Patterson, and Albert Nzula, a Zulu intellectual who was national secretary of the South African Communist Party. A high point of Haywood's visit occurred in 1927 when he met Stalin at a relatively small party given at the Kremlin during an international congress of trade unions. Josiah

Gumede, president of the African National Congress, and a descendant of Zulu chiefs, was also present. This visit to the Kremlin would not be Haywood's last; for he would play a conspicuous role at the Sixth Congress of Comintern in 1928 and would become vice-chairman of the Negro sub-committee of its Eastern (Colonial) Secretariat.

Haywood completed his studies at the Lenin School in June 1930, but stayed in Moscow for the meeting of the Fifth Congress of the Red International Labor Union held in August that same year. Six other black Americans attended: Ford, Padmore, Williams, and three new arrivals, Helen McClain, Ike Hawkins, and Arthur Murphy. In November Haywood returned to New York and resumed working for the Party. He worked as an organizer in different parts of the country and was a high official until 1938, after which he was at odds with the leadership in the American Communist Party. Although he was officially expelled from the Party in 1959, he remained a loyal communist and Stalinist throughout his life. He visited the Soviet Union twice after his student years: in 1932 on his own, and in 1943, when he stopped in Murmansk while serving in the wartime merchant marine.[15]

The final impressions of George Padmore, who began his sojourn in the Soviet Union in 1929, were similar to Patterson's and McKay's, although Padmore's visit ended in a very unpleasant manner. In fact, Padmore's experiences demonstrate, better than any of those presented, just how powerful the Soviet mystique could be.

Padmore was born Malcolm Ivan Meredith Nurse in Trinidad. He moved to the United States in the early 1920s, at first aiming toward medical training. However, after completing a sociology course at Columbia University, he decided to pursue preparatory studies for law school at Fisk University, where he enrolled in 1925. In 1926 he moved back to New York, possibly because as an outspoken student leader he had run afoul of the Ku Klux Klan in Nashville. By then he had joined the Communist Party; and upon its instructions, he moved to Washington, D.C., to study law at Howard University and to engage in party activities among the highly cosmopolitan student body there. Howard at the time had, perhaps, the largest percentage of foreign students in the country, mainly from British dependencies. By 1928 he had assumed the name George Padmore as a cover in his political work. It appears to have worked to some degree. Ralph Bunche, one of his instructors at Howard, recalled him quite well, but was unaware of his connection with the Communist Party.[16]

Initially, Padmore travelled extensively for the party within the United States. It was Padmore's work in the presidential campaign of William Z. Foster in 1928 that led directly to Padmore's trip to Russia. Foster decided to take Padmore with him to Moscow where Foster was to give a report. The circumstances surrounding Padmore's departure suggest the depth of Padmore's commitment to the communist cause. First of all, he was interrupting his final year at Howard. Second, upon receipt of his tickets, he discovered that they were one-way only for him and his wife. It was then that he realized Comintern expected him to remain abroad. His wife thereupon refused to go, never having condoned Padmore's political activities. He then left the United States without being able to obtain a re-entry permit, because he was a quota U.S. entrant going to unrecognized communist Russia. As it turned out, Padmore was never to return to the United States.

While abroad, he quickly became a prominent figure in Profintern, Comintern's trade union component, also known as the Red International of Labor Unions. He was made secretary of its International Trade Union Committee of Negro Workers, edited its *Negro Worker*, and contributed articles to the English-language *Moscow Daily* and other periodicals. He also lectured at Far East University and had an office in the Kremlin. As a further indication of his status, Padmore was given a place on the reviewing stand in Red Square for May Day, 1930. And he was elected to the Moscow Soviet in the company of Joseph Stalin, among others. On one occasion, he was introduced in this capacity to a group of British visitors, who were reminded that such status would have been impossible for a person of his color in Trinidad. Padmore was also sent on recruitment trips, perhaps including clandestine ones to Africa. He attempted to attract other young colonials to the party; among those he approached were the East African Jomo Kenyatta and the West Indian C. L. R. James, one of Padmore's boyhood friends.[17]

Early in 1930 Padmore was transferred to Vienna, Austria, as his base of operations. From there he continued to frequent the Soviet Union, parts of Europe, and other foreign destinations in connection with his organizational work for Negro worker international affairs. He contributed to a number of journals and wrote pamphlets on the subject. This went on until 1933, when he was jailed briefly in Germany and then deported to England as Hitler rose to power. Meanwhile, his sudden expulsion from Comintern, which did not become official until 1934, was apparently already in the works. He began to be accused of anti-party activity in some of the official publications. He was accused in particular of stressing race rather than class in his interpretations on current issues. Finally, in June 1934, he was expelled from the party and, as far as it was concerned, Padmore ceased to exist. Otto Huiswood replaced him as editor of the *Negro Worker*.

The party's rationale for having expelled Padmore notwithstanding, a more convincing explanation of his expulsion is that he was not willing to curtail his anti-imperialist activities in line with the party's policy at the time, which featured a relatively conciliatory attitude toward the Western powers. Padmore continued his work on his own and remained unequivocal on the theoretical issues involved until he died in 1959.

Despite his rejection by the party, the strength of the positive impression Padmore gained from his stay in the Soviet Union outweighed any resentment he might have felt. Throughout his career his writing reflected an unwavering admiration for the Soviet system as a model for socialist development. A prime example of his belief can be found in his book, *How Russia Transformed Her Colonial Empire.*

Further evidence that Padmore's treatment by the Communist Party was administered primarily as a matter of expediency is provided by the misadventure of a group of twenty-one Negroes and one white, who came to Russia in 1932 upon the invitation of Comintern to participate in one of its projects. In early 1932, Comintern decided to dramatize the American race problem by making a film in English called "Black and White." A sponsoring committee was formed to recruit black actors and it found a positive response among some black Americans. The poet Langston Hughes was enlisted as a consultant. Most of the volunteers were not actors, but, rather, curious intellectuals, including recent college graduates from Howard University and other black colleges.[18] There were no working class people in the group except for its one white member, who was also the only communist. Most envisioned the trip as just a summer frolic. They set out together first by ship to Europe, then by train through Berlin.

Even if they were not political activists, some members of the group clearly placed special significance on their visit to Russia. Upon arrival within the Russian border, in a gesture reminiscent of Patterson's in Mexico, a few stepped off the train to kiss the Soviet earth.[19] For its part, Soviet officialdom also deemed the arrival a cause for celebration. The handful of Negroes then living in Moscow had been rounded up as a special welcoming party. The film cast was quartered in the finest hotel in Moscow, one block from the Kremlin. At the time the Scottsboro case was being given wide press, further augmenting the polite treatment the group encountered in Russia at every turn. There was, however, one note of disappointment expressed by the Russians during the welcome. They had expected all of the Negroes to be dark-skinned with calloused hands. In fact, none of them met these criteria.

Langston Hughes, as a consultant, made a hundred times more than he could have earned in one week in any other country; however, he found that he was actually supposed to do very little. The script for the film was already written; he was asked only to advise. The plot

The American poet Langston Hughes toured Central Asia during his visit to the Soviet Union in 1932. (Courtesy Rose McClendon Memorial Collection Photos by Carl Van Vechten, Moorland-Spingarn Research Center, Howard University)

was set in Birmingham, Alabama, and centered on labor organizing at a steel mill. The one white cast member was to play the role of the organizer. When Hughes received an English copy he discovered that the script was ludicrous. The general plot was plausible; but nearly all the details were wrong. The basic problem was that the writer, who had never been to the United States, had depended on the very few books about American life that had been translated into Russian. The result was pure fantasy, whereas the objective was to create a film which could meet the standards of realism of the Constantine Stanislavsky school. The characterization of Negro manners and mentality was apparently taken from *Uncle Tom's Cabin*.[20]

The one element of the script which was usable was the proposed inclusion of Negro music. The cast therefore set about rehearsing Negro spirituals while the script was to be rewritten. But even here there was a problem. Shattering yet another stereotype, the cast discovered that few of them could carry a tune. However, with practice and the help of one professional singer in the group they improved. Meanwhile, they spent much of their time learning more about life in the Soviet capital. Hughes was particularly interested in learning about Negroes in Russia. He estimated that there were no more than half a dozen, besides his group, who were actual residents of Moscow. He was told about Negro students at the Lenin School, but never saw them.

Hughes uncovered a revealing portrait of life in Moscow through conversations with Emma Harris, a sixty-year-old American Negro from the South who had spent many years in Russia. Very dark-skinned and talkative, she had been affectionately dubbed the "mammy of Moscow" by American southern whites in Moscow. A former actress, at the time she often would give speeches at rallies concerning the Scottsboro boys. But after denouncing lynch law and American justice, she would step down and sigh under her breath that she wished she was back home. Then, in the next instant, she might share with Hughes an anti-Stalin joke. Before the Revolution, Harris had been a duke's mistress with six servants and a footman. Now she had no visible means of support except a ration card. Yet, she still had an elderly, part-time servant and through knowing all "the angles" ate better than anyone in the city.[21]

After a few months in Moscow, the film cast was sent to Odessa for what they were told would be a short vacation. En route in Kiev they by chance met a native Russian Negro, who had apparently not seen another Negro for many years. He was tall and dark, spoke only Russian and seemed to be frightened of the group of Negroes. He worked as a fireman in Kiev, and the group was unable to determine where he had come from. Hughes theorized that he was one of the Abkhazian Negroes.

The vacation in Odessa was genuine. The group reveled in the beauty of the Black Sea coast, marveled at the wholesome attitude regarding the practice of nude bathing, and for a time forgot why they had come to Russia. However, they were sharply brought back to reality when one of them noticed in a Paris newspaper that their film project had been cancelled. The unbelieving group returned to Moscow to check with the authorities, only to confirm that what they read was true. Hughes also noticed that this time the group was housed in a third-rate hotel. However, they were all paid in full just as if they had completed the film and were given their fare home, with the choice of returning through Europe or Asia. Another option was that they might remain and work in the Soviet Union as long as they wished. Three of them elected to stay. The group was never given a satisfactory explanation for the abandonment of the film project. A formal complaint lodged with Comintern went unanswered. The group was left to speculate, along with the international press, that the project had been sacrificed in line with the agreement between Stalin and President Franklin Roosevelt that promised U.S. diplomatic recognition of the Soviet Union. One stipulation, however, was that the Soviet Union would temper its world-wide, anti-American propaganda.

Hughes and others in the group elected to tour Central Asia before returning home; Hughes, however, remained there alone to write after the others had left. To his surprise, he encountered still other American Negroes in Uzbekistan. The first was Bernard Powers, an engineering graduate of Howard University, whom he met at the train station in the capital city of Tashkent. From him Hughes learned of a group of more than a dozen Negroes who were working at an experimental cotton farm about forty miles from Tashkent. Hughes had thus stumbled onto the largest organized group of Negroes—other than his own—who travelled to the Soviet Union for employment or permanent residence.

The origins and fate of this group throw even further light on the nature of the Negro "pilgrimages" to Soviet Russia of the 1930s. The main organizer of this contingent of agricultural experts was John Oliver Golden, a classmate of Harry Haywood. Also the son of a former slave, Golden had worked on cotton plantations as a boy and managed to enroll in Tuskegee Institute. He was expelled, however, after a quarrel with a white official. Also like Haywood, he had worked for a time as a dining car waiter. After confronting racism in every trade he attempted, he eventually turned to socialism as a possible solution to the problem of racial and social oppression. Recruited from the streets of Chicago by Fort-Whiteman, he made his first trip to the Soviet Union in 1925 in the group that included Otto Hall. His wife Jane, who was not a communist, had also gone, but died in Moscow the following year.[22] Haywood remembered Golden as the star pupil in their class on Marxist economics, although he had known nothing of the subject before.

Golden returned to the United States after two years of study and formed a group of Negro agricultural experts, which included plain cotton farmers as well as graduates of Tuskegee, Hampton Institute, Wilberforce University, and other colleges. They signed a contract with the USSR Ministry of Agriculture and set out for Uzbekistan. Among the other members of the group were Bernard Powers, John Sutton, George Tynes, Joseph Roane, C. T. Hopkins, Charles N. Young, Frank Faison, Welton Curry, and A. M. Overton. Young was the son of the famous Colonel Charles Young, the West Point graduate whose career was plagued by racial bias. Roane and Faison were accompanied by their wives. Golden brought along his second wife, who was of Polish-American descent. At the experimental station near Tashkent the group grew cotton, sugar beets, peanuts, and other crops. They were responsible for introducing at least one important new strain of cotton to the area and to the Soviet economy. Golden became an instructor at the Tashkent Institute of Irrigation and Mechanization of Agriculture and thereby made a substantial contribution toward modernizing agricultural production in this region. In tribute, he was soon elected to the Tashkent Soviet. He died in Tashkent in 1940.[23]

Another group member who remained permanently in the Soviet Union and gained a wide reputation was George Tynes. The son of a Negro preacher and a Dakota Indian, Tynes was born in Roanoke, Virginia. When he graduated from Wilberforce University with a degree in vocational agriculture education in 1929, he was also listed on the *Pittsburgh Courier* All-American football team. For his athletic prowess he was called "Whirlwind" Tynes. Upon graduation, having found absolutely no job opportunities, he met John Golden and was immediately attracted to the plan to go to the Soviet Union. It was not until 1936, after returning again to the United States, that Tynes decided to stay in Russia, where he found life to be much more congenial for him as a Negro. He recently recalled of his years in Central Asia that

> Down there they thought I was a Uzbek, a little bigger and a little darker than most, but they tried to talk Uzbek to me.[24]

In 1939 Tynes became a Soviet citizen, having already married a Russian, by whom he was to have three children. He was drafted into the Soviet Army during World War II, but spent the time as director of a collective farm. After working in Georgia, the Crimea, and the Volga region, he became chief of a large duck-breeding farm near Moscow, until his retirement in 1974. His work there earned him three medals from the All-Union Agricultural Exhibition.[25]

Not all of the original group of agricultural workers chose to renew their contracts after the initial two-year stint. Some found that they simply lacked sufficient pioneer spirit after it became apparent that they had moved into living conditions even more austere than those they fled. Another difficult problem was a high incidence of malaria. In any case, most members of the group had planned to stay for only a brief period of time.

Joseph J. Roane, a former high school mate of Tynes, who completed his training in agricultural science at Virginia Normal College, provided a good illustration of what an extended stay in Russia was like before returning home. Roane was actually of Irish and American Indian

descent, rather than African. His family had been landowners in
Virginia dating back to the eighteenth century. However, his career
pattern was quite comparable to the others in the group who went to
Russia since he was considered colored. His wife, Sadie, from Norfolk,
Virginia, was of Afro-American descent. When they set out on their
Russian adventure in 1931, they had recently married and graduated
from college. Recalling the experience in the Soviet Union some fifty
years later, they still considered it to be one of the most exciting
periods of their lives.[26]

It would seem that Roane was destined to visit Russia. He was
actually born in Kremlin, Virginia, in 1905. However, the immediate
inducement to go there was much more mundane. With a new bride
and a new degree, and in search of a job, he was readily recruited by
Golden. In Central Asia, the young couple found themselves treated
like high-level executives. The Soviet authorities were determined to
provide them the type of lifestyle they believed scientists enjoyed in
the United States. Sadie Roane and the other wives did not work
outside the home and were given Russian servants. In addition, housing,
food, child care, and medical care were free; plus Roane received a
salary equivalent to six hundred dollars per month. When these
circumstances were contrasted with the opportunities available to a
"colored" scientist in the United States, and with conditions during
the existing Great Depression, it is understandable that the Roanes
renewed their contracts until 1937, when they finally returned home.
Even then, reentry into the American economy was a shock, as Roane
took a teaching job at ninety dollars per month, and without any
socialistic provision of life's essentials.

Although the Roanes left the Soviet Union during Stalin's purges,
their leaving had no direct connection with these events. They had
spent two years in Central Asia and their remaining years in the
northern Caucasus and the Ukraine, supporting various types of
agricultural development. They left with an overall positive impression
of Soviet society, having been especially impressed by the prevailing
spirit of collective effort. Like Tynes, they also noted the apparent
absence of any racial bias directed toward them. Roane, too, was at
times taken for an Uzbek. When their son Joseph was born in Tashkent
they allowed Soviet officials to provide middle names, which were
required for the birth records. The predictable first choice was, of
course, "Stalin," and that was the name he carried into kindergarten.
The Roanes found that the only constant reminders of racism were
remarks by Russians about American events like the 1932 Scottsboro
case in Alabama, which was followed so closely by the Russian press.
The Roanes were surprised that the Russians made such an issue of
this event, since black Americans were so familiar with lynch law
that it was almost considered normal.[27]

Another "pilgrim" to the Soviet Union who returned to the United States after several years was John Sutton. Born in Texas, Sutton had attended Tuskegee and became a protege of George Washington Carver. Carver had recommended Sutton to the Soviet government after he himself declined a Soviet offer of a huge sum of money to come to the Soviet Union and work in agricultural research.[28] Sutton went in 1931 and worked in Uzbekistan until 1938. A 1938 report on his experiences attributed to him the development of a jute-like fibre from rice straw, which could have relieved the Soviet Union of the necessity of importing jute for making rope and other uses. Sutton reportedly claimed that the project was thwarted by corrupt Soviet officials for personal gain. According to the same report, Sutton opined that the purge of that era was justified and that the people who were punished for sabotage were guilty.[29] Back home again, Sutton encountered years of difficulty in finding employment because of his association with the Soviet Union. He eventually became a successful science teacher in New York City.

In addition to the organized groups affiliated with the film project and the agricultural station, Negroes in the 1930s came, individually, in unprecedented numbers to work in the Soviet Union. Homer Smith, who devoted a book, Black Man in Red Russia, to this subject was the most informative participant.[30] As a journalism student at the University of Minnesota at the beginning of the 1930's, Smith knew that, even after graduating, he would have no real chance of realizing his ambition to land a job on one of the major newspapers. He had good reason to suspect that his post office job, with which he was supporting his education, would be as good as he could hope for regardless of a college degree. Aware that twenty Negroes had been lynched in the United States in 1930 alone, Smith heard that Moscow was a place where he could "walk in dignity." In response to his inquiry, the Soviet government offered him a position as consultant to the Moscow Post Office at a salary higher than he was receiving in Minneapolis. Smith also persuaded the Negro press to allow him to represent them as their correspondent in Russia. In this capacity, he sent back a number of articles under the pen name Chatwood Hall.

Smith settled in Moscow in 1932, in the Mininskaia Hotel just off Red Square. In contrasting what he saw in Moscow to what he had been accustomed to in the United States, he saw poverty all around the Russian city except at the tourist hotels and official facilities. He observed that machinery was being given priority over food and consumer needs. As a consequence, many Russians courted friendship with foreigners in order to gain access to such luxuries as cigarettes and chocolate. Smith lived temporarily in a suburb of Moscow that he called a slum. There were outhouses, no running water, and a high crime rate. Smith was also surprised to meet one family of gentry descent, which had been dispossessed by the government and seemed to be starving. Smith likened this situation to the kind of discrimination he had sought to escape. On the other hand, he also met descendants of Alexander Pushkin, whose aristocratic origins were certainly not held against them. Nevertheless, they too lived in very meager circumstances. To place Smith's observations in proper context, it should be noted that, during these years, there was severe famine in some parts of the Soviet Union, including the most vital agricultural region, the Ukraine.

In spite of the faults he noted in Soviet Russia, Smith found conditions highly favorable for him and other Negroes, at least for his first several years there. They experienced a kind of racial inequality in reverse. They would be called to the head of the interminable lines that were almost a way of life for the Soviet citizen in acquiring essential goods and services. Very often the Negro guests were not even allowed to pay. It is small wonder that Smith remained for thirteen years. This special treatment did not mean, however, that the Negro residents were totally isolated from the main currents in Russian life. While the black Americans who were there to work were distinguished from those from various places in the political schools, there was some effort to indoctrinate the so-called "non-politicals." Smith recalled that Lovett Fort-Whiteman, in particular, engaged in proselyting.

Perhaps the best proof that the Negroes were involved in internal Soviet life is that some were swept up in some of its dominant developments. Fort-Whiteman disappeared about a year after the beginning of the Stalinist purge trials in 1936. Later an escapee from the Kolyma slave labor camp told Smith he had seen black men there, some of whom spoke English. Although Smith was uncertain about the reliability of his source, there was a similar report from a totally unrelated source. In 1951 an escaped refugee from behind the "iron curtain" related hearsay evidence to the effect that a number of American Negroes were living in "indescribable filth" in a Soviet prison camp near Warsaw.[31]

Smith also eventually became caught up in Soviet events. His disillusionment began with the assassination of the popular communist leader Sergei Kirov in 1934; it intensified when his boss, the postmaster, was liquidated. Afterwards, Smith was picked up and searched by the NKVD (People's Commissariat of Internal Affairs). In 1935, he did not renew his contract and remained only as a foreign correspondent. During the Second World War, he found that his nationality, not his color, gave rise to problems for him and his family. His Russian wife lost her job and his family was placed under surveillance. At that point Smith began making plans to leave Soviet Russia, although he did not do so until the war was over.

The experience of a Negro who went to Russia during the 1930s on his own and remained there for decades is best illustrated by that of Robert Robinson, a Jamaican-born naturalized American citizen from Detroit. In 1930 he left a job with the Ford Motor Company to accept a contract as a specialist in engineering offered him by the Soviet Union. While working at developing the Soviet tractor and motor industry, he furthered his own education and became a leading inventor and a senior engineer at the State Ball Bearing Plant in Moscow. One source credits him with no less than twenty-seven industrial inventions. In 1934 he was elected to the Moscow Soviet, along with such notables as Stalin, Nikita Khrushchev, and Viacheslav Molotov.[32]

There was one incident soon after Robinson's arrival in the Soviet Union that shows that the Negro "pilgrims" were still to some extent participating in a broader American experience by coming to Russia. Robinson's first assignment in the Soviet Union was at a tractor plant at Stalingrad where three hundred American engineers and mechanics worked among its employees. When two of the white Americans ejected Robinson from the mess hall because he was a Negro, they were arrested and charged with white chauvinism, a crime more serious than assault. After the trial in a Soviet court, the two were ordered out of the country. The case drew widespread attention in both the Soviet and international press.[33] This occurrence, coupled with the subsequent news about the Scottsboro case, helped explain the high level of genuine sympathy the Russians expressed towards the Negroes in their country and the preferential treatment that they gave them.

One category of Negro immigrant who settled in the Soviet Union which is worthy of mention is what is called the "professional Negro." Robert Ross from Butte, Montana, who moved to the Soviet Union in 1927 and lived quite well as a movie actor and lecturer, fit this category well. He played Negro roles in Soviet films and lectured on Negro life in America, although he never returned to the United States to update his conception of it.[34] Soviet recruitment of Negro technicians did not end in the 1930s. In 1945 the chairman of the All-Union Central Council of Trade Unions of the USSR invited the pilots of the Negro 99th Fighter Squadron to come to Russia for postwar jobs.[35] It was obvious that racism in the United States would preclude any employment for Negroes as flyers there. The invitation also welcomed all other skilled workers. The Soviet Union was, of course, resuming its intensive development, which had been interrupted by the war, and was now faced with the task of rebuilding the nation after the damage the war caused.

The attraction the Soviet Union held for Negro artists is shown most notably in the careers of Paul Robeson and Wayland Rudd. Both came to Russia for the first time in the early 1930s. One of the lures was a chance to work with the great filmmaker Sergei Eisenstein. Rudd had first come to Soviet Russia in 1932 with the "Black and White" cast, and then returned to live there permanently in 1934, after having visited the United States and deciding that it was simply too stifling for a Negro artist. Rudd eventually became a Soviet citizen and died in the Soviet Union in 1952. Robeson, however, never stayed for more than a few weeks at a time, but visited the country a countless number of times, mainly between 1934 and 1938. His reverence for the Soviet Union as an ideal society, and his admitted compulsion to return again and again for inspiration, made him perhaps the best example of the true "pilgrim." However, since he and Rudd were primarily artists, a fuller discussion of them appears in Chapter Ten: The Negro in Soviet Art.

W. E. B. Du Bois was another great Negro American who enjoyed a prominent association with the Soviet Union in the postwar era and who, like Robeson, received more unreserved respect abroad than at home. Although an erstwhile socialist very early in life, Du Bois did not actually profess communism until his tenth decade. He first visited the Soviet Union in 1926, then returned in 1936, 1949, 1958, and 1959. From these glimpses, he concluded that the Soviet Union, though not perfect, offered more promise than dismay. He said that he felt more comfortable and inconspicuous in Russia than in any other country.[36] In 1959 Du Bois was awarded the International Lenin Peace Prize. At his request, the award was presented in the United States the following year.[37] In a long interview with Premier Nikita Khrushchev, Du Bois suggested that the Soviet Academy of Sciences establish an institute for the study of Pan-African history, sociology, and other like disciplines. He viewed the later creation of the Africa Institute under his friend Ivan Potekhin as the realization of his initial suggestion.

Beginning in the late 1950s, an unparalleled level of interest in Africa also led to the greatest influx ever of Negroes into Russia. The chief cause: the education of thousands of African students in Russia. The relaxation of the "cold war" proved to be another determining factor in the increase of blacks in Russia, as well as a general opening up of the Soviet Union to foreign tourism. Figures are not available; but, undoubtedly, more Negro Americans are visiting the Soviet Union today with the same old curiosity, than ever before. Furthermore, the 1960s and 1970s appeared to mirror the zeal of the 1920s and 1930s. For instance, a 1962 *New York Times* article describes a black family in Newark, New Jersey, which was attempting to move to the Soviet Union. The family had already sent their teenaged daughter to school in Moscow, "away from Jim Crowism."[38]

In 1971 publisher George Murphy realized a life-long dream by

A 1940s meeting of Paul Robeson, W. E. B. Du Bois and U.S. Congressman Vito Marcantonio of New York. While Robeson and Du Bois ended as outcasts in the United States because of their sympathy for Soviet ideals, these prominent black Americans had earlier enjoyed acceptance in the highest circles. (Courtesy Moorland-Spingarn Research Center)

visiting the Soviet Union for the first time. He had first considered it in 1927 when he graduated from college, having become very bitter over racial injustice and having read much about the new Soviet state. The reports of Chatwood Hall (Homer Smith), which had appeared in Murphy's family's newspaper, the *Afro-American*, had further stimulated his interest. Murphy concluded from his visit that Soviet life was all that he had hoped it would be. In his opinion Smith defamed the true image of the Soviet Union in his book. For Murphy, the Soviet experiment holds the key to world peace and sets the example for ending interracial and international strife.[39]

Another black American, who recently realized a lifelong ambition to visit the Soviet Union, is Icabod Flewellen, founder of the Afro-American Cultural and Historical Society Museum in Cleveland, Ohio. A retired maintenance worker, and among the most energetic individual collectors of materials on black history, Flewellen has long promoted the idea of staging a grand Alexander Pushkin festival in the United States. This is a dream he shared with the late popularizer of black history, J. A. Rogers. Flewellen is attracted to Pushkin not only because he was a genius of African descent, but also because of his image as a champion of liberty. In Flewellen's view, Pushkin within his historical context suffered just as Robeson did in his for carrying his art too far into the political arena.

In 1980 Flewellen succeeded in obtaining a planning grant from the National Endowment for the Humanities as the first concrete step toward organizing a festival. This allowed him, along with a Russian scholar, to visit the Soviet Union to gather materials and to invite the participation of Soviet museums. In the United States, the planners arranged for various types of events including concerts, lectures, films, plays, and a symposium featuring a dozen Pushkin scholars.[40] This project eventually fell victim to an economic recession and accompanying cutbacks. However, it is a good illustration of the persistence of interest in things Russian in the American black community. It is also interesting to note, that despite Pushkin's unquestioned importance in world literature, no fitting tribute has yet been staged for him in the United States.

CHAPTER EIGHT

THE SOVIET PERCEPTION OF THE AMERICAN "NEGRO QUESTION"

> . . . if I were a Negro, . . .
> I would learn Russian
>   just because
>   Lenin spoke it.
>
> Vladimir Mayakovsky
> from "Nashemu Iunoshestvu" (1927)
> (To Our Youth)

Soviet leaders and intellectuals have never doubted that the example of the Soviet Union holds special significance for Negroes struggling for equal rights in various parts of the world. At the same time, this Negro struggle has been consistently reckoned as an integral factor in the achievement of Soviet global objectives. Soviet writers have devoted considerable attention to Negro liberation since as far back as Lenin's reference to the subject in his "Capitalism and Agriculture in the United States." Variously called "the Negro question," "the Negro movement," or "the Negro problem," this theme was a direct outgrowth of deliberations on opposition to colonialism. Therefore, conceptualization of the problem was on an international scale from the outset, although before the emergence of numerous black African liberation movements, attention centered mainly on the Negro in the United States.

In order to consider meaningfully the Soviet perception of the "Negro question," it is necessary to define more clearly the Soviet viewer as percipient and the Negro, who is the perceived object. Here, the perceptions of the leadership of the Communist International are of greatest interest. They include purely theoretical ideas about the "Negro problem" and actual developments in different societies. As will be seen, frequent disparity between the abstract and the real caused no little consternation. Comintern was, of course, dependent for its main contact with the American Negro upon the American Communist Party. This was the prism through which Soviet leaders peered at the American reality, as well as the main agency through which physical ties with Negro Americans were established. The American Communist Party, in turn, also had to correlate theory and reality in order to formulate the image it transmitted to Comintern. A final complicating factor was that Comintern, at times, dictated to its affiliates what was to be considered reality and insisted upon unquestioned conformity of belief in that reality. These considerations help to explain the formulation and evolution of the Soviet perception of "the Negro question."

This topic was formally introduced into Soviet councils at the Second Comintern Congress in 1920, where Lenin's own agenda specified "the Negro question" as one on which he wanted opinions and suggestions in relation to the "colonial and national question." The American journalist John Reed reported on the subject and it was decided that a commission of Negro revolutionaries would be invited to visit Russia. This was the background of the initial invitation to Claude McKay to visit the Soviet Union. McKay contributed considerably to making the issue more public. In reply to questions he posed to Trotsky at a meeting of the Moscow Soviet, the following letter was published in *Pravda, Izvestiia,* and other Soviet newspapers:

Dear Comrade McKay:

1. What, practically, can be done in order to keep France from using blacks in European conflict?—this was your first question.

It is necessary to set the blacks themselves against this. It is necessary to open their eyes to the fact that, by aiding French imperialism to enslave Europe, the blacks are enslaving themselves by supporting the dominion of French capital in Africa and other colonies.

The working class of Europe, especially of France and Germany, is deeply interested in this work of educating dark-skinned people.

The time for general resolutions about the rights of colonial peoples to self-determination, the equality of all people regardless of their skin color, and so on and so forth, has passed. The time for direct, practical action has arrived. Every group of ten Negroes attracted to the revolutionary banner, united into a group for practical action among dark-skinned people, is one hundred times more important than a group of ten principled resolutions in which the Second International was so rich. A communist party which would limit itself in this area to Platonic resolutions, without applying all its energies to practically conquering the largest number of progressive Negroes for its ideas in the shortest span of time, would not merit the name of a communist party.

2. There can not be any doubt that the involvement of colored troops in the imperialist war—and now in the business of occupying German territory—represents a well thought-out and carefully implemented attempt by European (and especially French and English) capital to find for itself armed forces outside of an aroused Europe, and thus to keep open the possibility of relying, in case of need, on mobilized armed, and disciplined Africans or Asians against the revolutionary masses of Europe. Thus, within the question about the use of colonial reserves in imperial armies lies hidden the question of revolution in Europe; i.e., the question of the fate of its working class.

3. There can be no doubt that the involvement of colonial masses who are more backward in economic and cultural respects in world imperialist conflicts, and more especially in European class conflicts, represents an extremely risky experiment from the point of view of the governing bourgeoisie themselves. Dark-skinned peoples, like natives of the colonies in general, preserve their conservatism and intellectual immobility only to the extent that they remain in their customary economic conditions and daily routine. When the hand of capital and, all the more so, the hand of militarism mechanically uproots them from their customary conditions of existence and compels them to risk their lives for complex and new problems and conflicts (conflicts between the bourgeoisie of different nations, conflicts between classes in one and the same nation), then their stubborn, conservative states of mind break down at once, and revolutionary ideas find quick access to a consciousness thrown off its equilibrium.

4. That is why it is so important to have immediately some progressive Negroes—even if only a small number—who are young, self-sacrificing, deeply interested in raising the material and moral level of the Negro masses, and capable, at the same time, of linking their fate with the fate of the international working class.

The training of black propagandists is the most imperative and extremely important revolutionary task of the present time. . . .[1]

This letter shows more fully why the recruitment of Negro students for the political schools in Moscow was carried out with a real sense of urgency. Meanwhile, the American Communist Party set about reorganizing itself to facilitate inclusion of Negroes in the party's work. The reorganization of the American party in 1925, in accordance with Comintern's instructions, created a Negro department.

As for the Negro response to all these developments, first it should be noted that there was lively interest among some Negroes in the Russian Revolution and surrounding events. The clearest manifestation of this was the founding of *The Messenger*, a monthly covering the period 1917–28.[2] Established by A. Philip Randolph and Chandler Owen, the publication was initially socialist in orientation and attempted to spread radical socialist thought among American Negroes in direct support of the Russian Revolution. However, no revolutionary organizations formed in response to *The Messenger's* appeals. Moreover, its leadership was suspicious of the American communist movement, although supportive of communist revolutions in Europe. A major reason for this was that the American communists adhered to the general socialist tradition of subordinating the race problem to class struggle. Nevertheless, the *Messenger* group contributed two of the earliest American Negro communists.[3] The first was Otto Huiswood, who has already been mentioned in connection with Claude McKay. Huiswood, a native of Dutch Guiana, was a printer in New York and had been active as a socialist in Harlem before joining the communists. The second Negro communist, formerly associated with *The Messenger*, was Lovett Fort-Whiteman, the publication's first drama critic.

The attitude of *The Messenger* toward the Communist Party emphasis on class struggle before racial equality is illustrative of a vital and unresolved issue Comintern faced in attempting to attract American Negroes. In 1925 the five Negroes who had come from the United States to study at Far East University were invited to tea by Stalin. There he expressed the view that since Negroes were the most oppressed segment of the American working class, they should have constituted the majority of the American Communist Party. Otto Hall responded, as he had a few years earlier to his brother Harry, that the Communist Party itself had racial discrimination within it. He said that the Southside branch in Chicago had been formed in 1922 with about seventy-five Negro members; but they soon left because of patronizing attitudes of whites. Part of this problem seems to have stemmed from the largely immigrant composition of the American Communist Party in the 1920s. One source estimates that in 1925 only one member in twelve spoke English. There was, incidentally, also friction between American and West Indian Negro communists. One reason the American Negroes wished to go to Russia was that they regarded the Russians as neutral arbiters.

In an effort to promote mass Negro involvement in communism, the American Negro Labor Congress (ANLC) was founded in 1925 as a communist front organization designed for workers and farmers. Fort-Whiteman returned from Moscow to become its national organizer. However, although over forty delegates met in Chicago in October 1925, few represented trade unions and none were farmers. The organization survived for five years, never gaining more than a few dozen members. One of the few Negro communist leaders recruited from its ranks was James Ford, who later authored many communist writings and was the American party's vice-presidential candidate in

1932.[4] Thus, even with the demise of the competition for mass allegiance, represented by the Garvey movement, the communists made no significant gains.

Furthermore, it became embarrassingly obvious that it was among black intellectuals, and not the masses, that the communists could hope to enlist the most support. Hence, when a coalition organization, the League of Struggle for Negro Rights, was formed in 1930 from the dormant ANLC, the league appealed to the black bourgeoisie while simultaneously castigating it. Under Langston Hughes, its elected president, the league was a conglomeration of groups with contradictory goals. At most, the Communist Party controlled its national council.[5]

When the Comintern adopted its official program at its Sixth Congress in 1928, it tacitly admitted that the Negro question had to be addressed in terms of race as well as class. For the Garvey movement had demonstrated the depth of nationalistic feelings among the black masses. The Russian experience with the nationalities question had also shown Soviet leaders the potential disruptive power of nationalism. The existence of black American ghettos and race riots suggested possible advantages of encouraging the depiction of Negroes as a colonized people within the United States. In addition to these considerations, the most important in dictating the new approach toward the Negro was the fact that the earlier tactic—that portrayed class struggle as the root problem for the worker—had proven ineffectual among blacks.

James Ford, a delegate at the Sixth Congress, voiced an implicit indictment of Comintern's misconception of the relationship between black nationalism and communism when he criticized the moderate tone of the moribund Second International's positions regarding racism and colonized peoples. To emphasize his point, Ford read from a resolution passed the previous year in Brussels by representatives of colonial peoples attending an international conference. While Ford stated that it was a congress of the Second International, he probably meant the First World Anti-Colonial Congress, which met in Brussels in February 1927, called by the German Communist Party. The resolution denounced the point of view:

> ... that the entire race question can be reduced to class struggle between the proletariat and bourgeoisie, and that there is no need to struggle for social equality of oppressed races; that such struggle even becomes harmful at the moment it becomes mixed with class struggle."[6]

Further, Ford pointed out the existence of assumptions of racial and cultural superiority in certain socialist attitudes, for example, those in the "renegade" Karl Kautsky's notion that the proletariat in the "civilized" world has a mission to bring the "backward" colonized

James Ford, American Communist Party candidate for vice-president of
the United States in 1932. (Courtesy Moorland-Spingarn Research Center)

peoples up to their level. Ford added that he had found this type of
thought "even in our own ranks." Ford concluded that the importance
of the nationalistic movements could not be overemphasized and that
they could be considered allies of the socialist revolutionary movement
because the two were confronting the same opposing forces. He
reminded the congress that the last world war was touched off by
nationalism and conjectured that the next, which he believed was
imminent, would also involve nationalism. In this event, he warned,
even more colonial troops and American Negroes would be hurled
against Russia than in the last war and Civil War combined. It was,
therefore, imperative that these millions be influenced to join the
ranks of the socialist proletariat by addressing their concerns through
Comintern's policies.[7]

The American Negro now came to be defined as an oppressed nation
and the slogan "self-determination in the black belt" became an official
policy of the Communist Party. It promoted establishment of a Negro
Soviet republic in the "black belt," defined basically as the southern
states.[8] Although the official policy emerged in Moscow, some Negro
communists had previously been involved in nationalistic activities
and must have contributed significantly to the new stance. Cyril Briggs

and Richard Morris, two American Negro communists, had joined the party from the African Blood Brotherhood, which had been founded by Briggs in 1919. The Brotherhood had urged the establishment of an independent Negro nation in the western or northwestern United States. Alternative sites later considered were South America, the Caribbean, or Africa. Haywood and Otto Hall also came into the Communist Party through the Brotherhood.[9]

Haywood, after his transfer from Far East University to the Lenin School in 1927, was chosen by the Soviet leadership to champion the new policy. He was to apply the definition given the problem by Stalin in his "Marxism and the National Question." Haywood had his own interpretation of the black liberation movement, which even he never succeeded in articulating clearly. However, his stance was attractive to the Comintern leadership because he, at least, opposed the moderate blacks, and some Russian theorists who saw the movement in America as just a liberal opposition to racism. Haywood was convinced that somehow the black movement was a revolutionary movement in its own right and went beyond even socialist opposition to racism, which most blacks in Moscow preferred it to be. Haywood was more optimistic than most other black communists about the possibility of uniting the black and white working class, which was stressed in the communist theory.[10]

The other Negroes at the Sixth Comintern Congress were opposed to the interpretation of self-determination adopted. Although Ford had won his point, the decision taken was not based on the practical realities of the society in question. The Negroes viewed the idea of a Negro Soviet republic as a kind of reverse Jim Crowism in revolutionary garb.[11] The National Association for the Advancement of Colored People (NAACP), the premier black liberal organization, voiced a similar opinion, terming it "Red segregation."[12] Nevertheless, the stance remained an official position, advanced with varying levels of intensity, until 1959. During the 1930s, when such stances as the "popular front" and "collective security" prevailed, the provocative "self-determination" slogan would be played down. Those communists, black or white, who wanted to remain in the good graces of the party had to endorse this policy whether they believed in its feasibility or not.

The rationale favoring such a policy derived from the notion that Negroes in the United States had the attributes defined by Stalin as constituting a nation:

> A nation is a historically evolved, stable community of people, formed on the basis of a common language, territory, economic life and psychological make-up manifested in a common culture.[13]

In 1920 Lenin had also described American Negroes as a nation, although he never took the further step of suggesting a specific policy of the type later adopted. Lenin contended that:

> ... it is necessary for the Communist Parties to render aid to the revolutionary movements in the dependent and subject nations (for example, in Ireland, the Negroes in America, etc.).[14]

In arguing for the policy adopted at the Sixth Congress, the white American communist John Pepper contended that industrialization had created a potential organizing base among Negroes for working class leadership. Actual separation of the Negro republic from the United States would be left up to the Negroes. The doctrine of "self-determination in the black belt" remained essentially symbolic throughout its existence. While accepting the doctrine, the American Communist Party did not stress this tactic as a practical approach.

The strategy approved at the Sixth Comintern Congress linked the Negro question in all parts of the world, and a leading role was assigned to the Negro in the United States. He was viewed as being the most advanced in revolutionary consciousness because he was subjected to capitalism and imperialism in their most fully developed forms. This was the rationale behind training Negro leaders in Moscow and, in some cases, sending them abroad to work for the party outside the Americas. George Padmore's assignments offer the clearest example of this procedure. A lecturer at Far East University, an official in Profintern, and an erstwhile unofficial emissary to Africa and elsewhere, Padmore's was a career pattern the Soviet leaders would surely have liked to duplicate many times over with other capable Negro communists. However, Padmore's independence of mind and his insistence on unswerving opposition to imperialism and racism above all other issues also suggested to Comintern's leaders possible pitfalls in generating a corps of black leaders.

At the same time, that particular issue may have been largely academic; for in the first instance, a major difficulty for the party in general was attracting black members. At the Sixth Comintern Congress in 1928, James Ford estimated that there were only fifty Negro communists in the United States. Cyril Briggs a year later said that Ford's estimate exceeded the mark by forty. Another source estimated that in 1930 there were not more than a thousand Negro Party members. Although during the 1930s the party recruited thousands of Negroes, few remained for very long. In 1939 one observer noted that over fifteen hundred Negroes had left the Communist Party in New York State.[15] Besides a simple lack of sustained interest in political activity, the most striking reasons for Negro disregard toward the party was the Soviet sale of oil to Italy during her war against Ethiopia in 1935, and the Nazi-Soviet pact in 1939.

Ironically, as Padmore's experience shows, some Negroes with the greatest potential for leadership, and the sincerest commitment to the communist ideals, consequently found it all the more difficult to remain in the good graces of the party. The gifted writer Richard Wright left a sensitive testimony regarding his personal attempt to be a loyal Communist Party member without sacrificing his own integrity and individuality in the process. He joined the party in 1933 through his membership in a John Reed Club in Chicago. What appealed to him about the party was quite simple:

> It was not the economics of Communism, nor the great power of trade unions, nor the excitement of underground politics that claimed me; my attention was caught by the similarity of the experiences of workers in other lands, by the possibility of uniting scattered but kindred peoples into a whole. It seemed to me that here at last, in the realm of revolutionary expression, Negro experience could find a home, a functioning value and role.[16]

However, in his three years of association with the party, Wright passed through several phases of disillusionment. First he discovered that even there his color made a difference. On the one hand, he was a symbol of an oppressed minority; but that distinction did not prevent his encountering great difficulty in finding housing when he was sent to New York as a delegate to a communist writers congress. White communists apparently welcomed him into the party more readily than into their homes.

Other types of disappointment greeted him during his activities among Negro communists on Chicago's Southside. He was shocked when some Negroes he addressed ridiculed his "bookish" manner of speaking and considered him strange and "intellectual," despite his being self-taught and having only a grammar school education. Furthermore, he found the Negro masses conservative and timid before the prospect of challenging the established order in even the most innocuous fashion. On one occasion, a group of Negroes in a theatre company threatened his life because he was attempting to have them act in a play depicting aspects of racial oppression. These experiences pointed up some of the difficulties inherent in Stalin's notion about Negroes constituting a nation.

Wright soon learned that the party was also suspicious of "intellectuals." It did not welcome individual initiative and would not tolerate independent thinking on issues. He found himself a lonely dissenter when the John Reed Clubs were dissolved in 1935 by a party directive. Although fully committed to the communist cause, he wanted to

The American writer Richard Wright was among those who were attracted by the communist ideals but eventually repelled by Communist Party practices. (Courtesy Rose McClendon Memorial Collection. Photos by Carl Van Vechten, Moorland-Spingarn Research Center, Howard University)

make his contribution in his own way, as a writer. He even declined an opportunity to visit the Soviet Union because of his work on a manuscript. Unable to reconcile himself to the specific demands the organization placed upon him, he was ostracized from the party against his will.[17]

To evaluate fairly Soviet overtures to the Negro masses during these years, it should be noted that no other party or movement was able to win any firm ideological loyalty from them either. The Democratic Party owed its success among Negroes primarily to the direct material relief provided by the New Deal.[18] Other socialist efforts realized even less success than the communists. For example, Leon Trotsky, through his "Fourth International," attempted to offer the Negro a revolutionary role tailored more closely to his reality. Interestingly, Trotsky's views on this subject did not differ sharply with Stalin's even after the former's exile. In Prinkipo, Turkey, in 1933, Trotsky stated:

> The Negroes are a race and not a nation:–Nations grow out of the racial material under definite conditions. The Negroes in Africa are not yet a nation but they are in the process of building a nation. The American Negro will develop leaders for Africa, that one can say with certainty and that in turn will influence the development of political consciousness in America.
>
> We do, of course, not obligate the Negroes to become a nation; if they are, then that is a question of their consciousness, that is, what they desire and what they strive for. We say: if the Negroes want that then we must fight against imperialism to the last drop of blood, so that they gain the right, whatever and how they please, to separate a piece of land for themselves. The fact that they are today not a majority in any state does not matter. It is not a question of the authority of the states but of the Negroes. That in the overwhelming Negro territory also whites have existed and will remain henceforth is not the question and we do not need today to break our heads over a possibility that sometime the whites will be suppressed by the Negroes. In any case the suppression of the Negroes pushes them toward a political and national unit.[19]

Trotsky's splinter group from the Comintern had organized support in America in the form of the Communist League of America—an expelled faction of the American Communist Party. However, the League was unable to devise an appeal to the Negro that was any more effective than the party's.

The most obvious and promising tactic for attracting Negro allegiance to the communist movement was the organization of relief from the suffering engendered by the depression. This prospect raised a paradox which is inherent in Marxist movements: it would mean allaying the very pressures which were supposed to facilitate the revolution. Nevertheless, the Communist Party did resort to this type of activity, and in some instances achieved considerable success. However, the vagaries of the party line here also tended to dissipate mass support just as it was about to be captured. A case in point involved the Sharecroppers Union in Tallapoosa, Alabama, from 1931 to 1936. After becoming very strong, the Union was dissolved in 1936 by directives from Moscow. Its members were instructed to join other organizations. By 1936 its membership was estimated to be three thousand, including some whites.[20] It is very likely that when the Communist Party called for a "united front" with other "progressive" forces in 1936, the Sharecroppers Union was already moving toward affiliation with established national unions. By 1937 its former members had joined the Farmers Union and the newly organized Farm Laborers and Cotton Field Workers Union. However, even if it were true that the success of the Sharecroppers Union destined it for eventual affiliation with more traditional labor organizations, the coincidence of the communist strategy encouraging this trend represented forfeiture of possible communist control of this segment of the Negro workers.

Later, however, the Second World War was to preoccupy the Soviet leaders with concerns far more vital than the Negro question, and, in any case, the war salvaged the American economy to such an extent that the conditions occasioning much of the interest shown by Negroes toward communism were improved. Although Comintern did not survive the war, the "self-determination" doctrine was revived upon the instructions from the Moscow party Politburo as the Cold War began. The American Communist Party, which had temporarily disbanded, again took up the call. After 1959 and the turn to "peaceful co-existence," the "self-determination" slogan was abandoned; but the American party, as well as the Soviet leadership, continued to give special attention to the situation of the Negro.

Since the 1950s, developments in the civil rights movement in the United States have provided an enormously rich store for Soviet anti-capitalist propaganda. Events such as the school desegregation in Little Rock, Arkansas, ghetto riots, violation of Negro voting rights, and desegregation of public facilities became major staples in Soviet newspapers and other Soviet news media. After the 1965 Watts riot in Los Angeles, the millions of *Pravda* readers all over the Soviet Union were met by pictures borrowed from American newspapers showing Negroes being abused by white policemen. These events, and the many subsequent ones occurring in the United States over the next few years, were from the Soviet standpoint tantamount to the fulfillment of prophecy. In late 1965 it would have been extremely difficult to disabuse the Soviet citizen of his commonly held view that the Negro in America was treated no better than a caged animal, and, in this instance, he was cordoned off from the rest of society in despicable slums, which he would rather burn down than continue to inhabit.

That this image of American society remained implanted in the minds of the Soviet public in the 1970s was evident in Soviet reaction to the famous case involving the American Marxist professor Angela Davis, who for a time had been a fugitive from American justice. Her case became the subject of Soviet radio and television shows and also received full treatment in the press. Furthermore, nearly every type of public organization in the Soviet Union passed resolutions supporting

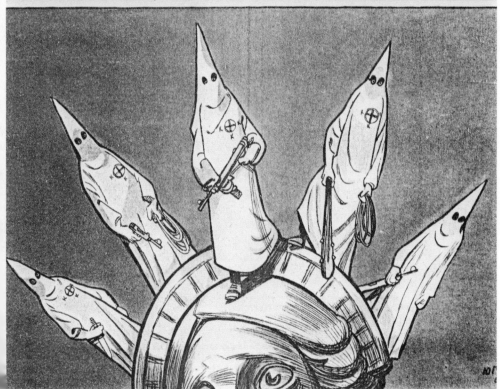

"The view from the sea ... and from closeup." *Krokodil*, 10 October 1961.

"School——A black child and dark characters." Reprinted from *Krokodil*, 30 September 1956.

her. It was a major event when she finally visited the Soviet Union in 1972.

Scholarly studies on the Negro question published in the 1960s and 1970s suggest that the Negro experience has become a permanent element in Soviet communist revolutionary theory. Compared to earlier Soviet treatises, these works also show a more sophisticated grasp of the Negro experience and American history. In addition to discussion of Marxist ideology and economics, they attempt a more comprehensive treatment of sociology, psychology, and religion in the American setting.[21]

A more thorough Soviet analysis of the Negro question has been made possible by increased Russian familiarity with American developments generally. Such a heightened awareness was helped by the vast increase in scope and militancy of the civil rights movement since the Second World War and the advent of notable black revolutionary movements. Whereas in the 1920s, the leaders of Comintern could have the temerity to formulate in Moscow a slogan for the Negro in the United States and have some degree of confidence it would be accepted there, communist leaders in the 1960s and 1970s were confronted by a Negro movement with its own well-articulated and divergent strains. In part exemplifying the impact of Soviet history on Negro thinkers, some black political groups even aspired to promote Marxism-Leninism, although no major thrust of this kind has been socialist or communist. The main role of Soviet thinkers, and more immediately the American Communist Party, has been to critique both the Marxist-Leninist interpretations advanced and the various other directions the American movement has taken.

In general, Moscow has applauded the continued growth of Negro protest against racial injustice and imperialism. It has been a constant reminder of the chronic ills engendered by capitalism. However, some of the main specific lines of Negro protest have been inconsistent with official communist doctrine. The most difficult issue to resolve has been the adoption of a workable position on nationalism. At the root of the problem is the fact that most Negroes have continued to view their situation primarily in racial terms, while the communists insist that it must be perceived primarily as a matter of class divisions. The Soviet view is that the American Negro problem is essentially a manifestation of fundamental contradictions of state-monopolistic capitalism. Racism is seen as having arisen as a justification for slavery, with the idea of innate inferiority surviving slavery because capitalism creates inequalities which reinforce racist ideology. The urbanization patterns which have created black ghettos, for instance, present the misleading illusion that the problem is racial, while it is really the Negro's status as part of the lower class, not his color, that explains his plight.

The practical implication of this line of reasoning is that the Negro should shape his struggle along class lines in close unity with poor whites. For this reason, Soviet scholars have praise for Martin Luther King, Jr., and W. E. B. Du Bois, who in different ways supported combined mass struggle. One Soviet author quotes King's statement that the slogan "black power," which gained prominence in the 1960s, should have been "power to the poor."[22] By the same token, black nationalists in the tradition of Marcus Garvey and Pan-Africanists of recent years, such as Imamu Amiri Baraka (Leroi Jones) and Stokely Carmichael (Sekou Touré) are strongly denounced. Their main fault in Soviet eyes lies in trusting nationalism rather than scientific social laws to fulfill the aspirations of the black masses.

In discussing black nationalist groups, Soviet critics have singled out the Nation of Islam, the so-called "Black Muslims," for special assault. Even more objectionable than the religious nature of the movement under Elijah Muhammad was its racist ideology. With the exception of the course taken by Malcolm X in his final years, Soviets have charged the Muslims with promoting passivity rather than political activity through their belief in the inevitable destruction of the established order. This movement's leaders have also been characterized as black bourgeoisie who cannot compete in the open market with monopoly capitalism and therefore attempt to make the black community their captive market.[23]

It is interesting to consider current Soviet thought on black nationalism against the background of earlier communist positions. Somewhat surprisingly, Soviet scholars never do; and, in fact, some current Soviet authors seem unaware of earlier official views. For instance, one work finds black nationalism to be reverse discrimination, the same charge critics made against the now defunct communist doctrine of "self-determination in the black belt." Another work calls black nationalists twentieth century "Uncle Toms" for advocating separate institutions.[24] Those who demand an autonomous region within the United States are described as the worst of all. The basic drawback of nationalism in the Soviet view is that it is static and conservative rather than social and revolutionary. Communist theorists apparently feel, therefore, that the kinds of concessions that were made to nationalist sentiment in the 1920s and 1930s can no longer be afforded.

Nevertheless, there is tacit admission that black nationalism is radical in one sense: it is perceived as radical in the black ghetto and thus helps to raise political consciousness. Soviet writers attribute a similar positive function to the Black Panther Party. This organization was generally viewed as the most hopeful of all those that have been spawned by the Negro liberation struggle, primarily because the Panther leaders at least espoused Marxist theory. However, their Marxism is adjudged to have been inadequate because it contained elements of the romantic and the anarchistic and borrowed piecemeal from Marxist principles to suit the needs perceived by the Panthers. Soviet objections are provoked in part by the attraction of some of the black Marxists to the writings of Mao Tse-tung and other sources besides Marx and Lenin. The Panthers' turn in the 1970s toward alliance with black business and churches, and involvement in electoral politics, was seen as proof of their inability to formulate a strong practical revolutionary program.[25]

In the face of such sweeping Soviet criticism of the dominant trends in the existing Negro struggle for recognition of full manhood, one would expect an equally comprehensive prescription for such leaders in the struggle to follow. The essence of the Soviet advice is that the Negro protest movement should follow the lead of the American Communist Party. However, it remains unclear how that party is now to gain the allegiance of the Negro masses that has, thus far, eluded it. There is no new Soviet guidance showing how Negroes are to be convinced that disadvantages they experience in American society stem from class rather than color. Furthermore, there is still disagreement among communists as to the exact status of the Negro as a group in American society.

Some communists allow that the analogy comparing the American Negro situation with a colony is appropriate, given a proven measure of social, economic, and political exclusion of Negroes from leadership roles. Others insist that the Negro struggle in the United States is a peculiar form, not to be likened to liberation movements in Asia, Africa, and Latin America. One Soviet study contends that it has been the growing consciousness of being an integral part of the American nation that explains the intensification, in the last two decades, of Negro demands for full rights.[26]

Meanwhile, a kind of symbiotic relationship that has long existed between Soviet Marxist theory and the general Negro movement continues. The depressed social status and social composition of the Negro population in the United States make it an ideal target for Soviet interest. Consider, for example, the fact that 90 percent of the Negro population falls into the Soviet definition of the worker class; and, as recently as 1985, more than 20 percent of that population was involuntarily unemployed. The National Urban League estimated the level of unemployment in 1984 at 33 percent. In addition, the conspicuous location of this large group of Negroes within the world's leading capitalist society, makes it a small wonder that Soviet theorists would recognize the potential of this group as a universal symbol and model of the manifestation of revolutionary socialist principles—if only it could be brought to evolve along the appropriate path.

More immediately, Soviet championing of the Negro cause, as well as other liberation struggles on an international scale, has enhanced Russia's image, especially in Africa. The Negro cause has, therefore, been useful regardless of how it has turned out. This point also reveals how the Negro struggle has benefitted from its association with Soviet social and political theory. Soviet interest has also been a constant buttress for the Negro movement by providing it an international forum. The consequent pressure on the United States government has been one of the main determinants of the political and economic gains Negroes have made in recent decades. The Communist Party, through actions (such as its role in the Scottsboro case), helped give an edge and a scope to Negro protest which the black community alone could never have achieved. Even allowing for periods when anti-American propaganda in the Soviet Union was curtailed for political expediency, Soviet vigilance has consistently assured a worldwide audience for any significant adverse development concerning the condition of the Negro in the United States.

Soviet theory regarding the Negro has been erroneous in many particulars and unclear in others. However, much like Du Bois and other pioneer Negro Pan-Africanist thinkers, Soviet theorists had the prescience to anticipate that the American Negro movement was international in many respects. They knew that American Negroes could be instrumental in generating black leadership in Africa, although they perhaps did not foresee the tremendous impact the emergence of black African nations would have on the consciousness of Negro Americans. In any case, the main point here is that such interrelatedness was recognized. Therefore, the Soviet theory in question is more valuable because of its effort to show such relationships than in any specific demonstration of the validity of Marxian historical laws.

CHAPTER NINE

THE USSR
AND
BLACK AFRICA

Soviet interest in black Africa has reflected a considerable degree of continuity with the former tsarist policies and attitudes. This is to be expected given the close territorial identity and inherently similar geopolitical circumstances faced by the two otherwise contrasting Russian regimes. However, both the objectives and activities of the Soviet government in Africa have been far more extensive than those of its tsarist predecessor. The ultimate Soviet aim is to facilitate the revolutionary role that Africa is to play in the universal defeat of capitalism. The primary method for achieving this goal has been to exploit strong African nationalist sentiment in order to weaken the colonial powers. In this approach clear parallels with the Comintern policies in America are evident, including the dilemma of how to reconcile nationalism and communism. Discussion in the previous chapter of Soviet deliberations on the Negro question has shown that resolutions at the Fourth and Sixth Comintern Congresses provided the main policy definition on this subject. These deliberations were aimed at Africa as well as America. However, Russian observers had a clearer understanding of the African situation than they did the American.

The history of Russian involvement in Africa, which included efforts to limit the imperialist endeavors of other European powers, provided a tradition and a literature from which to draw perspective. In addition, the Soviet leadership bore a certain justified siege mentality as it emerged from the Russian Civil War and from the Allied intervention in the early 1920s. Consequently, as mentioned previously, one of the Soviet Union's chief concerns was the potential use of Negro troops against it, as the French had done in one instance during the Civil War. This threatened a dreadful distortion of class lines in lieu of the anticipated Marxist revolutionary upheaval. It, therefore, became particularly urgent that the African masses be won over to the communist cause.

In this same setting, Soviet leaders also evinced a fleeting interest in the Garvey movement and in the budding Pan-African movement, both of which featured radical demands consistent with Soviet doctrine and were international in scope. However, the tendencies which Moscow favored in these movements were not the ones which predominated as the movements further evolved. More precisely, black nationalism proved to be too strong for Soviet appetites.

Official denunciation of Garveyism surfaced at the Sixth Comintern Congress in 1928. The movement was criticized as a utopian Zionism which would damage the cause of world revolution by advocating removal of American Negroes from their location in American society where they could be a most effective disruptive force. However, this same congress then signalled its acknowledgment of the power of nationalism by proposing that independent Negro republics be established in South Africa and in the southern United States. This proposal, which had no practical foundation in either continent, apparently grew out of the concept of union republics adopted in Russia to solve the nationalities problem on her own soil. This measure caused factionalism to emerge within the American and South African Communist parties and practically destroyed the latter. Part of the difficulty here was that the white membership feared black domination of the party.[1]

While the proposals for Negro republics in the United States and South Africa are similarly utopian, significant differences between them should not be ignored. Moreover, although the idea of such a republic in South Africa was equally as impracticable as a separate Negro republic in America, the former was a more practical idea. The Negro peoples of South Africa, unlike their American counterparts, constitute an overwhelming majority of the population and, at least in their historical memories, had previously experienced political, social, and economic organization independent of the colonialist powers. Furthermore, the manifest power of nationalism, as witnessed in Europe's previous hundred years, suggested that Africans could achieve some form of independence in the foreseeable future. Against the varied array of independent African states, which did eventually emerge, the Soviet proposals do not appear so far-fetched.

The most crucial practical problem confronting Soviet leaders with regard to the African situation was the same one they faced in America: identification and recruitment of Negro leaders. It was all very well to embrace in Moscow Lenin's observation that countries with a proletarian dictatorship might directly aid non-industrialized societies toward socialism. It was yet another matter to expect Africans to trust leaders whose skin color they identified with their colonial oppressors. Black leadership was all the more imperative given the preponderance of the Negro population. This factor also meant that the appeal for black and white unity, so prominent in the American strategy, was subordinated to nationalism, which clearly had a stronger basis for a real mass movement.

Since the global scenario suggested to Soviet theorists that the American Negro was a more advanced group than the African in terms of revolutionary consciousness, the direct use of American blacks in leadership positions in Africa still seemed plausible to the Soviets. And, indeed, the example of George Padmore's activities proved that such intervention could be very effective, with or without Soviet backing. On the other hand, it must be noted that at the very moment it elevated Padmore to prominence in 1929, Comintern announced its shift away from the notion that American Negroes would be the vanguard of revolution in Africa. Thus, it was already clear to Soviet leaders by the time of Comintern's Hamburg Conference of Negro Workers in 1930 that they must rely upon African Negroes to lead their own revolution in Africa.

Padmore was, nevertheless, a pivotal figure for the Soviet policy, for what he symbolized as well as for what he did. He and James Ford played guiding roles in the formation of the International Trade Union Committee of Negro Workers, which became the most important formal agency for promoting revolution among Negro populations around the world. Even though Padmore did not enjoy field grade rank in the Red Army, nor command hundreds of secret agents, as one source contends, his influence was considerable.[2] Ranging from his office in the Kremlin, to travels to Western Europe, and secret trips to Africa, Padmore established contacts which proved vital to Moscow's ties both with African events generally and, more importantly, with the budding African liberation movements.

With respect to Comintern's objectives in Africa, it is significant that there were more African than American Negro leaders present at the Hamburg conference. Among those in attendance were Jomo Kenyatta of Kenya, E. F. Small of Gambia, and I. T. A. Wallace-Johnson of Sierra Leone. After the conference, several of the Africans accompanied Padmore to Moscow to attend the Fifth Congress of the Red International Labor Union. Soviet access to African leaders had been facilitated by Comintern's virtual control of the League Against

Imperialism, which had been formed at the World Anti-Colonial Conference held in Brussels in 1927. The calling of the conference itself had been instigated in part by Comintern, working through the German communists who organized the conference, and it had attracted an impressive representation from black Africa among a sizeable Third World contingent. One prominent figure at the conference sessions was Lamine Senghor, a leading West African nationalist, who died in November 1927 after a brief imprisonment by the French upon returning home. The Soviet support given the League Against Imperialism is another illustration of Soviet acknowledgement of the necessity of a role for nationalism. Another non-communist organization aiding Soviet efforts in Africa was the nationalistic, Paris-based League for the Defense of the Negro Race, which showed kinship to the Garvey movement and existed under various other names in the 1920s and 1930s. The league was a chronic source of discomfort for French authorities in colonial Africa. The Negro Welfare Association based in London similarly plagued the British. Despite the Soviet concession to nationalism, another problem the communists faced in Africa as well as in America, was the need to rely heavily on the Negro bourgeoisie for leadership rather than on the black masses. The key black spokesmen turned out to be those educated in European culture, often in Europe. This fact, in part, dictated the tactics employed by communists involved in the liberation movements.[3]

The main tactic Comintern implemented through its various agencies was literary propaganda. This meant not only disseminating Comintern's newspapers and pamphlets for its organizations such as Padmore's Committee of Negro Workers, but also providing funds for distributing periodicals such as the League for the Defense of the Negro Race's *La Voix des Negres* (Voice of the Negro), labor union materials, and political flyers. For non-communist organizations, the Soviet leadership did all it could to shape the views of the leaders, including, on occasion, provision of financial support. The period during the late 1920s and early 1930s was a very favorable one for this tactic. The depression deeply affected the great colonial powers and, therefore, their African holdings. Meanwhile the Soviet Union, not yet as embroiled in the world economy, could not only decry the ills of capitalism, but hold itself up as a shining example the African peoples should seek to emulate when they built their independent states. To this end, the Soviet leaders were able to use even the racial incident involving Robert Robinson and the three white American workers to glorify the Soviet attitude against racism.

Scholars who have argued that Soviet policy toward black Africa during this period was based on expediency dictated by current Soviet needs have compelling evidence for their case. Until the mid-1930s the effects of the German-Russian accord, signalled by the Treaty of Rapallo, were felt in Africa, as former German colonies were spared the critical attention the French and British colonialists received from the Soviets. In a dramatic turnabout in the mid-1930s, Germany came to be considered the major threat to the interests of world communism, and the Soviet Union decided to cooperate with England and France in common opposition to Germany's new fascist regime. This new stance became official doctrine at the Seventh Comintern Congress in 1935.

The most conclusive evidence that the new stance signalled a change in the struggle against African colonialism was George Padmore's involuntary departure from the party. Also, the International Trade Union Committee of Negro Workers, Comintern's main executive agency in this area, was temporarily disbanded. Padmore made it clear on more than one occasion that the main reason for his treatment by the Soviets was his insistent emphasis on the struggle against colonialism. This position was not consistent with the new, moderate Soviet approach. For Negroes around the world, yet further doubt was cast on the status of anti-colonialism among Soviet priorities when the Soviet Union, despite its vigorous vocal support for Ethiopia against invasion by racist Italy, sold fuels to Italy. The Nazi-Soviet pact in 1939 could, of course, only make the situation all the more uncertain. And, indeed, documents now available show that Soviet discussions with Germany, concerning spheres of influence, included the partitioning of Africa. In these talks, Soviet spokesmen were willing to agree to Hitler's control of Central Africa and Mussolini's territorial ambitions in the north and northeast, in exchange for support of Soviet aspirations in the Indian Ocean.[4]

In the years just preceding the war, the apparent break which these developments showed in the Soviet commitment to the creation of independent black African states is perhaps the main reason for the general false impression held that Soviet involvement in Africa began only after the war. This situation was prolonged during the war by the necessity of Soviet alliance with the other great powers. The Russians also participated in the various summit conferences which attempted to design the postwar globe. Finally, owing to the nature of the new Soviet involvement in world affairs, Comintern became one of the war's casualties. This, in effect, removed what had been the main vehicle for Soviet activities in Africa.

When in the 1950s the Soviet Union again directed concerted attention to black Africa, it found that the liberation movements had progressed even further along their strongly nationalistic lines. Now, it was the Soviet leadership's turn to accuse black African leaders of collaborating with colonial regimes because, in some cases, they entered into electoral politics and became involved with non-communist parties.[5] On the other hand, the Soviet leaders could have taken some satisfaction in the earlier contributions they had made and upon which the black leaders had continued to build. For example, Soviet encouragement of the Africans to promote their political interests through organized labor had been highly beneficial.[6] Continuity with what Comintern had initiated was also manifested in the presence and wide-ranging influence of George Padmore, the communist outcast who had become almost legendary on his own through continuing what he had begun under Comintern. When Ghana became independent in 1957, it was a fitting tribute that he became an official adviser in the government of his former protege, Kwame Nkrumah.

However, although the considerable Soviet contribution to the African liberation movements was appreciated by Africans despite the suspicious Soviet behavior in the late 1930s and 1940s, the Africans correctly felt that they were winning their liberation themselves. Therefore, when the Soviet Union approached Africa in this new era of independence, it was still as an outsider, albeit without the stigma of having been one of the colonial powers, who, at the time, were being ousted. The first step toward insuring that communism would have a dominant influence in the emerging free Africa would be the establishment of positive relations with the new independent states while continuing to support those liberation struggles still in progress. Heads of African states now visited the Soviet Union frequently and were accorded the appropriate official formalities. Even leaders of liberation movements not yet in power were warmly welcomed. At the Twenty-fourth Communist Party Congress in 1971, for example, the Guinean leader Amilcar Cabral spoke, as did Agostinho Neto of the Popular Movement for the Liberation of Angola. There were also delegations from the Mozambique Liberation Front and other African revolutionary parties. It is significant that such full recognition of the importance of black Africa did not occur in the United States (the other principal exponent of universal democracy) until the late 1970s.

At the beginning of 1956, Ethiopia was the only black African country with which the Soviet Union had diplomatic ties. By 1966 there were twenty-five, and the number has continued to grow. The approach chosen to establish these connections has followed the same pattern that had been set during the entire century of Russian ties with Africa: The Soviet Union offered technical assistance in exchange for goodwill and the hope of future communist allies in world affairs. The impact of this strategy became ever broader under Leonid Brezhnev, as Soviet surrogates from the Warsaw Pact, Cuba, and North Korea, also provided aid to African states. By the end of the 1970s, non-military advisory personnel sent to sub-Saharan Africa was estimated by United States intelligence to number around eight thousand. At

Kwame Nkrumah, who once considered the Soviet political structure as a model for West Africa. (Courtesy Moorland-Spingarn Research Center, Howard University)

the same time, there were probably over forty thousand Cuban and ten thousand Russian military personnel there. In the period from 1955 to 1978, an estimated ten thousand Africans, mainly from Somalia, Tanzania, and Ethiopia,[7] were trained in the Russian military system.

One of the main forms of assistance to Africa has been in the area of education.[8] This aspect of Soviet policy deserves special attention for two reasons. It has brought thousands of black Africans to the Soviet Union for periods of up to six years and it has, incidentally, led to allegations that racism has manifested itself in the Soviet Union against the Africans. While the attendance of foreign students from

"The Colonizers: He isn't yet mature enough for independence." Reprinted from *Krokodil*, 30 July 1960.

"They have him surrounded." Reprinted from *Krokodil*, 10 April 1962.

communist countries at Soviet universities began soon after World War II, Asian, African, and Latin American countries joined the program only in 1958. The political schools founded in the 1920s had not survived Stalin's regime. Most of the students were now attending regular Soviet universities. Meanwhile, on the international plane, Africa was becoming the main area of concentration for all communist countries promoting educational and cultural exchange. The formation of the Africa Institute in 1959 was an indication of this new interest within the Soviet Union.

The creation of this special institute within the Academy of Sciences

"Entrance for colored—This is the way the American racists wanted the entrance to the UN to look." Reprinted from *Izvestiia*, 15 October 1960.

demonstrated the Soviet awareness that Russia needed to learn more about this part of the world if she was to succeed in gaining dominant influence there. Soviet leaders, therefore, drew upon the tradition of African studies which extended back to tsarist times and adapted it to new purposes. African language studies had experienced especially strong continuity. N. V. Yushmanov had taught Ethiopian linguistics and Hausa at Leningrad University as early as the 1930s. In the same era, D. A. Ol'derogge taught Swahili and Zulu there. Ivan Potekhin, the first director of the Africa Institute, studied Swahili under Ol'derogge while completing his studies in social anthropology. These two scholars combined efforts to edit an ethnographic survey, *Narody Afriki* (Peoples of Africa), published in 1954, which outlined the basic Soviet approach toward Africa in the Cold War era. It was directed against both colonial rule and "bourgeois" scholarship, which characterized African culture

"They (Mobutu, Tshombe) are coming into power (Congo sovereignty trampled underfoot)." Reprinted from *Krokodil*, 10 October 1960.

as inherently inferior. In this, the Soviet position was a step ahead of Western scholarship, which at times stated explicitly that Africa had no history. However, while subjecting African history to the same Marxist analysis by which they scrutinized all other history, communist leaders still failed to offer Africans a picture or plan consistent with African perceptions of reality. The Africa Institute was far more successful within the Soviet Union, training many more specialists and spreading the awareness of Africa among the general public. The latter is facilitated by the fact that, more than in the West, Soviet scientific scholarship has been systematically published for a popular audience as well as for scholars.[9]

Taking stock of the new world situation, and the irrelevancy of ideology to some of the African settings, the Soviet leadership shifted priority away from the training of communist cadres to the preparation of leaders for non-communist organizations, such as trade unions, student agencies, and professional academies. Toward that end, for example, trade union schools for Asians, Africans, and Latin Americans were founded both in Soviet bloc nations and in Africa. However, the main institution founded to advance this new approach was the Friendship University established in Moscow in 1960. The initial enrollment in 1961 showed the largest number of students (191) to be from Latin America. The region next most represented was Africa with 140.[10] The emphasis placed on black Africa became evident not only in the composition of the student body, but also in the university's name change in 1961 to Patrice Lumumba University, in honor of the slain Congolese leader.

The course descriptions and admission requirements for the university, announced in 1960, reveal why the new Soviet education program became very popular for students from the developing nations. The subjects in the curriculum included engineering, agriculture, medicine, mathematics, physics, chemistry, biology, economics, law, history, literature, and Russian language. The course of study in medical training lasted five years; it spanned four years for all other fields. Anyone under thirty-five years of age was eligible for admission regardless of sex, race, nationality, or religious conviction. Students from Asia, Africa, and Latin America were invited to submit applications either directly to the university or through Soviet embassies or consulates abroad. Those having less than a high school level of preparation might be admitted into a special preparatory program for up to three years of preliminary training. All students lacking a knowledge of Russian would be so enrolled for up to a year.

The government assumed all the student's educational expenses, including housing and medical care. In addition, it paid for the student's travel from home to Russia and back, provided a monthly stipend for living costs, and financed an annual vacation. Under such terms it is not surprising that, between 1961 and 1966, the number of university students from African countries in the Soviet Union increased six-fold to about four thousand students, with the largest contingent at Lumumba University. In 1960 alone there were over forty-three thousand applicants for the five hundred slots available. By way of comparison, it can be noted that this number of African students was still lower than the number studying in the United States, and was not even half the number in Britain and France. As foreign students in the Soviet Union began to number in the thousands, they were placed in various schools and institutes throughout the country according to their planned fields of specialization. At the same time, the program grew to include students who received scholarships provided by their own governments and who were partially aided by the USSR. However, mainly those who attended Lumumba University were directly and principally funded by the Soviet government.

The new Soviet policy appeared to be progressing well until an incident occurred in 1963 which was highly unusual in the Soviet Union and which jeopardized the program's reputation. It began with the mysterious death of a twenty-nine-year-old Ghanaian medical student, Edmond Asare-Addao, who was found dead near a train track on the outskirts of Moscow in sub-zero weather. African students who knew him claimed that he had been murdered by Russians who objected to his proposed marriage to a Russian woman. Soviet authorities conjectured that he had been drinking and that he had collapsed and frozen to death. In response, about five hundred African students scuffled with police in staging the first mass protest in Red Square since the late 1920s when Trotsky's supporters had objected to his removal from leadership status. Among the placards carried by Africans was one that read, "Moscow, a second Alabama," and another which said, "Friend today, devil tomorrow." The march ended when a delegation of students was received by the minister of higher education. The students demanded investigation of Asare-Addao's death and expressed general complaints about racial hostility from Russians.[11]

This episode turned out not to be totally unique. In fact, already in 1960, a group of Somalis abandoned their studies in Moscow because, they alleged, "the Russians consider us an inferior race and treated us accordingly."[12] In April 1965 in Baku, the unexplained death of another African student led to protest and the departure of some students when their requests to be moved to another university were refused. Most of these students were Kenyans. They complained of intolerable race discrimination, and some said they had been attacked by gangs. Baku has continued to carry rumors of mysterious African deaths. In November 1969 a Kenyan student was found murdered in Kiev, and the Kenyan *Daily Nation* reported on November 22d that other Africans in Kiev went on strike demanding more personal security. Yet *Newsweek* reported another such death in its issue of September 16, 1985.

Similar ripples of discontent surfaced in Czechoslovakia and Bulgaria, where other sizeable communities of African students existed. About seventy Africans left Bulgaria in 1965 complaining of racial discrimination and segregation. One recurrent issue in the 1960s among the African students there was the refusal of the authorities to allow African students to form their own separate union.[13] There was a similar demand involved in the 1963 protest in Moscow. However, since the 1970s the authorities have been more responsive to such requests from the students.

Through occasions such as the social depicted here, the Soviet government has sought to convince African students that there is no racial discrimination in Russia. (SOVFOTO)

African students have published numerous accounts of their experiences in the Soviet Union. If we keep in mind that most of those who published were those who had negative experiences, an examination of some of these writings can provide the basis for a better understanding of an ostensibly racial problem. One such writer was Michel Ayih-Dosseh from Togo, who studied at Moscow University from 1958 to 1960. One of the first ten Africans to study at Moscow University, he came with positive preconceptions, but he left bitterly disillusioned, complaining of racism, injustice, and a lack of freedom. He was sent home after two years, having been a leader in an African students organization of which the government did not approve. According to him, the organization was prohibited because it was organized on a regional basis. While the government permitted organizations defined by country, there was only one country with more than two students there at the time. In 1961 Ayih-Dosseh published a warning to other Africans that communism in practice was not consistent with its theory and cautioned against choosing the Soviet Union as a model.[14]

Another student in this same group was Andrew Amar from Uganda. Amar had initially gone to Russia on his own, without a scholarship.

He noted that the Soviet government gave preference to students applying directly from their native countries, without having visited any other Western countries. Amar had been studying in England from 1957 to 1959 and had been active there in an African students' organization. After some early bureaucratic difficulties, he was eventually admitted to Moscow University, and, curiously, without ever filling out any forms. Furthermore, he was granted one of the regular nine-hundred rouble-per-month scholarships and an extra winter clothing allowance. Russian students, who received only about a third as much as the foreigners, were resentful. Most African students in Moscow at the time lived in the Russian Language Institute. Each dormitory room included at least two Russians. A major grievance for Amar was that he felt the African students were used by the Soviet government for political purposes. He recounted that the Africans were ordered to greet Krushchev's motorcade whenever he was returning home from some state visit. Then the whole scene would be photographed. Amar left the Soviet Union in the summer of 1960 and resumed his studies in England.[15]

Another member of this first group of African students left the most detailed account of what they experienced. Everest Mulekezi and a cousin had travelled all the way from their native Uganda to Cairo seeking access to an education. There they were enthralled by a Soviet embassy official's description of the new program, promising in addition to everything else a free trip home every other year. Mulekezi had once been offered a one-year scholarship at an American university, but was denied a passport by British officials because he lacked the money for travel.

Upon arrival in Moscow, Mulekezi was surprised to discover that the thousand or so foreign students were housed a mile away from the university, separate from the main student body, although they had Russian roommates. He was also disturbed to find that their five-story dorms had guards at the doors and that all students were required to show passes in order to enter the dorms and the campus. This practice also restricted their contacts with Russians they might meet outside the university. Mulekezi generally had a favorable impression of the Russian people, finding them among the friendliest he had ever met. However, he also recalled racial incidents, including intimidation and beatings.

Meanwhile, he quickly concluded that the educational program was a ruse and that he and the other Africans were being used as "stooges." He described one celebration of "Uganda Day," where:

> In our name a stranger called for a vote on a resolution demanding immediate independence for Uganda, serverance of all ties with Great Britain, and alliances of friendship with the Soviets. Before we could open our mouths, a roar of approval went up. Cameras snapped as the

Russian actors gathered around to congratulate us on our "action." Tape
recordings were made for broadcasts to be beamed back home. Suddenly
it was over, and we Ugandans were left dumfounded and angry.[16]

There were similar fetes held for Nigeria, Guinea, and the other African
states, as well as an "All-Africa Day." In Mulekezi's opinion, most of
the black African students there at the time were anti-Soviet. The
pressures placed upon them, both in the classroom and outside, served
only to harden their negative reactions. Hence their efforts to organize
their own student union against government wishes. They also enraged
the authorities by attracting Russian students to jazz music, which
was considered decadent by official Soviet standards, and by engaging
the Russians in long discussions, which included much anti-Soviet
debate.

Mulekezi surmised that the decisive development precipitating his
departure from the Soviet Union was the government's decision to
open Friendship University. The students were under the impression
that it would be for foreigners only; they objected to this as harmful
segregation. The black students' union appointed one of their own,
Stanley Okullo from Uganda, to write a letter to the Ministry of Higher
Education protesting the discrimination they had suffered. Okullo was
thereupon expelled from the Soviet Union for "immorality, drunken-
ness, and joining the imperialist camp." This led Ayih-Dosseh, Amar,
Mulekezi, and other members of their union to leave Russia. Mulekezi,
studying at an American university a year later, estimated that there
were about one hundred African students who had also left Moscow
and were wandering in Europe, not as fortunate as he in finding a way
to continue their education.

One student who studied in a city other than Moscow, Nicholas
Nyangira, encapsuled his impressions in the title of an article appearing
in the New York Times Magazine on May 16, 1965, "Africans Don't
Go to Russian to Be Brainwashed." Nyangira was one of twenty-nine
Kenyans sent home before finishing their courses, following the
protests which were mounted in the wake of the unexplained African
death in Baku, capital of the Azerbaijan Soviet Republic, in April 1965.
After his registration and receipt of a passport in Moscow, Nyangira
had been sent to Baku. He recalled being disappointed by what appeared
to be slum conditions there, accompanied by a scarcity and poor
quality of food. This Caspian Sea port with its majority Azerbaijani
population was quite different from European Russia. The stipend in
Baku was eighty roubles per month, a sum he found to be inadequate.
However, he noted that the average Soviet citizen was paid only
seventy roubles per month.

Although the Africans were welcomed by a large Komsomol gathering upon their arrival in Baku, they soon encountered great hostility.

They were refused service by restaurants and taxis. They noticed that Russian men were cruel to Russian women seen talking to Africans. On occasion, local youth would attack Africans with bottles and stones, and officials would take no action on African complaints. Nyangira added, however, that the Russians were somewhat friendlier than the Azerbaijanis.

Nyangira also found the quality of education deplorable. He said that *Pravda* was the textbook for language study and the technique featured much rote learning. Also, sixteen to eighteen hours per week of Marxism-Leninism was mandatory. Nyangira incurred the ill will of Komsomol by refusing to make certain anti-imperialist speeches. Lectures were often preempted by "spontaneous" demonstrations, that is, except the lectures on Marxism-Leninism. Nyangira also complained that in some cases students with five years of education were grouped with others with twelve; both would presumably be trained as doctors or engineers in another four or five years. Some of the African students soon concluded that their training in Baku was strictly indoctrination. They began to protest by boycotting lectures. They were then refused contact with their embassy and at times found their mail had been read or seized. They were eventually expelled and sent home, rather than to another Soviet city as they requested.

These personal accounts are fairly representative of the type of publicity this Soviet policy received abroad during its beginning phase in the early 1960s. Numerous articles on the subject can be found, for example, in the *New York Times* from 1960 through 1963. The picture that emerges is that of a program which featured both special, favorable treatment of African students and very real encounters with racist attitudes in the Soviet Union. Displaying their passionate desire for education, hundreds of African youths travelled hundreds of miles, sometimes on foot, to make contact with the Soviet orbit, often leaving their native region illegally. Notwithstanding the legitimacy of the complaints such as those enumerated here, the majority of the students apparently achieved their educational objectives in Russia. What is less clear, however, is whether they returned home afterwards and whether their having been trained in the Soviet Union worked to Soviet advantage. Their Soviet academic credentials appear to be respected in the socialist states, but are a liability in pro-Western regimes. There is, of course, no complete answer to these questions at present, since the training program and the process of state formation in Africa are still in progress. There are now approximately six thousand graduate and undergraduate students at Lumumba University, with the largest contingent from Africa. Each year, six thousand more apply for seven hundred available openings.[17] Several thousand other foreign students continue to study at other Soviet institutions.

Meanwhile, the presence and nature of whatever racism there is in the Soviet Union continues to raise important questions for the future of Soviet links with black Africa. In response, Soviet leaders mounted a concerted effort to erase the effects of the events of 1963. In 1965, a new campus was opened for Lumumba University in a different part of Moscow where there was no prior contact with foreigners. African student unions organized in accordance with nationality also became acceptable. African protests against indoctrination at the expense of their regular education have apparently ceased. It is not clear how many other measures were taken. Some success is evident in that there have been few incidents since 1965 suggesting significant African discontent in the Soviet Union. However, the foreign press continues periodically to detail some cases. For example, the *Washington Post's Potomac* magazine in January 1976 cited an occasion when African students in Kiev rioted after the Czech government withdrew a scholarship from a Czech woman when she married a Nigerian.[18]

Considering the relatively stable situation that has been achieved regarding what seemed to be such a volatile racial issue in 1963, it would appear that only part of what the Africans complained of could truly be attributable to racism. A large part of what occurred was a result of a clash between the expectations of the Africans and the Russians from the program. There was, of course, an element of cultural shock on both sides.[19] This was especially true of the Russian public, which had not been prepared in any way for the African presence and usually found the Africans inconsistent with their preconceptions. This may help explain why the Africans in the south of Russia, further away from the outside world, and among the non-European nationalities, encountered more hostility. Instead of the primitives they anticipated, the Russians encountered Africans who were often more sophisticated in Western dress and manner than they. Moreover, rather than being humble and grateful toward their Soviet hosts, some were arrogant, even belligerent in their insistence on being allowed the freedoms they thought appropriate. For their part, the Africans had already had some exposure to Europeans. However, they entered the Soviet Union with no sound concept of Soviet life. Taking at face value the Soviet promise that the program had no strings attached, they accepted benefits superior to those provided most Soviet citizens and then had the temerity to make even further demands.

It would seem that this circumstance was the basic cause of the antagonism which developed between the general Soviet public and the African students. The Soviet government might have helped matters by explaining to the public that not all of the students were on Russian stipends. But the government preferred to boast of its generosity. The material advantages afforded the Africans continue to be a source of resentment among the Russians. That this economic factor can lead to racist attitudes is quite apparent when one considers that Russian women, as well as men, might be attracted to African students because of their larger stipends and access to foreign currencies and rare goods from abroad. Widespread resentment of a group easily identified by color can easily evolve into racist sentiment even though it may not have been racist at the outset. In any case, it would appear that such racism as exists in the Soviet Union is of the individual, rather than the systematic, variety. Racism has not been made official policy, as has historically been the case in many other countries.

However, as one African who studied for seven years in the Soviet Union observed, even the official Soviet stance may represent a dangerous flirtation with racism. In the Soviet news, entertainment media, and educational system, the oppression and misery of people of African descent around the world is highlighted. There is no coverage of great achievements by black Africans or black Americans who live in capitalist nations, for obvious ideological reasons. As a result, there is little opportunity for the Russian public to see evidence showing blacks to be their equals in intellectual ability.[20] It would seem then that the Soviet public is conditioned more toward pity than respect for their African brothers and sisters. Firmly cautioned against the evils of racism, the Soviet public may inadvertently be led to believe in a false inferiority. When the factor of skin color is part of this equation, racism is inescapable. Those inclined toward racial biases, buoyed by the usual skepticism the public has for official pronouncements, will find it all the easier to denigrate the darker races.

Andrea Lee, a black American who accompanied her husband during his ten months as an exchange student in Russia in 1978–79, elicited the following comment from an Ethiopian she met:

> Most of my African classmates hate it here because of the climate, because we live here under miserable conditions, and because the Russian *narod*, the masses, call us black devils and spit at us in the streets.[21]

Lee was apparently not recognized as black by Russians because of her light complexion. She was, therefore, privy to the most candid expressions of racial attitudes by Russians. She observed several clear signs that strong negative racial feelings toward blacks as well as other non-Russian nationalities persist in Soviet society.[22]

The issue of racism is by no means merely academic for Soviet interests. It has particular significance owing to the rivalry between the USSR and China for influence in Africa.[23] That the Chinese are themselves colored enhances still further the appeal they already have in African eyes for being non-Western and former victims of Western colonialism. However, even the hint of Soviet racism would be disastrous for Soviet objectives in the so-called Third World in general, and in American Negro communities in particular.

The resilience of the Soviet role in black Africa can be explained largely in terms of its diversity. As the years have passed, that role has evolved to combine diplomatic ties, trade, military training and supply, joint economic ventures (such as fishing and communications), and scholarship aid. It is not likely that failure could occur in all of these areas at once. This lesson was perhaps learned in the 1960s, when, in a number of instances, individual leaders backed by Moscow fell, and Soviet fortunes with them.[24] While the Kremlin still may err in choosing sides in civil conflicts, as in its backing of Joshua Nkomo over the victorious Robert Mugabe in Zimbabwe, the consequences for its influence in an entire region will not be as great.

It is still too early to make a reliable assessment of Soviet achievements in black Africa. Nevertheless, a few observations concerning the pattern of developments may be instructive. In comparing the Soviet role in Africa to that in America, it seems apparent that the Kremlin's understanding of black Africa was, from the very beginning, much more sophisticated than its grasp of black America during the same period. Perhaps the most important reason for this was the greater direct contact between Russians and prominent leaders from the African Negro population than from the American.

However, this more sophisticated understanding of Africa has not led to greater certainty of Soviet success. There has been a high degree of unpredictability in the fate of Soviet efforts. The areas wherein the most effort was invested have not been those where the greatest success has been achieved; and success has often proved ephemeral. The initial Soviet choice to concentrate its critical attention on British and French colonial Africa was sound for still other reasons besides the vagaries of Russian foreign policy that have been mentioned earlier. These colonial areas had the highest degree of organized labor and a larger class of educated blacks. It was through these two channels (labor and education) that Comintern and its successors could best penetrate into Africa. However, nationalism has been so strong that it precludes dominant Soviet influence even in those emergent African states which espouse socialism, whether Leninist or some other type. They insist upon the right to develop an independent form of socialism, as characterized by Euro-communism, or by Algeria's pragmatic state capitalism. At the same time, the African socialist states see no inconsistency in borrowing their state model and material support from the East while simultaneously taking capital and technology from the West.[25]

Although some African states have maintained close ties with the Soviet Union, including long-term agreements, these relationships have proven to be tenuous.[26] The sudden break in 1977 with Somalia is a case in point. This resulted, at least in part, from the resumption of the centuries-old courtship between Russia and Ethiopia, who still possesses some of the same allurements that drew the Russian tsars to her, the foremost being her strategic location. Also, reminiscent of Eastern Orthodoxy, there is again an ideological linkage: the new military regime in Ethiopia has proclaimed itself socialist, like its Russian ally.[27]

On the whole, the Soviet experience in black Africa has shown that the communist appeal is greatest to revolutionary movements before they assume power and head a state. This explains the continued Soviet influence in Angola and Mozambique and less Soviet prominence in more stable African states. Given the many causes of unrest on the continent, this also means that the prospects are very good for continued and successful Soviet involvement, especially surrounding the intransigent, racist Union of South Africa.[28] It is very likely that much of Africa will eventually adopt some form of socialism. It is equally improbable that any will adopt the official Soviet version of communism. The Africans view socialism as a useful means of organizing and unifying on some type of national scale. However, they insist upon using or not using it only as they see fit. They appear responsive to Leopold Senghor's admonition to stay close to their own cultural roots while borrowing from modern advances.[29] Future Soviet endeavors in black Africa will have to address this reality. There is indication that they already have begun to do so. In 1979 the new director of the Africa Institute, Anatoli Gromyko, counted over a dozen "socialist-oriented" states in Africa, but admitted that existing social and economic structures prevent their immediate transition to socialism.[30]

CHAPTER TEN

THE NEGRO IN SOVIET ART

Known artists and entertainers were among the most conspicuous of the Negroes who left Russia to escape the Revolution and Civil War. However, others remained and represented a direct continuity between Negro contributions to the arts in tsarist and in Soviet society. A good example was the singer Coretta Arli-Titz. Born in Mexico in 1894 to a family of poor farm workers, she was raised in New York. She settled in Russia in 1913, after having moved to Germany to pursue an operatic career in a Negro opera company that proved to be short-lived. A number of the other Americans joined her in the move to Russia. During the Civil War, she performed in a troupe for Red Army units on the southwestern front. After the war, she furthered her musical training by studying under the composer Michael Ippolitov-Ivanov, and graduated from his Tchaikovsky studio in Moscow in 1923. Thereafter until her death in 1951, she devoted herself to concert singing and earned high critical acclaim for her fine soprano voice. She was married to Professor Boris Titz, another accomplished musician. Her repertoire encompassed Russian and Indian songs as well as distinctively Negro pieces. Among her admirers was the famous writer Maxim Gorky, who with her made an exception to his general dislike of women singers. During the Second World War, Arli-Titz was again a prominent performer for the Russian troops.[1]

Wayland Rudd, who successfully pursued his stage career in Russia after tiring of his struggle against racism in the United States. (Courtesy Moorland-Spingarn Research Center, Howard University)

Arli-Titz's career reflected both the old and the new Russia. However, more characteristic of the Negro artistic role and its effect on the general mood of Soviet society were the experiences of the American actors Wayland Rudd and Paul Robeson beginning in the early 1930s. Rudd was raised in an American orphanage from the age of nine. Later, although working at such jobs as mining and delivering messages, he developed an avid interest in the theatre and joined an amateur troupe. He became embittered upon finding that, even there, he would be relegated to menial roles. His fortunes brightened when he was noticed by Jasper Deeter, a disciple of Stanislavsky who featured Rudd in Negro lead roles in his Hedgerow Theatre in Rose Valley, Pennsylvania. Rudd received wide acclaim for his performance in Eugene O'Neill's "Emperor Jones."[2]

However, this limited success only heightened Rudd's frustration over the obstacles racism posed for his development. It was out of this frame of reference that he sailed for Russia in 1932. Reflecting upon his initial impressions two years later, during a brief visit home before moving permanently to Russia, he observed:

When I left America two years ago I was told by most of my intimate
friends that I was a fool to go away just at the time the dawn of the
Negro actor's day was breaking. I was reminded that America was
looking to the Negro to give the theatre resuscitation, and I believed it
myself. I left the Statue of Liberty behind me with strange misgiv-
ings. ... Came ... the opening of the Moscow theatre season, and I
confess that there has never been anything in my histrionic experiences
so thrilling and absorbing as the moments the theatre afforded me there
unless it is my present imagination of what the theatre in America
could be like if it were liberated as the Russian theatre is liberated. ...
The Negro has long since had something vital to give theatre but theatre
hasn't wanted it, or rather it has only wanted the "song and dance." ...
Theatre has been quite certain that its public only wanted to laugh at
the Negro, and has refused to take him seriously.[3]

Rudd's views, as noted above, were not as naive as they might
appear. He had measured his words:

There are those who have heard of the strict censorship placed upon
theatre in Russia and will arch their eyebrows at my use of the word
liberated. But the strict censorship in the Soviet theatre only gives it a
definiteness that theatre no place in the world can boast of. Fancy an
American director having a script put into his hands and being told that
the sky was his limit for production expenses and not to cut down the
cast. ... Yet that is the glorified privilege of the Russian director: to
work unhampered by expense limitations, though he must worry about
what the play says. The government which subsidizes all theatres in the
Soviet says, "we'll make up all deficits, but your plays must be healthful
to our society." Broadway Angels say: "look out for our pocketbooks,
society be d——ned." And because they were never interested in society
nor the play, nor the actor, but in their pocketbooks, the theatre in
America is almost dead. ... And when I look at the way "the Negro is
saving the American theatre" I am ashamed for both the Negro and the
theatre, because if the Negro had been awake to himself he might have
saved the theatre in America; and if American theatre had given him a
chance he might have saved it anyway.[4]

Rudd was understandably mesmerized by all the excitement of
experimentation current in the Soviet theatre at the time. Most
impressive for him was the fact that here there was an equal role for
the Negro. In his determination to gain support for the theatre, he
apparently never questioned whether governments are the best judges
of what is "healthful" for society. He also seemed to find no difficulty
in associating with opposing schools of theatre. He first worked in the
Vsevelod Meyerhold theatre and at the same time made some films.
He graduated from the Theatrical Art Institute in Moscow and then
joined the Stanislavsky Opera and Drama Theatre. (Meyerhold's approach to theatre opposed Stanislavsky's in many respects. Both had
been pioneers in experimental theatre working with the Moscow Art
Theatre founded in 1898. However, whereas Stanislavsky's approach

stressed psychological realism, Meyerhold's stressed spectacles and special effects.) Over the years Rudd played in a number of Soviet films, among them one called "Tom Sawyer." He was also a frequent lecturer on the problem of racism in the United States.

The disfavor into which the Meyerhold school fell in the 1930s did not adversely affect Rudd. Meyerhold's quarrels with the Soviet leadership led to the closing of his theatre and his arrest in 1939. He died in a concentration camp. After the German invasion of Russia, Rudd enlisted in a theatre company which performed at the front lines. Returning to Moscow after the war, he resumed his stage career. He was outstanding in the role of Othello and became the first Negro actor to play it in Russian. During this period, he also headed a drama company and did some directing. One of the company's plays was "Deep are the Roots," in which Rudd played a Negro war veteran grappling with racism in the United States. Rudd died in Moscow in 1952.

THE IMPACT OF PAUL ROBESON

In spite of the fact that he never actually lived there, the Negro artist who has made by far the greatest impact on Soviet society was the gentle giant Paul Robeson. Robeson's experience in Russia is an example of the most obvious proof that the significance of the Negro in Russian history and thought cannot be measured merely in terms of the Negro population as a whole. Yet another son of a former slave, Robeson was born in 1898 in Princeton, New Jersey, and, like the other "pilgrims" to Russia, he had battled racism throughout his life. As a student at Rutgers University, he already showed great potential, having surmounted formidable obstacles to become a Phi Beta Kappa and a football All-American. He later earned a law degree at Columbia University.

Robeson's serious interest in the Soviet Union dated from the time he began his acting and singing career in New York. In addition to his friendship with William Patterson, in theatrical circles he found a number of radical thinkers. John Reed's *Ten Days that Shook the World* was a much discussed and influential work among Robeson and his contemporaries. Many Americans were fascinated by this sympathetic eyewitness account of an early phase of the Russian Revolution. In the late 1920s in England, Robeson further developed his own social thought. Singing his favorite folksongs in Wales, he discovered the close similarity between the aspirations of the workers there and those of the Negro in America. This convinced him that the struggle for human rights had to be universal.

Paul Robeson in stage garb. (Courtesy Moorland-Spingarn Research Center, Howard University)

From the time of his first visit to the Soviet Union, Robeson was seemingly enchanted by it. In fact, he may have predisposed himself to have a favorable impression of Russia even before the visit. According to one report, while residing in London, Robeson was invited to come to Moscow to sing the lead role in the opera "Boris Godunov."[5] In a 1931 interview in London, Robeson said of his current study of Russian culture:

> I found at once that the language and the music seem to suit my voice, and I think there is a psychological explanation. There is a kinship between the Russians and the Negroes. They were both serfs, and in the music there is the same note of melancholy touched with mysticism. I

have heard most of the great Russian singers on the gramophone, and have occasionally found whole phrases that could be matched in Negro melodies. . . .[6]

Other newspapers avidly pursued his further comments on this topic. For example:

Isn't it strange that while I can interpret Moussorgsky and other great Russian composers so as to move a Russian audience to tears I never could feel and render Brahms, Wagner and Schumann. . . .[7]

and:

I do not understand the psychology or philosophy of the Frenchman, German or Italian. Their history has nothing in common with the history of my slave ancestors. So I will not sing their music, nor the songs of their ancestors. . . .[8]

After Robeson actually visited Russia, with his wife, Eslanda, accompanying him, it was clear in his mind that all he had seen more than confirmed his expectations:

The workers are alive. You sense it in the streets, everywhere. You see it in their bearing. . . . In the factories, handling the most up-to-date machines, I saw men who obviously had been ignorant peasants a few years ago. In the universities and schools were students born in savage tribes that up to a decade ago were still in the stone age. The theatres and opera houses packed every night by workers. On the trains you see men and women studying works on science and mathematics. In the Soviet Union today there is not only no racial question; there is not even the concept of a racial question. Black, white, yellow—all were part of a whole, and no one thought of the question. . . .[9]

In an interview with a Soviet newspaper decades later, Robeson retained the same level of enthusiasm:

In the Soviet Union I felt like a person for the first time. This was not theory, but reality. I visited many schools, watched the pupils and saw in their eyes that the children in your country are taught a very important thing: that it is necessary to treat people equally, regardless of their skin color. . . . I again and again come to the conclusion that socialism is the key to the resolution of all the problems.[10]

In subsequent interviews over the years he spelled out more clearly what some of the problems were for him personally:

The world must not be deceived by references to Marian Anderson, Joe Louis, Dr. Ralph Bunche and myself as proof of opportunities for and fair treatment of Negroes in the United States. Only a small group of well-known Negroes are tolerated in the United States. The Negroes of the south are oppressed and no Negroes, including famous ones, are

secure from lynching. Only in the Soviet Union . . . did I feel like a man.
Here I found joy and happiness and I strove to instill a love of the Soviet
Union in my son. . . .[11]

To accomplish the latter, Robeson enrolled his son, Paul, Jr., age nine,
in a Moscow public school at the beginning of 1937. His father visited
periodically from London while on tour or vacation. According to
Homer Smith, who sent out press dispatches on the Robesons at the
time, Paul, Jr. was warmly received by the Russians and did very well
in school. However, the Robesons returned to the United States in
1938 after Robeson correctly sensed that the clouds of war were
gathering.

There were apparently times during the 1930s when Robeson toyed
with the idea of moving to the Soviet Union; but he denied ever
wishing to change his citizenship:

> At present I have my son in a soviet school in an environment completely
> devoid of all prejudice or racial differences, for my present attitude was
> made possible through the teachings of Russia. But I do want Paul Jr.,
> to return to America often enough to become familiar with its traditions
> as far as the Negro is concerned, because he is, first of all, an American.
> My reason for coming back here to live is that I have realized the more
> I live abroad, the more convinced I am that I am an American and this
> is where I belong—my roots are here—the material for my career is
> here. . . .[12]

In considering Robeson's infatuation with Russia, it should be noted
that this was a consistent part of his broader notion of the universality
of the human condition. The Soviet Union for him was just the place
where the most progressive steps had been taken toward achieving
the ideals he promoted. At one point he had considered spending the
rest of his life abroad in various areas where there are colored peoples,
especially Communist China and Africa, in addition to Soviet Asia.[13]

Robeson's high regard for the Soviet Union did not immediately
cause him any problem, even when he moved back to the United
States in 1939 after more than a decade's residence in London. During
the war years he was a leading celebrity in patriotic endeavors. All
this, however, occurred while Russia was an ally of the United States
against fascism, which Robeson viewed as one of the worst evils on
earth. The cold war, however, brought about a new climate and with
it the confrontation with his government toward which Robeson had
been headed for a long time. Negro Americans, already treated as
inferior, had to be extremely careful about expressing positive sentiment about the Soviet Union.

This repressive atmosphere did not silence the effusive humanist
Robeson; and he suffered the consequences. The decisive event was a
speech he gave at the Paris World Peace Conference in April 1949. In

extemporaneous remarks, he questioned the propriety of young American Negroes, treated as second-class citizens at home, taking up arms against Soviet Russia in the event a war should occur between the two super powers:

> It is unthinkable . . . that American Negroes would go to war on behalf of those who have oppressed us for generations . . . against a country which in one generation has raised our people to full human dignity of mankind.[14]

In subsequent interviews Robeson would defend all aspects of the Soviet system, including the concentration camps.[15] It is not clear, however, whether or not he had known how extensive they were. To this day there is also controversy concerning his knowledge about, and silence regarding, Soviet persecution of Jews in the Soviet Union. Among those saying he had such knowledge is his son, Paul.[16] It is a measure of Robeson's prestige that he could arouse equal passion by either speaking out, as he was wont to do, or by remaining silent. During the same time as his Paris speech, Robeson drew fire from Padmore in West Africa, who said Robeson had erred in castigating the South African regime's racial policies at a meeting in London. In Padmore's opinion, such harsh criticism would alienate sympathetic white Africans, and Robeson should restrict his political statements to his music.[17]

From Paris, Robeson travelled to Moscow to participate in the sesquicentennial of Pushkin's birth. It was only after he arrived home in June that he discovered what extreme punishment had been determined for him as a result of his Paris remarks. On the one hand, all doors were now closed to any pursuit of his livelihood in the United States. At the same time, the U.S. State Department informed him that in order to maintain his passport he would have to sign an affidavit certifying that he was not a member of the Communist Party. This he refused to do as a matter of principle. His great talent, universally acclaimed for the dramatic stage, film, and concert performances, was consequently stifled, thus limiting what would surely have been one of his most creative decades. He had to struggle against this ruling until 1958, when the Supreme Court ruled in his favor.

When he was again allowed to travel abroad, Robeson renewed his association with the Soviet Union and became, of course, a greater hero than ever there. Now he was a martyr in the truest sense. There is no evidence that he ever did join the Communist Party; but every other conceivable honor was given him in the Soviet Union. In 1952 he was awarded the Stalin Peace Prize, which carried with it $25,000. At about the same time, a 13,000-feet-high mountain in the Tian Shan range was named after him. In 1958 he was made an honorary professor at the Moscow State Conservatory of Music.[18] Upon his return to the Soviet Union, he was entertained personally by Premier Khrushchev. For the remaining two decades of his life, Robeson periodically received collective tributes from the Soviet public; and he reciprocated with personal communications on various state occasions.

Notwithstanding his social and political activism, Robeson's impact should not be dismissed simply as a propagandistic ploy. There was a genuine mutual love between Robeson and the Soviet Union, which goes beyond the very real politics which were also involved in the relationship. He may have been the most popular visitor in Soviet history. As an artist, apart from his role as activist, he had a deep appreciation for Russian folk music. Russian audiences proved that he was quite correct in his conviction that his renditions had special power for stirring their emotions. He took this as further confirmation of a theory he advanced describing the existence of a structural universality in all folk music, based on a pentatonic scale.[19] Moreover, his boundless success in the Soviet Union—matched by similar experiences in such dissimilar places as the United States, Wales, and Spain—was not only living proof for him supporting his theory of the universality of music, but also served as evidence for his more general beliefs about the universality of the human condition. This is why, even apart from politics, Robeson was repeatedly drawn to Russia to sing. His repertoire would include such American labor songs as "Joe Hill," other protest songs from various cultures (including some Negro spirituals), and traditional Russian songs such as the "Volga Boatmen," and "Evening Bell," as well as patriotic Russian songs. The Russian audiences were even more thrilled by his performance of the traditional, sentimental Russian songs than they were by those having clear political implications. He was not aware that some of these songs were no longer in official favor, because the new regime sought a new, truly Soviet form of music for what was intended to be a truly new kind of society. He therefore brought to the general public some of their own culture—and under official sponsorship—that they could not experience in such high quality in any other way.

If Robeson had a weakness for things traditional, the Soviet leaders were willing to forgive him because he had so many redeeming characteristics. He was internationally renowned, a member of an oppressed people, and highly sympathetic to socialism. Even his philosophy of art was consistent with the Soviets'. As has been shown, very early in his career he decided that his artistic talents should be used consciously to promote the advancement of humanity. Here he was showing an attitude about the social role of art that was similar to that adopted by Rudd and, with respect to Russia, had been present in the Russian intelligentsia extending back to Vissarion Belinsky, a renown literary critic in the early nineteenth century. The rest of Robeson's career bears out his sincerity in this approach.

His first visit to the Soviet Union in 1934 followed several years residence in England, where he had found a more suitable milieu for furthering his career despite brilliant performances on the American stage. Robeson's path to Russia bears a haunting similarity to Ira Aldridge's nearly a century earlier. How strange it is that the two greatest Negro actors in American history should have received their widest recognition in Russia. There was also a personal link between the two. In 1930 Robeson studied voice and diction with Aldridge's younger daughter, Amanda Ira Aldridge. Like Ira Aldridge, Robeson went to Russia in response to an invitation which promised to further his professional development. Robeson was invited by Sergei Eisenstein to read for the lead role in a projected film on Toussaint L'Ouverture.[20]

The Soviet government, of course, sought to take full advantage of Robeson's visit for its propaganda value. His music was already known to some Russians even before his first visit. The Soviet radio stations played Robeson's songs to celebrate his coming to Russia. Even Negro spirituals were played, but with the explanation that such phrases as "Steal Away to Jesus" were a code language for rebellion. Apparently, however, these explanatory remarks were not sufficient to keep a number of broadcast personnel from being fired for airing a song about Jesus in a society dedicated to atheism.[21] For his part, Robeson was favorably impressed by all he saw.

This attitude, what Robeson symbolized for Soviet ideology, and the power of his music combined to make Robeson the instant and lasting hero he became in the Soviet Union. At the same time, he saw Soviet Russia as the one major state which seemed to put real institutional commitment behind the same democratic and humanitarian goals Robeson himself pursued. Here was an entire society which espoused the philosophy of art which he had earlier reached on his own—that art should be utilitarian and aimed toward improving society. If Robeson was aware of any shortcomings of Soviet practice, as compared to theory, he apparently decided that any such failings were temporary and of secondary importance. After regaining his passport in 1958, Robeson returned to the Soviet Union on a number of occasions before retirement due to an illness which was to end his life in 1976. Robeson's career inspired a number of tributes from Soviet artists as well. One is a play by Iu. Krotkova, "Dzhon, soldat mira" (John, soldier of peace). The hero of the play is a Negro singer.[22]

Notwithstanding Robeson's strong sympathies for the Soviet cause and all the accolades Russia gave him, it is erroneous to characterize him as a dupe of the Soviet Union, as has often been done. He was perhaps quixotic, and surely mistaken at times; but he was not merely a pawn. An occurrence in 1959 in Moscow shed light on an aspect of Robeson's character often missed. Invited by the Soviet Writers Union to participate in a celebration of the centennial of the Jewish writer Sholem Aleichem's birthdate, Robeson, as usual during a performance, accompanied his singing with commentary. The event was planned as a gesture of goodwill toward Soviet Jews; however, the authorities failed to anticipate the innocent frankness of Paul Robeson's remarks. To the audience's delight and the officials' chagrin, he began by saying that Jews and Negroes share a common fate. Then, among other complementary remarks about Jewish culture, he mentioned the Jewish actor Schlomo Mikhoels, a victim of Stalin's purges whose name was still considered taboo.

Robeson also sang in Yiddish. In addition to folksongs, he sang one stirring Jewish fighting song, "The Song of the Jewish Partisans," from the heroic struggle against the Nazis in the Warsaw ghetto. A witness later recalled:

> In a spellbound hall, Robeson sang in Yiddish: "Never say this is the final path I tread." I shall never forget those moments, nor will the thousands who were present. It seemed as though Robeson sensed the significance of the unusual tension in the hall and that he utterly surpassed himself in the power of the feeling he poured into this superb war song.
>
> When he finished, there was a long moment of silence. The audience was too deeply moved. Then, all of a sudden, like an approaching storm, there arose a thunderous wave of applause, and it went on and on, and it would not end, it would not end, it seemed as if it would never end. All their suffering, pain and humiliation, all their yearnings and longings, were put into their clapping hands; and in the rhythmic pounding of thousands of hands, the audience let everyone know what they bore in their hearts and minds.[23]

On the occasion of his seventy-fifth birthday, thousands of Soviet citizens mailed letters of greeting to Paul Robeson through Radio Moscow. A poem from one of these describing another of his concerts shows how strikingly similar was his affect on all who heard him:

You appeared on stage,
Head bowed, eyes lowered

The pianist struck a chord
And, gently, your wonderful voice overflowed.

Then the hall and the pit fell silent
And only your voice was heard.
And in the spellbound stillness
It charmed and conjured . . .

When it was done
And your head was again bowed low,
An expectant hush
For a moment lingered on . . .

And suddenly, spontaneously, thundering applause shook the hall,
Like the thunder accompanying a cloudburst
Sweeping past in a clear sky
And sprinkling the earth with rain.

And everyone wanted to hear again
Your wonderful voice without ending . . .
And, instead of a fine bouquet,
To place at your feet our hearts!

Elizabeta Nikolaevna Demidova[24]
Novosibirsk, Siberia

There are a number of other Negro artists who have gained considerable renown in the Soviet Union. One is Tito Romalio, a Brazilian-born variety actor. Having originally come to Europe on a tour just before World War II, Romalio was imprisoned by the Nazis in Lithuania. He was freed by the Soviet Army and subsequently became a Soviet citizen. He starred in a number of Soviet films and travelled in shows which included Brazilian music. Another notable Negro artist, ballerina Ulamei Scott, was born in Moscow in 1933. She graduated from the Bolshoi Theatre School and then joined the famed Bolshoi Ballet. Later, she earned a diploma from the Theatrical Art Institute and published her thesis, "Dances of the Peoples of Africa."[25]

Lloyd Patterson, a 1931 graduate of Hampton Institute in Virginia, literally made his contribution to the Russian arts "behind the scenes." He originally came to the Soviet Union with the ill-fated propaganda film project in 1932 and decided to stay. His first job was to paint the gold- and silver-leaf work that decorated the interior of the Metropol Hotel in Moscow. Later he designed stage sets for the Meyerhold Theatre. After the theatre was closed following Meyerhold's demise, Patterson became a journalist for Radio Moscow. He died in combat during the Second World War.[26]

NEGRO THEMES IN SOVIET ART

In addition to the direct participation of Negroes in the arts, the Negro is prominent as a theme in Soviet works of art. A number of examples have already been cited, and the Negro appears as a subject in the theatre, film, painting, literature, and music. Among the top-rated films listed for 1977 in the magazine *Soviet Screen* included one about Abram Hannibal, entitled "How Tsar Peter Married Off an *Arap*." Among selected foreign literature translated and published for the Soviet public have been works by black Americans. An example is the

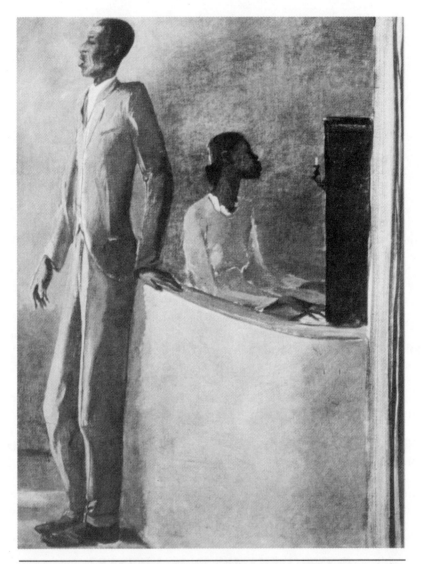

A Negro Concert, by Aleksandr Deineka, 1935. Deineka captured this scene during a visit to the United States. Reprinted from Deineka, *Iz moei Rabochei praktiki* (Moscow, 1961).

novel by John Oliver Killens, *And Then We Heard the Thunder*, which treats the subject of racism. Outstanding examples of the depiction of blacks in Soviet painting can be found among the works of Aleksandr Deineka.[27]

In music, the most important Negro influence is found in the very

A Negro Youth, by Aleksandr Deineka, 1935. Reprinted from Deineka,
Iz moei Rabochei praktiki.

considerable impact of jazz on Soviet society. Despite an awkward,
ambivalent attitude toward it by the Soviet government, this distinctive, twentieth century music form, which originated in the United
States, has enjoyed persistent and wide popularity in the Soviet Union,
just as it has in other parts of the world. A taste for jazz in Soviet
society had in some ways already been induced by Russian society's
earlier exposure to the cakewalk—a dance first performed by American
Negroes. With the advent of films, ragtime and jazz provided favorite
background music. Once the Russian public became acquainted with
the new dances associated with a particular type of music its popularity
was assured. Vsevelod Meyerhold took a major step in that direction

by staging a full jazz band in some of his productions in the early 1920s. To avoid any chance of arousing official displeasure, the music had to be presented as symbolic of capitalist decadence. Within a few years hundreds of Russian musicians were playing the new music, including the young Dmitri Shostakovich.[28] As in the evolution of American jazz, Jewish promoters and performers were very prevalent in the early development of Soviet jazz. Examples are Valentin Parnakh, Alexander Tsfasman, Leonid Utesov, and Polish-born Eddie Rosner. Some of these men, along with others, became enormously wealthy from the new music.

Although the first performances of jazz in Russia were by Russians, there can be little doubt that most Russians associated jazz with Negroes. According to a recent study:

> A St. Petersburg confectioner exploited the notion of ragtime as black music by issuing the latest hits on records pressed into discs of hard baker's chocolate. Since none of these discographic gems has survived, it can be assumed that the listening public eagerly consumed them.[29]

A decade later, Harry Haywood recalled that once, in 1926, when he and three other Negroes were walking down a main street in Moscow, a group of Russian children followed shouting "jass band . . . jass band!" He concluded that the children associated them with the Leland and Drayton revue, which had toured the Soviet Union for six months the previous year. Haywood had encountered the revue in Berlin on his way to Moscow.[30] The Leland Drayton revue was the first black jazz group to make the journey to Russia. Also during 1926, thirty-three other black American jazz musicians, dancers, and singers arrived for a three-month tour: Sam Wooding and His Chocolate Kiddies variety show. The same year, a contrasting style of jazz was introduced to the Soviets by Benny Peyton's seven-piece New Orleans Jazz Band. The band included the legendary saxophonist Sidney Bechet, another black American who had earned great renown in Europe while remaining relatively unknown at home.[31]

The period between 1925 and 1928—the final years of Lenin's conciliatory New Economic Policy—signalled a greater cultural freedom. However, as Stalin consolidated a more coersive, repressive regime, its force was felt on the arts as elsewhere. The tone of the official position regarding jazz was set in a 1928 article by Gorky, who called it degenerate, bourgeois music.[32] The music was considered all the more dangerous because a significant part of the public viewed it as refreshing and liberating. Unable to eliminate it completely, the government retreated to attempting to create a peculiarly Soviet style, more controlled, both musically and politically. There were eventually state jazz orchestras in various republics. At the same time, some elements in the government continued to try to discredit the music. Here Paul Robeson lent his hand, expressing his own prejudice against jazz in an article in *Sovetskaia Muzyka* (Soviet Music).[33]

The nature of modern communications has made it impossible for the Soviet government to eliminate jazz by force. Cognizant that many citizens were secretly following Voice of America and British Broadcasting Corporation programs for jazz, the government decided to allow it locally in order to curtail the exposure to the political message accompanying the music on foreign broadcasts. The especially heavy proliferation of movie theatres in the Soviet Union, and more recently television, has further exposed the population to the music. It has not mattered much whether top officials, like Nikita Khrushchev, opposed the music or admired it. In the 1960s and 1970s American jazz musicians were again welcomed in Russia after a break of some two decades during which the Russians and other Europeans had continued to develop the music in the Soviet Union. Black musicians who visited Russia during this period include Earl "Fatha" Hines in 1966, the Charles Lloyd Quartet in 1967, Duke Ellington in 1971, and B. B. King in 1979. One older Russian man attending the King concert in Leningrad remarked to an American present that:

> B. B. King astounded me. This blues music—it's not like jazz. He poured his whole heart and soul out there on the stage. Such feeling is very Russian—we believe in emotion, in the soul. I never thought that an American could feel that way.[34]

Meanwhile in the 1970s, rock music, another form which had drawn its original inspiration from black artists, began to be favored by Soviet youth as it had been earlier by their American counterparts. In the Soviet Union, this may have been in part a reaction against jazz having come too much under the control of the government authorities, who thereby tainted the aura of freedom which made the music so attractive. Not to be outdone, the government moved quickly to monitor the progress of rock music as well. A Soviet-American cultural exchange, on May 28, 1983, offers a good illustration of the success and failure of the Soviet regime in its love/hate relationship with jazz and rock music. During a rock festival held in California, televised greetings were simultaneously exchanged by satellite between many of the three hundred thousand fans present and an audience of three hundred in Moscow. An hour of cultural discussion preceded an hour of exchanging rock music.[35]

Soviet literature features a number of works that provide insight concerning the image of the Negro projected in the Soviet Union. Boris Kornilov's poem "Moia Afrika" has been mentioned earlier. One of the poem's messages offers an affirmation of the ubiquitous nature of class struggle. Praising the black colonel from Africa, who lost his life in fierce, conspicuous battle for the Red cause in the Civil War, Kornilov wrote:

> He was black,
> With thick lips
> He was from Africa—killed on the spot,
> But like we,
> From the Don and Kuban,
> He fought for our Russia,
> Not for medals—
> In order to give it to
> The African bourgeoisie, African capitalists,
> In the Neck, as we do in Russia.
>
> . . . .
> Ah, remember, Russia,
> Mother Volga.
>
> . . . .
> Moscow and Tula,
> Please remember always
> That he, of course,
> Was a Negro by birth,
> But completely Russian.[36]

Another particularly interesting source are the writings of the Russian Negro poet James Patterson, the son of Lloyd Patterson and his Russian wife. James Patterson, born in 1933 in Moscow, attended primary school in Sverdlovsk in the Urals, attended naval schools, and then pursued a naval career. He began writing poetry in 1956 and in 1957 graduated from the Literary Institute. He published in such journals as *Moskva* (Moscow), *Ogonyok* (Fire), *Sovetskii Voin* (Soviet Soldier), and *Sovetskaia Ukraina* (Soviet Ukraine). The main theme of his work is Russia and Africa; and he wrote one poem of that title which included these lines:

> But I recall,
> How two old women anxiously
> Sang something beside my cradle.
> And they bent over me, their skins different in color,
> Somehow very similar and dissimilar,
> And their hands rocked me as one,
> And they radiated to me a simple warmth.
>
> . . . .
> But I recall,
> How Russia and Africa with deep feeling
> Sang something to me at my cradle.[37]

Patterson's work also reflects a more specific identification with his Afro-American heritage. One of his most popular poems, entitled

"Schoolgirl," was inspired by the celebrated school integration battle in Little Rock, Arkansas, in 1957. While the motivations for Patterson's interest in Negro themes are quite obvious and personal, what he expresses is nonetheless characteristic of Soviet writers in general. Earlier cited films and plays with Negro themes, which were not written by Negro authors, have the same tone as Patterson's work.

This is also true of more illustrious Soviet writers' expressions on Negro themes. The source of interest in such topics for at least two famous Soviet poets was their undying reverence for Pushkin. The two are Vladimir Mayakovsky (1893–1930) and Marina Tsvetaeva (1892–1941). In contrast to the prevailing sentiment in tsarist Russia, in Soviet Russia Pushkin is universally regarded as a Negro. This is somewhat curious, since this was not Pushkin's view and since it is based on a uniquely American definition of Negro. However, for the poets in question this is a positive attribute. The often irreverent Mayakovsky in "Iubileinoe" (Jubilee) hails Pushkin, the "arap," and "Afrikanets," as a beloved and kindred spirit.[38]

The highly original Tsvetaeva in "Moi Pushkin" relates how the story of Pushkin's life and visits to his monument in Moscow fed her childhood fantasies. The darkness of the bronze statue further reinforced her feeling that he was a Negro, notwithstanding his light-colored hair and eyes. In her words, "Pushkin had side whiskers (NB! only Negroes and old generals have them) ..." While Tsvetaeva's elusive prose style defies specific interpretation and, thus, could be quoted out of context, "Moi Pushkin" (My Pushkin) reveals an indelible impression of a "Negro" Pushkin on the author and a consequent deep involvement with the issue of "black" versus "white" in many other aspects of her life. In yet another work, her poem "Petr i Pushkin," (Peter and Pushkin) shows further that Tsvetaeva's interest extended back to Abram Hannibal as well.[39]

It should be reiterated that while the Russian writers mentioned represent cases of spontaneous interest in the Negro theme, there were also institutional efforts at promoting such interest both within the Soviet Union and abroad. It was such efforts which convinced McKay, Robeson, Rudd, and other Negro artists to visit the Soviet Union. There is evidence that there was an especially intensive Soviet campaign in the 1920s to establish strong cultural ties between the Soviet Union and Negro America. In 1926 the American Negro Arna Bontemps was awarded the Pushkin Prize for literature. At about the same time, scores of prominent Negroes received invitations from the Soviet Cultural Relations Society to visit the Soviet Union, among them the entire executive staff of the National Association for the Advancement of Colored People. Most Negroes, however, must have concurred with the sentiment expressed by NAACP Executive Secretary James Weldon Johnson to a colleague in 1927: ". . . I fully agree with you that our job is in the U.S. and not in Russia."[40]

Over the decades, the number of Negroes actually involved in Soviet literature and the arts has not grown significantly. However, the Negro as a theme has continued to be constant and probably will remain so as long as the Soviet Union is interested in the developing world.

CONCLUSION

The collective experience of Negroes in tsarist Russia suggests this was for them a land of opportunity where they could not only survive, but could attain high social position. Slaves, servants, other immigrants, and visitors all were received rather well. This is striking not only because of the absence of the stigma attached to their color as in the United States and certain other places, it is also significant that this group was not part of the regular upper class and was conspiciously non-Russian. It is true, as shown by the episodes concerning the African visitor Abakari's color, that there was some ambivalence in the Russian attitudes toward Negroes. This was even true of Alexander Pushkin, who once poetically referred to himself as an "ugly offspring of Negroes," which at least implies that such ancestry caused his "ugliness." At the same time, some of his contemporaries saw in traits such as his violent temper what they viewed as African characteristics. Other evidence of stereotyping surfaced surrounding Ira Aldridge's appearances as Othello, evoking allusions to the "beauty and the beast" concept. However, offsetting this type of thought was the relatively progressive stance against Negro slavery and a respectful attitude toward black Africa. Besides, although there are signs that negative images do exist in Russian attitudes about the Negro as an abstraction, the concrete experiences in tsarist society showed that such attitudes did not prevent a high level of social acceptance and achievement for Negroes.

The experience of Negroes in Soviet Russia, while promising, has not been as uniformly positive as that under the tsarist regime. The attraction for Negroes to the new Russia has remained, as before, their quest for a society offering them a better life free of racial discrimination. A particularly bright lure in Soviet society was the promise of artistic freedom, during the 1920s and 1930s, when cultural links between the arts in the United States and Russia became apparent. Claude McKay, Wayland Rudd, Langston Hughes, Richard Wright, Paul Robeson, for example, had much in common with Vladimir Mayakovsky and other Soviet artists in their dedication to utilitarian art expressed in the folk medium. The instant popularity of jazz among the Russian public is just as understandable as the appeal of Mayakovsky, and more consistent with the entire Soviet mood than the government's attempt to proscribe it. Perhaps the Negroes and the Russians were misled by the seeming similarity of forms like Eugene O'Neill's naturalism and Soviet realism. However, their common view of the universality of the basic human condition was the main binding tie. Consider the remarkable resemblance between Gumilev's and Kornilov's poetry about Africa and that of the contemporary Negritude poets. The honors bestowed upon the Negro guests represented both sincerely held sentiments as well as propaganda.

The Soviet interest in Africa has been even more concentrated, more extensive, and more successful than was the tsars'. At the same time, due to the nature of Soviet ideology, communist interest in the Negro has truly become worldwide in scope. Given the importance of Marxist ideology in the Negro experience with the Soviet Union, it may provide some clues to what Negroes can anticipate as they have now begun to look toward other socialist societies, such as China, Cuba, and African socialist states, in their continued search for a truly free society. Soviet society has not proven to be a panacea for the Negro, as indicated by the literature sampled from some of the African students' experiences there. However, the fact remains that, regardless of Soviet motives, their championing of Negro rights and those of colonialized peoples on the international level as well as at home has brought benefits to the Negro. A good example is the pressure this placed on the United States government to show better progress in making Negroes full citizens.

How are these conclusions to be reconciled with the conventional negative depictions of both tsarist and Soviet Russia? Tsarist Russian society is usually regarded as "backward," an environment from which to flee, and, decidedly, not a place to seek refuge. This is the view that was projected by some elements within the Russian intelligentsia as well as the Western observers. The concept of "backwardness" may be instructive if it is used in a non-pejorative sense, meaning "less advanced along the usual Western path to modernization." And how has Soviet Russia, often characterized in the West as one of the most oppressive regimes, been able to come as close as she has to her ideals in the treatment of the Negro?

The present study underscores the need to refine the criteria for answering such questions; for, in all fairness, Russia's society must be compared to other societies rather than to abstract ideals. The questions this raises are extremely complex. For example, in considering Russian attitudes toward Negroes, Pushkin was not considered a Negro in Russia; but he would have been considered one in parts of the United States and would have suffered for it. Does this mean that, in this regard, autocratic Russia was more enlightened than democratic America? That this question has no simple answer is evident in the fact that while an American slave might take to sea and make his fortune in Russia, the Russian proprietary serf could do likewise in America if only he could reach it. Similarly, a Soviet Jew can emigrate to the United States to what he hails as a better life, just as a few American Negroes have moved to the Soviet Union. Soviet leaders must have been painfully reminded of these ironies in July 1984, when the black American presidential hopeful, Reverend Jesse Jackson, appealed to them to allow the ailing dissident Andrei Sakharov and his wife, Yelena Bonner, to leave the Soviet Union. On an issue less sensitive for current Soviet policies Jackson's public appeal to universal humanitarian values might have proven irresistible.

While it seems clear that a non-pejorative "backwardness" perspective is of some value for studying Imperial Russian society, new approaches are also needed.[1] Among the topics that must be addressed is the peculiar mixture of attitudes which made Russians relatively blind to skin color, opposed to slavery, and yet, until the 1860s, supportive of a form of serfdom approximating slavery.

For tsarist society, part of the explanation for the positive treatment Negroes experienced there seems to lie in the very rigidity of Russian society, which is sometimes cited as one of its negative features. It should be noted that at the time, Russians in general did not have specific civil rights; but certain classes had designated privileges. The Negroes from abroad did not fit clearly into any of the numerous well-defined social categories and, thereby, enjoyed a certain unusual degree of freedom. The Abkhazian Negroes, once they came under Russian rule, were at least treated like all other subject peoples. The timing of the main influx of Negroes into Russia from abroad was also a factor in their experience. This was the period when modernization was taking hold—with all the social and economic diversification that that entails. It was a time when new roles and new concepts were more likely than ever before to be acceptable.

Regarding the status of Negroes in tsarist society, it appears to have been largely dependent, at least initially, upon Russian sponsors. These were most often members of the upper classes or the tsar. Hence, a servant or guest of a nobleman drew enhanced status from that association. Later he might establish himself in the upper class. The Negro artists, athletes, and entertainers who came to Russia were special guests not only of their individual sponsors, but of the entire public they attracted; this also gave them special status. Their complete acceptance by the Russians was in sharp contrast to the type of race prejudice based on skin color, to which Negroes had become accustomed in the Western world. This may be accounted for by the absence of Russian involvement in the massive African slave trade. It may also have to do with the fact that Russia is in Asia as well as in Europe, which may have engendered a different attitude toward skin color. Given both the existence of slavery in Russia during earlier centuries and Russian imperialism in Asia, this does not imply Russia's moral superiority over the Western states who ravaged much of Africa. It did, however, contribute to better attitudes in Russia toward the Negro.

In Soviet society, unlike tsarist society a century earlier, citizens' rights were defined from the beginning, and Negroes were delighted to discover that the status of full citizenship could include them. This points up one of the advantages the Soviet Union derived from being a new and radically different kind of society: It did not have to contend with any of the remnants of slavery or colonization of Negro peoples. It could, therefore, offer Negroes full legal manhood status immediately, while in their own native societies, such as in the United States, Negroes found only various types of gradual emancipation still in progress. There were, to be sure, certain aspects of Soviet life which some of them found less than congenial. Padmore found himself an outcast when he was not willing to subordinate his personal beliefs on African liberation to current official doctrine and tactics. Homer Smith sensed a dimming of communist ideals the longer he remained in Russia. On the other hand, both these complaints could be made regarding any society.

What has most impressed Negroes about Russian society is the absence of institutionalized racism. There may be racist individuals; but if detected these persons are subject to crushing public opprobrium. The circumstances surrounding the African student protests in the Soviet Union suggest the conditions under which systematic racism might develop: increased competition for scarce commodities or privileges between Russians and a group easily identifiable by skin color. Such a situation is unlikely to occur because the Negro population in Russia shows no likelihood of any great increase in numbers. The Abkhazian Negroes have been encouraged to assimilate, and may soon be indistinguishable from the rest of the population. Likewise, Negro immigrants usually marry Russians; and many have eventually returned to their native lands. Quite apart from those who suffered disillusionment, others returned home either to continue the struggle for equal rights, or just because the homeland ties were too strong to break.

As a new "developing" nation, the Soviet Union could identify closely with other nations of the world that are categorized in that way. Such identification was mutual to some extent. Negroes saw the new Soviet state, especially during its first decade, as a bright, dynamic, democratic challenge to the oppressive status quo and, therefore, a champion of all oppressed peoples. The Soviet Union continues to draw upon the strength of that image as it continues to seek even today significant influence in black Africa. However valid, this image should not be allowed to obscure the more basic underlying causes for the persistent Russian interest in black Africa. These are geopolitical and, therefore, apply equally well for tsarist and Soviet Russia. The global strength and security of this land-and-ice-locked giant simply dictate a need for ties with black Africa. The convergence of European imperialism in Africa, the color problem, and Soviet ideology fuel a diplomatic strategy which would likely be employed by any Russian state.

It is within this framework that the current rapid changes in Soviet ties with African states can best be understood. At the same time, Soviet efforts at applying Marxist doctrine to Negro societies in Africa provide further evidence of some of the practical difficulties with which the twentieth century has confronted Marxism. The Russian Revolution was a spectacular demonstration that, contrary to Marx's vision, a society just beginning modernization is more vulnerable to a Marxian revolution than an advanced one. But in the attempt to turn this unexpected development to advantage, the Russian Revolution has yet to solve the riddle of how to expand worldwide. A central problem, which is further accentuated in the record of Soviet involvement with the American Negro question, is the ideological clash between various types of nationalism and the ideal of international socialism. The question of the potential for future Soviet success in guiding Negro revolutionary movements is inextricably tied to finding an accommodation between nationalism and international socialism.

NOTES

CHAPTER ONE

1. A good general description of Abkhazia may be found in Sula Benet, *Abkhasians The Long-Living People of the Caucasus* (New York: Holt, Rinehart and Winston, 1974), pp. 1–8.

2. These were later published in a volume by V. P. Vradii, *Negry batumskoi oblasti* (Negroes of Batumi province) (Batumi: G. Tavartkiladze, 1914).

3. F. Elius, "Chernokozhie rossiiane" ("Black-skinned Russians"), *Argus* 10 (1913). See also P. I. Kovalevskii, *Kavkaz* (The Caucasus), vol. 1 of *Narody Kavkaza* (Peoples of the Caucasus) (St. Petersburg: M. I. Akinfiev, 1914), p. 37.

4. Albert Parry, "Negroes in Russia," *Opportunity*, October 1925, p. 306; *Abbot's Monthly*, April 1931, pp. 11–16, 56–67; "Negroes Found Living in Russia," *New York Times*, 24 September 1931.

5. Some of these studies are enumerated in Lily Golden-Hanga, *Africans in Russia* (Moscow: Novosti Press, 1966).

6. Slava Tynes, "Many Africans Came to the Soviet Union During Turkish Rule," *The Afro-American*, 16 February 1973, Washington, D.C. edition.

7. Vradii, *Negry batumskoi oblasti*, pp. 16–17.

8. K. Gan, comp., *Izvestiia drevnikh grecheskikh i rimskikh pisatelei o Kavkaze* (Accounts of ancient Greek and Roman writers about the Caucasus), pt. 1 (Tiflis, Russian Georgia: Office of the Civilian Department Chief, 1884).

9. Patrick English, "Cushites, Colchians, and Khazars," *Journal of Near*

Eastern Studies 18 (1959): 49–53. See also Frank M. Snowden, Jr., *Blacks in Antiquity* (Cambridge: Harvard University Press, 1970), p. 270; and W. E. D. Allen and Paul Muratoff, *Caucasian Battlefields* (Cambridge: Cambridge University Press, 1953).

10. Golden-Hanga, *Africans in Russia*, p. 10.

11. Slava Tynes, "When Did Africans Get to the Soviet Union?" *The Afro-American*, 30 January 1973.

12. A. Lopashich, "Negro Community in Yugoslavia," *Man* 58 (1958): 169–73; Joseph E. Harris, *The African Presence in Asia* (Evanston, Ill.: Northwestern University Press, 1971), p. 76.

13. Philip D. Curtin, "The Slave Trade and the Atlantic Basin: Inter-continental Perspectives," in Nathan Huggins, ed., *Key Issues in the Afro-American Experience* (New York: Harcourt Brace, 1971), pp. 76–77.

14. Isidor Schneider, "A Negro Citizen of Soviet Georgia," *Opportunity*, May 1942, pp. 148–49, 157; reprint, *Soviet Russia Today*, February 1942.

CHAPTER TWO

1. M. Bogoslovskii, ed., *Petr I: Materialy dlia biografii* (Peter I: materials for a biography) (Leningrad: OGIZ-SOTSEKGIZ, 1941), pp. 267, 295, 402.

2. A. I. Uspenskii, ed., *Ikonopistsy XVII v.; Zapiski Mosk. arkhiol. Inst.* (Icon-painters of the XVII century; notes of the Moscow Archael. Inst.), vol. 2 (Moscow: A. I. Snegirevoi, 1910), p. 276.

3. D. A. Rovinskii, *Podrobnyi slovar' russkikh gravirovannykh portretov* (Unabridged dictionary of Russian engraved portraits) (St. Petersburg: Imperial Academy of Sciences, 1886–1889), vol. 3, col. 1560; George A. W. von Helbig, *Russiche Gunstlinge* (Russian favorites) (Tubingen: J. G. Cotta, 1909); M. Vegner, *Predki Pushkina* (Pushkin's ancestors) (Gorky: "Sovetskii pisatel'," 1937), p. 20.

4. Czeslaw Jesman, "Early Russian Contacts with Ethiopia," *Proceedings of the Third International Conference of Ethiopian Studies, 1966* (Addis Ababa: Institute of Ethiopian Studies, 1969), pp. 259–60.

5. *Autobiography of Andrew Dickson White* (New York: Century Co., 1905), vol. 2, p. 113.

6. *The Diary of John Quincy Adams*, ed. Allan Nevins (New York: Scribner, 1929), p. 96; Mina Curtiss, "Some American Negroes in Russia in the Nineteenth Century," *The Massachusetts Review* (Spring 1968): 268–78; Richard Field to Jonathan Russell, 3 August 1810, Jonathan Russell Papers, The John Hay Library, Brown University, Providence, Rhode Island.

7. W. H. Grimshaw, *Official History of Freemasonry Among the Colored People in North America* (New York: Broadway Publishing Co., 1903), pp. 84–98; Charles H. Wesley, *Prince Hall: Life and Legacy* (Washington: United Supreme Council, Southern Jurisdiction, Prince Hall Affiliation, 1977), pp. 20–23.

8. *Pennsylvania Historical Survey, Work Projects Administration Maritime Records Port of Philadelphia*, sec. 5, Alphabetical List of Masters and Crews 1798–1880, vols. 1–108 (Harrisburg, Pa.: WPA, 1942).

9. John D. Maxwell, *The Czar, His Court and People—Including a Tour to Norway and Sweden* (New York: Baker and Scribner, 1848), pp. 207–8.

10. Matthew Henson, *A Negro Explorer at the North Pole* (New York: Arno Press, 1912), p. 3; Bradley Robinson, *Dark Companion* (New York: R. M. McBride & Co., 1947), pp. 37–38.

11. *A Narrative of the Life and Travels of Mrs. Nancy Prince Written by Herself* (Boston: Nancy Prince, 1856), pp. 5–35 *passim*; Judith Zacek, "The Russian Bible Society and the Russian Orthodox Church," *Church History* 35 (December 1966): 411–37.

12. Nancy Prince, *Narrative*, pp. 26–27.

13. *Ibid.*, pp. 31–32.

14. Jesman, "Early Russian Contacts with Ethiopia," p. 260; Albert Parry, "Black Folk in Russia," *Abbot's Monthly*, April 1931, p. 11; Ralph G. Martin, *Jennie: Reminiscences of Lady Randolph Churchill* (Englewood Cliffs, N.J.: Prentice Hall, 1969), p. 233; A. Vrubova, "Vospominaniia" (Memoirs), *Novy Zhurnal* 130 (1978): 113.

15. Harold Nicolson, *The Age of Reason, The Eighteenth Century* (New York: Doubleday, 1961), p. 139; V. A. Nikolaev and Albert Parry, *The Loves of Catherine the Great* (New York: G. P. Putnam & Sons, 1982), p. 179.

16. B. Kozlov, "Kogda rodilsia praded Pushkina Gannibal?" (When was Pushkin's grandfather Hannibal born?), *Novoe Russkoe Slovo*, 11 January 1970.

17. M. Vegner, *Predki Pushkina*, p. 15.

18. Nikolai Gastfreind, *Pis'ma Abrama Ganibala (Arkhivnye dokumenty)* (Abram Hannibal's letters (Archival documents)) (St. Petersburg: "Sever," 1904), pp. 1–5.

19. N. Malevanov, "Abram Gannibal—Uchastnik Poltavskoi bitvy" ("Abram Hannibal—participant in the Battle of Poltava"), *Novoe Russkoe Slovo*, 7 May 1972.

20. Vegner, *Predki Pushkina*, p. 42.

21. Elena Kozlovskaia, "Muza Suida" (The Suida estate), *Novoe Russkoe Slovo*, 10 October 1975.

22. Vegner, *Predki Pushkina*, p. 42.

23. L. Abrusow, *Grundriss der Geschichte Liv-, Est- und Kurlands* (Outline of the history of Liv-, Est- and Courland) (Riga, Latvia: Jonck und Poliewsky, 1918), p. 339.

24. Gastfreind, *Pis'ma Ganibala*, pp. 12–13.

25. Vladimir Nabokov, *Pushkin, Eugene Onegin* (New York: Random House, 1964), vol. 3, p. 438.

26. A. S. Pushkin, *Polnoe sobranie sochinenii* (Complete collected works) (Moscow: Academy of Sciences, 1937–1950), vol. 12, pp. 310–14; B. L. Modzalevskii, *Rodoslovnaia Gannibalov* (The genealogy of the Hannibal family) (Moscow: Yakovlev, 1907); Henri Troyat, "Pushkin's Ethiopian Ancestry," *Ethiopia Observer* 1 (July 1957): 244–45.

CHAPTER THREE

1. Sergius Yakobson, "Russia and Africa," in I. Lederer, ed., *Russian Foreign Policy* (New Haven: Yale University Press, 1962), pp. 454–55.

2. V. Burtsev, "Russian Documents in the British Museum," *Slavonic Review* 4 (1925–26): 677; Cited in Yakobson, "Russia and Africa," p. 455.

3. C. Jesman, "Early Russian Contacts with Ethiopia," pp. 262–67; Edward Wilson, *Russia and Black Africa Before World War II* (New York: Holmes & Meier, 1974), pp. 10–17.

4. Wilson, *Russia and Black Africa*, p. 23.

5. M. P. Zabrodskaia, *Russkie Puteshestvenniki po Afrike* (Russian travellers in Africa) (Moscow: Geografiz, 1955); Discussed in *Russia Looks at Africa* (London: Central Asian Research Centre, 1960), p. 2.

6. Zabrodskaia, *Russkie Puteshestvenniki*, pp. 52–73.

7. Richard Hellie, "Recent Soviet Historiography on Medieval and Early Modern Russian Slavery," *Russian Review* 35 (January 1976): 1. For fuller treatment of Russian slavery, see Hellie, *Slavery in Russia* (Chicago: University of Chicago Press, 1982).

8. Yakobson, "Russia and Africa," pp. 466–67.

9. A. N. Radishchev, *Puteshestvie iz Petersburga v Moskvu* (Journey from St. Petersburg to Moscow) (Moscow: Gos. Khudozh. Lit-ry, 1966), pp. 128–29.

10. Alexander S. Pushkin, *Polnoe sobranie sochinenii* (Complete collected works) (Moscow: Academy of Sciences, 1937–1950), in "Dzhon Tenner" (John Tanner), vol. 12, p. 104.

11. Max M. Laserson, *The American Impact on Russia—Diplomatic and Ideological—1784–1917* (New York: Macmillan, 1950), p. 146.

12. Nicholas Turgenev, *La Russie et les russes* (Russia and the Russians) (Paris: Imprimeurs Unis, 1847), vol. 2, p. 228.

13. Quoted by M. Laserson, *The American Impact on Russia*, pp. 152–53, from *Liberty Bell*, 1853.

14. *Ibid.*, p. 154, from *Liberty Bell*, 1856.

15. Quoted in Laserson, *The American Impact*, p. 212; in A. Herzen, "Russian Serfdom," *Leader* (5 November 1953).

16. See Laserson, *American Impact*, pp. 246–47.

17. The installments were under the title, "Zhizn' v iuzhnyk shtatakh" (Life in the southern states), *Sovremennik* 67 and 68 (1858). Stowe's influence on the Russian public is mentioned in Andrei Klenov, "Garriet Bicher-Stou" (Harriet Beecher Stowe), *Novoe Russkoe Slovo*, 18 November 1983.

18. "Politika" (Politics), *Sovremennik* 1 and 2 (January/February 1863): 388.

19. *Sovremennik* 6 (June 1865): 265.

20. *Illiustratsiia*, 2 April, 1859.

21. Eduard Tsimmerman, *Soedinennye Shtaty Severnoi Ameriki* (The United States of North America) (Moscow: Grachev and Co., 1873).

22. See either of his two following works: Pavel G. Mezhuev, *Istoriia velikoi*

amerikanskoi demokratii (History of the great American democracy) (St. Petersburg: Akts. Obshch. "Brokhaus-Efron" 1906) or *Sotsiologicheskie etiudy* (Sociological studies) (St. Petersburg: Ts. Kraiz, 1904).

23. Nicholas Dobroliubov, "The Organic Development of Man in Relation to His Intellectual and Moral Activities," in Dobroliubov, *Selected Philosophical Essays* (Moscow: Foreign Languages Publishing House, 1956), p. 88.

24. William Cohen, *The French Encounter with Africans: White Response to Blacks 1530–1880* (Bloomington, Ind.: Indiana University Press), p. 85.

25. Wilson, *Russia and Black Africa*, p. 30.

26. Patrick J. Rollins, "Imperial Russia's African Colony," *Russian Review* 27 (1968): 432–51.

27. Wilson, *Russia and Black Africa*, p. 53.

28. *Ibid.*, pp. 82–84.

CHAPTER FOUR

1. It should also be noted that there is hardly any information at all on American immigrants to Russia. More research is necessary concerning the extent to which there was a continuation of westward expansion in America into Russia and Eurasia as a whole. U.S. consular records show that there were American settlers, for example, in Vladivostok. General Records of the Department of State, *Dispatches from United States Consuls in Vladivostok, 1898–1906,* Record Group 59, National Archives Microfilm Publication M486, roll 1. See also Albert Parry, "Yankee Whalers in Siberia," *The Russian Review* 5 (Spring 1946): 36–49.

2. *Peoples Advocate*, 24 February 1877.

3. R. H. Bruce Lockhart, *British Agent* (New York: G. P. Putnam & Sons, 1933), p. 71. According to Lockhart, Thomas was a British subject; but most sources say he was an American.

4. "Slukhi i fakhty" (Rumors and facts), *Novoe Russkoe Slovo*, 19 October 1965.

5. "The Saga of Jimmy Winkfield," *Ebony*, June 1974, pp. 64–70.

6. D. Aminado, *Poezd na tret'em puti* (The train on the sidetrack) (New York: Chekhov Press, 1954), p. 52; Harmon Tupper, *To the Great Ocean: Siberia and the Trans-Siberian Railway* (Boston: Little, Brown, 1965), p. 302.

7. Alexandre Tarsaidze, *Czars and Presidents* (New York: McDowell, Obolensky, 1958), p. 177; Charlayne Hunter, "New Museum Traces Black Stage History," *New York Times,* 9 July 1975; "Fisk Jubilee Singers," *Ebony*, November 1951, p. 70.

8. *Foreign Relations of the United States 1867* (New York: Kraus Reprint, 1965), vol. 1, 1867, p. 382; vol. 2, 1868, p. 87; Rayford Logan and Michael Winston, eds., *Dictionary of American Negro Biography* (New York: W. W. Norton, 1982), s.v. "T. Morris Chester," by Allison Blakely.

9. (St. Petersburg) *Golos*, 4 February 1867, p. 3.

10. *Harrisburg Telegraph*, 30 May 1867. In introducing this document, the editor claimed to have seen the original. I have been unable to locate it, and

therefore cannot say whether the roughness of its grammar and punctuation are attributable to its author or its translator. I am indebted to Richard Blackett for bringing this letter to my attention.

11. *Jack Johnson is a Dandy* (New York: Chelsea House, 1969), pp. 64–65.

12. General Records of the Department of State, *Dispatches from United States Consuls in Vladivostok, 1898–1906,* Record Group 59, National Archives Microfilm Publication M486, roll 1.

13. Donald W. Treadgold, *The Great Siberian Migration* (Princeton: Princeton University Press, 1957), p. 34.

14. Richard T. Greener to Booker T. Washington, 9 November 1906, Booker T. Washington Papers, Manuscript Division, Library of Congress.

15. For more on Greener, see Allison Blakely, "Richard T. Greener and the 'Talented Tenth's' Dilemma," *Journal of Negro History* 59 (October 1974): 305–21.

16. See, for example, *The Boston Globe,* 12 March 1904.

17. Tarsaidze, *Czars and Presidents,* p. 177.

18. Salim B. Abakari, "Safari Yangu-ya Bara Urusi na ya Siberia" (My journey to Russia and Siberia), in *Swahili Prose Texts,* trans. Lyndon Harries (London: Oxford University Press, 1965), pp. 268, 271.

CHAPTER FIVE

1. Pushkin, *Polnoe sobranie sochinenii,* vol. 2, pp. 139–40.

2. V. Nabokov, *Pushkin,* vol. 4, p. 388.

3. Pushkin, *Polnoe sobranie sochinenii,* vol. 2, pp. 322–23.

4. *Ibid.* p. 338.

5. Avrahm Yarmolinsky, ed., *The Poems, Prose & Plays of Alexander Pushkin* (New York: Random House, 1936), p. 754.

6. *Ibid.,* p. 782.

7. Nabokov, *Pushkin,* vol. 3, p. 436.

8. *Ibid.,* p. 435.

9. Henri Troyat, *Pushkin,* trans. Nancy Amphous (New York: Doubleday, 1970), p. 441.

10. A. S. Griboedov, *Gore ot uma* (Woe from wit) (Moscow: "Neva, " 1923), p. 63; Albert Parry, "Black Folk in Russia," *Abbot's Monthly,* April 1931, p. 12.

11. L. N. Tolstoy, *War and Peace,* trans. R. Edmonds (Baltimore: Penguin Books, 1957), bk. 2, pt. 4, p. 614.

12. F. I. Tiutchev, *Polnoe sobranie sochinenii* (St. Petersburg: A. F. Marx, 1913), pp. 2, 13.

13. N. Gumilyov, *Shatyor* (Revel: "Bibliofil," 1921), p. 5.

14. *Ibid.,* p. 51.

15. A. I. Uspenskii, *Ikonopistsy XVII v.,* p. 276.

16. D. A. Rovinskii, *Podrobnyi slovar' russkikh gravirovannykh portretov*, vol. 2, col. 753; vol. 3, col. 1560; vol. 4, col. 610; L. Polivanov, ed., *Al'bom Moskovskoi Pushkinskoi Vystavki 1880* (Album of the Moscow Pushkin exhibition 1880) (Moscow: I. I. Gagen, 1897); *Russkoe iskusstvo* (Russian art) (Moscow: State Publishing House, 1962), vol. 5, pt. 1, p. 175; *K. P. Briullov* (Moscow: "Sovetskii artist," 1964).

17. A. K. Lebedev, *Vasilii Vasil'evich Vereshchagin: zhizn' i tvorchestvo 1842–1904* (Vasili Vasil'evich Vereshchagin: His life and work 1842–1904) (Moscow: "Iskusstvo," 1972), pp. 234–35.

18. Yakov B. Kniazhnin, *Izbrannye proizvedeniia* (Selected works) (Leningrad: "Sovetskii pisatel'," 1961), p. 61ff.

19. Herbert Marshall, *Ira Aldridge the Negro Tragedian* (Carbondale, Ill.; Southern Illinois University Press, 1958), pp. 14–22.

20. Quoted in Marshall, *Ira Aldridge*, p. 277.

21. S. Durilin, "Ira Aldridge," trans. E. Blum in *Shakespeare Association Bulletin* 17 (January 1942): 37–38.

22. *Den'*, 29 September 1862, no. 39, pp. 17–18, quoted in Marshall, *Ira Aldridge*, pp. 265–66.

23. Theophile Gautier, *A Winter in Russia* (New York: Henry Holt & Co., 1874), pp. 151–53.

24. *Russkii Vestnik* (The Russian Herald), October 1862, no. 40, pp. 12–13, quoted in Marshall, *Ira Aldridge*, p. 273.

25. I. Kulinich, *Poet i tragik* (The poet and the tragedian) (Kiev: "Naukova dumka," 1964).

26. *Syn Otechestva* (Son of the fatherland), November 1858, quoted in Durilin, "Ira Aldridge," p. 34.

27. *Severnaia Pchela* (The Northern Bee), no. 259, 1858, quoted in L. Golden-Hanga, *Africans in Russia*, p. 13.

28. Gautier, *A Winter in Russia*, p. 153.

29. Marshall, *Ira Aldridge*, p. 239.

30. *Moskovskii Zhurnal Iskusstva* (Moscow Journal of Art), November 1862, quoted in Marshall, *Ira Aldridge*, p. 257.

CHAPTER SIX

1. Slava Tynes, "Many Africans Came to the Soviet Union During Turkish Rule," *The Afro-American*, 16 February 1973; S. Tynes, "Skin Color Creates No Barrier to Africans in the Soviet Union," *The Afro-American*, 17 February 1973.

2. Nutsa Abash, "V zashchitu moikh sestyor" (In defense of my sisters), *Pravda*, 29 September 1963.

3. Schneider, "A Negro Citizen of Soviet Georgia," pp. 148–49.

4. The book is L. Golden-Hanga, *Africans in Russia*. See also Svetlana Alliluyeva, *Only One Year* (New York: Harper & Row, 1969), pp. 9–10, 231–35.

5. "Negroes Found Living in Russia," *New York Times*, 24 September 1931.

6. Harry Haywood, *Black Bolshevik: Autobiography of an Afro-American Communist* (Chicago: Liberator Press, 1978), p. 197; Joel A. Rogers, *Sex and Race*, vol. 3 (New York: J. A. Rogers Publications, 1944), p. 291.

7. Milton Dickerson, interview with author, Washington, D.C., 11 May 1978.

CHAPTER SEVEN

1. Dillingworth Dilling, "What Are the Soviets," *Abbot's Monthly*, June 1932, pp. 6–7, 48. This estimate is probably not exorbitant. Another source, citing more concrete data, shows that thousands of Americans went to the Soviet Union in the early 1930s for employment opportunities. Sylvia R. Margulies, *The Pilgrimage to Russia: The Soviet Union and the Treatment of Foreigners, 1924–1937* (Madison, Wisc.: University of Wisconsin Press, 1968), pp. 227–28. See also Robert Dunn, "What I Did Not See in Russia," *The Labor Herald* 2 (August 1923): 14–15.

2. A. Verbitskii, "Negry v Sov. Soiuze" (Negroes in the Soviet Union), *Novoe Russkoe Slovo*, 20 July 1976.

3. Wilson, *Russia and Black Africa*, p. 95; Boris Kornilov, "Moia Afrika," in *Prodolzhenie zhizni: stikhotvoreniia, poemy* (Continuation of life: verses and poems) (Moscow: "Khudozhestvennaia Literatura," 1972), pp. 309–45.

4. Theodore Draper, *American Communism and Soviet Russia* (New York: Octagon Books, 1960), pp. 168–69.

5. Claude McKay, *A Long Way From Home* (New York: Arno Press, 1937), pp. 153–234.

6. Claude McKay, "Soviet Russia and the Negro," pt. 1, *The Crisis*, December 1923, p. 65.

7. Claude McKay, *The Negroes in America*, trans. Robert J. Winter, ed. Alan L. McCleod (1923; reprint, Port Washington, N.Y.: Kennikat Press, 1979).

8. McKay, *A Long Way From Home*, p. 206; McKay, "Soviet Russia and the Negro," pt. 2, *The Crisis*, January 1924, p. 117. On Huiswood see Gert Oostindie, "Kondreman in Bakrakondre. Surinamers in Nederland, 1667–1954" (Surinamers in The Netherlands, 1667–1954), in Gert Oostindie and Emy Maduro, *In het land van de overheerser, II, Antillianen en Surinamers in Nederland, 1634/1667–1954* (Antillians and Surinamers in The Netherlands, 1634/1667–1954) (Dordrecht: Foris Publications, 1986), pp. 62–65. I am indebted as well to Bert Altena for sharing unpublished, collected materials on Huiswood.

9. McKay, "Soviet Russia," *The Crisis*, December 1923, pp. 61–64; January 1924, p. 117.

10. James R. Giles, *Claude McKay* (Boston: Twayne Publishers, 1976), pp. 134–38.

11. William L. Patterson, *The Man Who Cried Genocide* (New York: International Publishers, 1971), p. 112.

12. Haywood, *Black Bolshevik*, p. 1.

13. *Ibid.*, p. 122.

14. Joseph Stalin, *Marxism and the National Question* (Moscow: Foreign Language Publishing House, 1945).

15. Haywood, *Black Bolshevik*, pp. 148–217.

16. James R. Hooker, *Black Revolutionary: George Padmore's Path from Comintern to Pan Africanism* (New York: Praeger, 1967), p. 6.

17. Wilson, *Russia and Black Africa*, pp. 211–23.

18. Among others in the group were Wayland Rudd, Henry Lee Moon, Ted R. Poston, Sylvia Garner, Taylor Gordon, Mildred Jones, Loren Miller, Lloyd Patterson, and Constance White. Langston Hughes, *I Wonder as I Wander: An Autobiographical Journey* (New York: Hill and Wang, 1956), p. 70; Haywood, *Black Bolshevik*, p. 383.

19. Hughes, p. 73.

20. *Ibid.*, pp. 76–77.

21. *Ibid.*, pp. 82–85.

22. Haywood, *Black Bolshevik*, pp. 153, 166.

23. Golden-Hanga, *Africans in Russia*, pp. 21–23.

24. Robert C. Toth, "Russian Negro from Roanoke," *San Francisco Chronicle*, 16 December 1974.

25. Toth, "Pensioner in Russia with Negro Nationality," *International Herald Tirbune*, 18 December 1974.

26. Joseph J. and Sadie Roane, interview with author, Kinsale, Virginia, 19 November 1983.

27. Joseph J. and Sadie Roane, interview with author. See also an article based on an earlier interview appearing in the *Richmond Times*, 3 April 1977.

28. John Sutton, conversation with author, 2 February 1978.

29. *Black Dispatch*, 4 June 1938; Elton Fax, *Through Black Eyes: Journey of a Black Artist to East Africa and Russia* (New York: Dodd, Mead, 1974), pp. 132–34.

30. Homer Smith, *Black Man in Red Russia: A Memoir* (Chicago: Johnson Publishing Co., 1964).

31. *Philadelphia Independent*, 16 June 1951.

32. Golden-Hanga, *Africans in Russia*, p. 20.

33. Walter Duranty, "Americans Essay Color Bar in Soviet," *New York Times*, 9 August 1930; Duranty, "Soviet Sees 2 Sides in Attack on Negro," *New York Times*, 13 August 1930.

34. William B. Davis, "How Negroes Live in Russia," *Ebony*, January 1960, pp. 65–69.

35. Henry Lee Moon, "Soviets Invite 99th Pilots to Postwar Jobs," *Chicago Defender*, 10 March 1945.

36. W. E. B. Du Bois, *The Autobiography of W. E. B. Du Bois: A Soliloquy on Viewing My Life From the Last Decade of its First Century* (New York: International Publishers, 1968), p. 40.

37. "Uil'iam Diubua: 'Vash opyt ukrepliaet veru v cheloveka" (William Du Bois: Your experience strengthens the belief in mankind), *Literaturnaia Gazeta,* 5 May 1959; "Primer muzhestva i besstrashiia: vruchenie mezhdunarodnoi Leninskoi premii doktoru Diubua" (An example of courage and fearlessness: Presentation of the International Lenin Peace Prize to Doctor Du Bois), *Pravda,* 25 June 1960.

38. "Newark Negro and Family Plan to Move to Soviet," *New York Times,* 12 April 1962; "Jersey Girl Going to School in Russia Seized in Newark," *New York Times,* 25 June 1964.

39. George Murphy, *A Journey to the Soviet Union* (Moscow: Novosti Press, 1974).

40. Richard M. Peery, "Pushkin Festival Planned Here," *Cleveland Plain Dealer,* 7 August 1981, p. 35.

CHAPTER EIGHT

1. McKay, *Negroes in America,* pp. 7–8.

2. Theodore Kornweibel, *No Crystal Stair: Black Life and the Messenger, 1917–1928* (Westport, Conn.: Greenwood Press, 1975).

3. Draper, *American Communism,* p. 320.

4. *Ibid.,* pp. 332–34.

5. Wilson Record, *The Negro and the Communist Party* (Chapel Hill: University of North Carolina Press), p. 78.

6. *Stenograficheskii otchet VI Kongressa Kominterna* (The stenographic record of the VI comintern congress) (Moscow: Government Publishing House, 1929), vol. 5, p. 207.

7. *Ibid.,* pp. 210–12.

8. A. Amo, *Negritianskie rabochie* (Negro workers) (Moscow: "Partiinoe izdatel' stvo," 1933), pp. 10–12.

9. Draper, *American Communism,* pp. 324–26. See also Haywood, *Black Bolshevik.*

10. Haywood, *Black Bolshevik,* pp. 218–80.

11. *Ibid.,* p. 348.

12. Record, *The Negro and the Communist Party,* p. 65.

13. Stalin, *Marxism and the Nationalities Question,* pp. 50–56. Trotsky, writing from Turkey in 1933, expressed a more cautious view on the question of whether Negroes constitute a nation. He saw them as a race, which might become a nation if it chose to. George Breitman, ed., *Leon Trotsky on Black Nationalism and Self-Determination* (New York: Pathfinder Press, 1972), pp. 12–15.

14. V. I. Lenin, *Collected Works* (Moscow: Progress Publishers, 1966), vol. 31, pp. 147–48.

15. Record, *The Negro and the Communist Party,* p. 62; William Nolan, *Communism Versus the Negro* (Chicago: Regency, 1957), p. 32; J. R. Johnson (C. L. R. James) statement in Breitman, ed., *Leon Trotsky,* p. 34.

16. Richard Wright, *American Hunger* (New York: Harper & Row, 1977), p. 63.

17. Breitman, *Leon Trotsky*, pp. 37–44, 60–135. C. L. R. James experienced a similar disenchantment with Trotskyism by the early 1950s. Interview with author, Washington, D.C., 7 June 1978.

18. Breitman, pp. 9–10.

19. *Ibid.*, pp. 12–13.

20. Record, *The Negro and the Communist Party*, pp. 73–78; Theodore Rosengarten, *All God's Dangers: The Life of Nate Shaw* (New York: Knopf, 1974), app.

21. Allison Blakely, "Recent Soviet Interpretations on 'The Negro Problem,' " *The Black Scholar* (March/April 1979): 56–65.

22. L. N. Mitrokhin, *Negritianskoe dvizhenie v SShA: ideologiia i pratika* (The Negro problem in the USA: Ideology and practice) (Moscow: "Mysl'," 1974), p. 161.

23. E. L. Nitoburg, *Chernye getto Ameriki* (America's black ghettos) (Moscow: Polit Izdat, 1971), p. 137.

24. B. P. Likhachev, *Negritianskaia problema v SShA* (The Negro problem in the USA) (Moscow: "Znanie," 1968), p. 26; A. P. Koroleva, *20 Millionov protiv Dzhima Krou: (negritianskoe dvizhenie v SShA na sovremennom etape)* (20 million against Jim Crow: The present stage of the Negro Movement in the USA) (Moscow: "Mysl'," 1967), pp. 120–21.

25. Mitrokhin, *Negritianskoe dvizhenie*, pp. 174–96.

26. Koroleva, *20 Millionov*, pp. 155ff.

CHAPTER NINE

1. Wilson, *Russia and Black Africa*, pp. 169–70.

2. See Wilson, *Russia and Black Africa*, pp. 221, 351.

3. *Ibid.*, pp. 150–51, 229–53.

4. Department of State, *Nazi-Soviet Relations, 1939–1941, Documents from the Archives of the German Foreign Office*, ed. Raymond James Sontag and James Stuart Beddie (Washington: Department of State, 1948), p. 257; Cited in Yakobson, "Russia and Africa," pp. 470–71.

5. Yakobson, "Russia and Africa," p. 472.

6. Wilson, *Russia and Black Africa*, pp. 290–97.

7. Richard Bissell, "Union of Soviet Socialist Republics," in Thomas H. Henriksen, ed., *Communist Powers and Sub-Saharan Africa* (Stanford: Hoover Institution Press, 1981), pp. 11–14.

8. Roger E. Kanet, "African Youth: The Target of Soviet African Policy," *The Russian Review* (April 1968): 161–75; "Communism in Africa; Reds Focus on Students in Drive for Control of New Nations," *The National Observer*, 29 April 1962.

9. David Morison, *The U.S.S.R. and Africa* (London: Oxford University Press, 1964), pp. 59–62.

10. U.S. Department of State Research Memorandum RSB-10, 25 January 1967; "Universitet Druzhby Narodov Zhdet Studentov" (Friendship of Nations University awaits students), *Komsomolskaia Pravda*, 24 March 1960; Seymour Rosen, "The Peoples' Friendship University in the U.S.S.R.," *Studies in Comparative Education*, U.S. Department of Health, Education, and Welfare, Office of Education, Division of International Education (April 1962), p. 8.

11. Theodore Shabad, "Soviet Warns Students from Africa on Protests," *New York Times*, 21 December 1963; Henry Tanner, "500 Africans Fight Police in Race Protest," *New York Times*, 18 December 1963.

12. "Commentary," January 16, 1970 (Radio Liberty Internal Document).

13. *Ibid.* See also Iu. Bolshukhin, "V Bolgarii zastrialo svyshe 300 negritian-skikh studentov" (More than 300 Negro students on strike in Bulgaria), *Novoe Russkoe Slovo*, 23 February 1963.

14. Branko M. Lazitch, *L'Afrique et les Lecons de l'Experience Communiste* (Africa and the lessons of the communist experience), Introduction by Michael Ayih-Dosseh (Paris: Edimpra editeur, 1961), pp. 5–12.

15. A. Amar, *A Student in Moscow* (London: Ampersand, Ltd., 1961).

16. Everest Mulekezi, "I Was a 'Student' at Moscow State," *Reader's Digest*, July 1961, p. 101.

17. "Friendship University," *Soviet Life*, September 1977, pp. 30–33.

18. "Blacks in Russia," *Potomac Magazine*, 25 January 1976.

19. The character of this phenomenon is captured well in Jan Carew, *Green Winter* (New York: Stein and Day Publishers, 1965).

20. Mr. Coulibaly Modibo S., interview with the author, Washington, D.C., 4 January 1984.

21. Andrea Lee, *Russian Journal* (New York: Random House, 1979), p. 155.

22. *Ibid.*, pp. 146, 158 and *passim*.

23. C. L. Sulzberger, "Racism in the Communist Orbit," *New York Times*, 5 June 1963.

24. Bissell, "Union of Soviet Socialist Republics," pp. 1–10.

25. David and Marina Ottaway, *Afrocommunism* (New York: Holmes & Meier, 1981), pp. 209–10.

26. Peter Osnos, "Podgorny Poised to Go to Africa to Boost Soviet Influence There," *Washington Post*, 18 March 1977; David Ottaway, "Podgorny Visit Consolidates Soviet Influence in Africa," *Washington Post*, 5 April 1977; Raymond Wilkinson, "Somalia Orders Soviet Advisors Out," *Washington Post*, 14 November 1977.

27. David Ottaway, "Soviet Weapons Begin Flowing to Ethiopians," *Washington Post*, 18 April 1977.

28. Thomas Henriksen, "Communism, Communist States, and Africa: Opportunities and Challenges," in Henriksen, ed., *Communist Powers*, pp. 111–30.

29. Leopold Senghor, *On African Socialism* (New York: Praeger, 1964).

30. Anatoli Gromyko, "Socialist Orientation in Africa," *International Affairs* 9 (1979): 95–104. See also Ottaway, *Afrocommunism*, p. 160.

CHAPTER TEN

1. Golden-Hanga, *Africans in Russia*, pp. 23–24.

2. *Ibid.*, pp. 24–26.

3. Wayland Rudd, "Russian and American Theatre," *The Crisis,* September 1934, p. 270.

4. *Ibid.*, p. 278.

5. *New York Times*, 19 January 1933, p. 11.

6. "Robeson in London," *Living Age,* September 1931, p. 85; Quoted from Lenwood G. Davis, *Paul Robeson: A Selected Annotated Bibliography* (Westport, Conn.: Greenwood Press, 1982), p. 157.

7. "Paul Robeson Interview," *Daily Gleaner* (Jamaica, British West Indies), 17 December 1932, p. 3; From Davis, *Robeson Bibliography*, p. 184.

8. "Paul Robeson Never to Sing in Italian, French or German Again," *Washington Sentinel,* 9 September 1933; In Davis, *Robeson Bibliography*, p. 185. Robeson may have said this, but he certainly did not keep the vow.

9. "Paul Robeson Tells of Soviet Progress," *Irish Workers' Voice* (Dublin), 23 February 1935; In Davis, *Robeson Bibliography*, p. 212.

10. "USSR—nadezhda chelovechestva: Beseda s Polem Robsonom" (The USSR—the hope of humanity: A conversation with Paul Robeson), *Trud,* 25 October 1957.

11. Joseph Newman, "Robeson Flies to Testify Here at Trial of Red; Tells Soviet Union He Loves It "More Than Any Other"; Fears for Negroes in U.S.," *New York Herald Tribune,* 18 June 1949, p. 8; In Davis, *Robeson Bibliography*, p. 216.

12. Chatwood Hall, "Robeson Vacations on Black Sea Coast," *Richmond Planet,* 9 October 1937, p. 1. Quoted in Davis, *Robeson Bibliography*, p. 215.

13. Hall, "Robeson Called "Comrade" by Russians," *Afro-American,* 12 January 1935.

14. Dorothy Butler Gilliam, *Paul Robeson All-American* (Washington: New Republic Book Co., 1976), p. 137.

15. E. P. Hoyt, *Paul Robeson: The American Othello* (Cleveland: World Publishing Co., 1967), p. 173.

16. Morris U. Schappes, "The Record—Paul Robeson Jr. Refutes Lloyd Brown," *Jewish Currents* (February 1982): 25–30; Lloyd L. Brown, "Telling the Truth About Paul Robeson," *Jewish Affairs* (January/February 1982).

17. George Padmore, "Robeson Songs Banned from South Africa," *West African Pilot* (Lagos, Nigeria), 10 May 1949, p. 1; Summarized in Davis, *Robeson Bibliography*, p. 390.

18. I. S. Kulikova, *Pol' Robson—borets za mir i demokratiiu* (Paul Robeson—fighter for peace and democracy) (Moscow: "Znanie," 1952), p. 31; *New York Times,* 2 October 1949, p. 37; *Afro-American,* 29 October 1949, p. 1.

19. Paul Robeson, *Here I Stand* (Boston: Beacon Press, 1958); On music theory, see app.

20. Hoyt, *Paul Robeson: The American Othello,* pp. 67–72; Marshall, *Ira Aldridge*, p. 2.

21. "Soviet Dismisses High Officials of Radio for Broadcasting of a Robeson 'Spiritual,'" *New York Times*, 2 January 1935, p. 1.

22. Kulikova, *Pol' Robson*, p. 31.

23. Ariel L. Eliaev, *Between Hammer and Sickle* (New York: New American Library, 1969), pp. 41–42.

24. "Tvoi chudnyi golos" (Your wonderful voice), Letters to Paul Robeson on the Occasion of His 75th Birthday, Manuscript Division, Moorland-Spingarn Research Center, Howard University, Washington, D.C.

25. Golden-Hanga, *Africans in Russia*, pp. 26–27.

26. *Chicago Defender*, 1 December 1934; Golden-Hanga, *Africans in Russia*, p. 27.

27. Deineka (Moscow: "Izobrazitel' noe Iskusstvo," 1973).

28. S. Frederick Starr, *Red & Hot: The Fate of Jazz in the Soviet Union* (New York: Oxford University Press, 1983), pp. 27, 50.

29. *Ibid.*, p. 33.

30. Haywood, *Black Bolshevik*, p. 170.

31. Starr, *Red & Hot*, pp. 54–78.

32. M. Gorky, "O muzyke tolstykh" (Degenerate music), *Pravda*, 18 April 1928, p. 4; Discussed in Starr, *Red & Hot*, pp. 90–91.

33. Paul Robeson, "Pesnia moego naroda," (Song of my people) *Sovetskaia muzyka*, July 1949, p. 104. See also Starr, *Red & Hot*, p. 222.

34. Lee, *Russian Journal*, p. 175.

35. Starr, *Red & Hot*, pp. 150, 287, 303, and ch. 13.

36. Boris Kornilov, *Prodolzhenie Zhizni*, pp. 338–41.

37. James Patterson, *Rossiia Afrika stikhi i poema* (Russia Africa poems and verses) (Moscow: "Molodaia gvardiia," 1963), p. 9.

38. V. Mayakovsky, *Stikhotvoreniia, poemy* (Verses, poems) (Moscow: "Khozdestvennaia literatura," 1975), p. 64.

39. M. Tsevetaeva, *Moi Pushkin* (My Pushkin) (Moscow: "Sovetskii pisatel'," 1967), pp. 34–50; See also "Petr i Pushkin" (Peter and Pushkin), pp. 177–80.

40. James Weldon Johnson to Moorfield Storey, 13 October 1927, Records of the NAACP, Manuscript Division, Library of Congress; See also in the same collection J. W. Johnson to James A. Cobb, 3 Obtober 1927.

CONCLUSION

1. This problem is treated for Russia in a discussion by three authors in the *Slavic Review* 4 (December 1961): 565–600. The participants are Cyril E. Black, "The Nature of Imperial Russian Society"; Hugh Seton-Watson, "Russia and Modernization"; and Nicholas Riasanovsky, "The Russian Empire as an Underdeveloped Country."

SELECTED
BIBLIOGRAPHY

BLACKS IN RUSSIA

Abakari, Salim B. "Safari Yangu-yu Bara Urusi na ya Siberia" (My journey to Russia and Siberia). In *Swahili Prose Texts*. Translated by Lyndon Harries. London: Oxford University Press, 1965.

Adams, John Quincy. *The Diary of John Quincy Adams*. Edited by Allan Nevins. New York: Scribner, 1929.

Abrusow, L. *Grundriss der Geschichte Liv-, Est- und Kurlands* (Outline of the history of Liv-, Est- and Courland). Riga, Latvia: Jonck und Poliewsky, 1918.

Allen, W. E. D., and Paul Muratoff, *Caucasian Battlefields*. Cambridge: Cambridge University Press, 1953.

Alliluyeva, Svetlana. *Only One Year*. New York: Harper & Row, 1969.

Amar, A. *A Student in Moscow*. London: Ampersand, Ltd., 1961.

Aminado, D. *Poezd na tret'em puti* (The train on the sidetrack). New York: Chekhov Press, 1954.

Benet, Sula. *Abkhasians The Long-Living People of the Caucasus*. New York: Holt, Rinehart and Winston, 1974.

Blakely, Allison. "Richard T. Greener and the 'Talented Tenth's' Dilemma." *Journal of Negro History* 59 (October 1974): 301–21.

———. "T. Morris Chester." In *Dictionary of American Negro Biography*. Edited by Rayford Logan and Michael Winston. New York: W. W. Norton, 1982.

Bogoslovskii, M., ed. *Petr I: Materialy dlia biografii* (Peter I: materials for a biography). Vol. 2. Leningrad: OGIZ-SOTSEKGIZ, 1941. Reprint. The Hague: Mouton, 1969.

Curtiss, Mina. "Some American Negroes in Russia in the Nineteenth Century." *The Massachusetts Review* (Spring 1968): 268–78.

Davis, Lenwood. *Paul Robeson: A Selected Annotated Bibliography.* Westport, Conn.: Greenwood Press, 1982.

Davis, William B. "How Negroes Live in Russia." *Ebony,* January 1960, pp. 65–69.

Debrunner, Hans. *Presence and Prestige: Africans in Europe. A History of Africans in Europe before 1918.* Basel: Basler Afrika Bibliographien, 1979.

Dobroliubov, Nicholas. *Selected Philosophical Essays.* Moscow: Foreign Languages Publishing House, 1956.

Elius, F. "Chernokozhie rossiiane" (Black-skinned Russians). *Argus* 10 (1913).

English, Patrick. "Cushites, Colchians, and Khazars." *Journal of Near Eastern Studies* 18 (1959): 49–53.

Fax, Elton. *Through Black Eyes: Journey of a Black Artist to East Africa and Russia.* New York: Dodd, Mead, 1974.

Gan, K., comp. *Izvestiia drevnikh grecheskikh i rimskikh pisatelei o Kavkaze* (Accounts of ancient Greek and Roman writers about the Caucasus). Pt. 1. Tiflis: Office of the Civilian Department Chief, 1884.

Gastfreind, Nikolai. *Pis'ma Abrama Ganibala* (Abram Hannibal's letters). St. Petersburg: "Sever," 1904.

General Records of the Department of State. *Dispatches from United States Consuls in Vladivostok, 1898–1906.* Record Group 59. National Archives Microfilm Publication M486. Roll 1.

Giles, James R. *Claude McKay.* Boston: Twayne Publishers, 1976.

Gilliam, Dorothy Butler. *Paul Robeson All-American.* Washington: New Republic Book Co., 1976.

Golden-Hanga, Lily. *Africans in Russia.* Moscow: Novosti Press, 1966.

Grimshaw, W. H. *Official History of Freemasonry Among the Colored People in North America.* New York: Broadway Publishing Co., 1903.

Harris, Joseph E. *The African Presence in Asia.* Evanston, Ill.: Northwestern University Press, 1971.

Haywood, Harry. *Black Bolshevik: Autobiography of an Afro-American Communist.* Chicago: Liberator Press, 1978.

Helbig, George A. W. von. *Russiche Gunstlinge* (Russian favorites). Tubingen: J. G. Cotta, 1909.

Henson, Matthew. *A Negro Explorer at the North Pole.* New York: Arno Press, 1912.

Hollander, Paul. *Political Pilgrims.* New York: Oxford University Press, 1981.

Hooker, James R. *Black Revolutionary: George Padmore's Path from Comintern to Pan-Africanism.* New York: Praeger, 1967.

Hoyt, E. P. *Paul Robeson: The American Othello*. Cleveland: World Publishing Co., 1967.

Hughes, Langston. *I Wonder as I Wander: An Autobiographical Journey*. New York: Hill and Wang, 1956.

Johnson, Jack. *Jack Johnson Is a Dandy*. New York: Chelsea House, 1969.

Kovalevskii, P. I. *Kavkaz* (The Caucasus). Vol. 1, *Narody Kavkaza* (Peoples of the Caucasus). St. Petersburg: M. I. Akinfiev, 1914.

Kulikova, I. S. *Pol' Robson—borets za mir i demokratiiu* (Paul Robeson—fighter for peace and democracy). Moscow: "Znanie," 1952.

Lee, Andrea. *Russian Journal*. New York: Random House, 1979.

Lockhart, R. H. Bruce. *British Agent*. New York: G. P. Putnam & Sons, 1933.

Lopashich, A. "Negro Community in Yugoslavia." *Man* 58(1958): 169–73.

McKay, Claude. *A Long Way From Home*. 1937. Reprint. New York: Arno Press, 1969.

Margulies, Sylvia R. *The Pilgrimage to Russia: The Soviet Union and the Treatment of Foreigners 1924–1937*. Madison: University of Wisconsin Press, 1968.

Martin, Ralph G. *Jennie: Reminiscences of Lady Randolph Churchill*. Englewood Cliffs, N.J.: Prentice-Hall, 1969.

Maxwell, John D. *The Czar, His Court and People—Including a Tour to Norway and Sweden*. New York: Baker and Scribner, 1848.

Modzalevskii, B. L. *Rodoslovnaia Gannibalov* (The genealogy of the Hannibal family). Moscow: Yakovlev, 1907.

Mulekezi, Everest. "I was a 'Student' at Moscow State." *Reader's Digest*, July 1961.

Murphy, George. *A Journey to the Soviet Union*. Moscow: Novosti Press, 1974.

Nabokov, Vladimir. *Pushkin, Eugene Onegin*. Vol. 3, App. New York: Random House, 1964.

Nicolson, Harold. *The Age of Reason, the Eighteenth Century*. New York: Doubleday, 1961.

Nikolaev, V. and A. Parry. *The Loves of Catherine the Great*. New York: G. P. Putnam & Sons, 1982.

Nyangira, Nicholas. "Africans Don't Go to Russia to be Brainwashed." *New York Times Magazine*, 16 May 1965, pp. 52–64.

Parry, Albert. "Abram Hannibal, The Favorite of Peter the Great." *Journal of Negro History* (October 1923): 359–66.

———. "Black Folk in Russia." *Abbot's Monthly*, April 1931, pp. 11–16, 56–67.

———. "Negroes in Russia." *Opportunity*, October 1925, p. 306.

Patterson, James. *Rossiia Afrika stikhi i poema* (Russia Africa poems and verses). Moscow: "Molodaia gvardiia," 1963.

Patterson, William. *The Man Who Cried Genocide.* New York: International Publishers, 1971.

Pennsylvania Historical Survey, Work Projects Administration Maritime Records Port of Philadelphia. Sec. 5. Alphabetical List of Masters and Crews 1798–1880. Vols. 1–108. Harrisburg: WPA, 1942.

Prince, Nancy. *A Narrative of the Life and Travels of Mrs. Nancy Prince Written by Herself.* Boston: Nancy Prince, 1856.

Pushkin, Alexander S. *Polnoe sobranie sochinenii* (Complete collected works). Moscow: Academy of Sciences, 1937–1950.

Robeson, Paul. *Here I Stand.* Boston: Beacon Press, 1958.

Robinson, Bradley. *Dark Companion.* New York: R. M. McBride & Co., 1947.

Rogers, Joel A. *Sex and Race.* Vol. 3. New York: J. A. Rogers Publications, 1944.

Rovinskii, D. A. *Podrobnyi slovar' russkikh gravirovannykh portretov* (Unabridged dictionary of Russian engraved portraits). Vol. 3. St. Petersburg: Imperial Academy of Sciences, 1886–1889.

Rudd, Wayland. "Russian and American Theatre." *The Crisis,* September 1934.

Russell, Jonathan. Papers. The John Hay Library, Brown University, Providence, Rhode Island.

"The Saga of Jimmy Winkfield." *Ebony,* June 1974, pp. 64–70.

Schneider, Isidor. "A Negro Citizen of Soviet Georgia." *Opportunity,* May 1942, pp. 148–49, 157. Reprinted from *Soviet Russia Today,* February 1942.

Smith, Homer. *Black Man in Red Russia.* Chicago: Johnson Publishing Co., 1964.

Tarsaidze, Alexandre. *Czars and Presidents.* New York: McDowell, Obolensky, 1958.

Teletova, N. N. *Zabytye rodstvennie sviazi A. S. Pushkina* (Forgotten family ties of A. S. Pushkin). Leningrad: Nauka, 1981.

Troyat, Henri. *Pushkin.* Translated by Nancy Amphous. New York: Doubleday, 1970.

———. "Pushkin's Ethiopian Ancestry." *Ethiopia Observer* 1 (July 1957): 244–45.

Tupper, Harmon. *To the Great Ocean: Siberia and the Trans-Siberian Railway.* Boston: Little, Brown, 1965.

Vegner, M. *Predki Pushkina* (Pushkin's ancestors). Gorky: "Sovetskii pisatel'," 1937.

Vradii, V. P. *Negry batumskoi oblasti* (Negroes of Batumi province). Batumi, Georgia: G. Tarvartkiladze, 1914.

Wesley, Charles H. *Prince Hall: Life and Legacy.* Washington: United Supreme Council. Southern Jurisdiction. Prince Hall Affiliation, 1977.

White, Andrew Dickson. *Autobiography of Andrew Dickson White.* Vol. 2. New York: Century Co., 1905.

Winter, Eduard. *Halle als Ausgangspunkt der deutschen Russlandkunde im 18 Jahrhundert* (Halle as the Point of Departure of German Russian Studies in the 18th Century). Berlin: Deutsche Akademie der Wissenschaften, 1953.

Yakobson, Sergius. "Russia and Africa." In *Russian Foreign Policy.* Edited by I. Lederer. New Haven: Yale University Press, 1962.

RUSSIAN IMAGES OF BLACKS

A. Deineka. *Iz moei Rabochei praktiki* (From my work experience). Moscow, 1961.

Deineka. Moscow: "Izobrazitel'noe Iskusstvo," 1973.

Du Bois, W. E. B. *The Autobiography of W. E. B. Du Bois: A Soliloquy on Viewing My Life From the Last Decade of Its First Century.* New York: International Publishers, 1968.

Durilin, S. "Ira Aldridge." Translated by E. Blum. *Shakespeare Association Bulletin* 17 (January 1942): 37–38.

Eliaev, Ariel L. *Between Hammer and Sickle.* New York: New American Library, 1969.

"Friendship University." *Soviet Life,* September 1977, pp. 30–33.

Gautier, Theophile. *A Winter in Russia.* Translated by M. M. Ripley. New York: Henry Holt and Co., 1874.

Golden-Hanga, Lily. *Africans in Russia.* Moscow: Novosti Press, 1966.

Griboedov, Alexander. *Gore ot uma* (Woe from wit). Moscow: "Neva," 1923.

Gumilyov, Nicholas. *Shatyor.* Revel: "Bibliofil," 1921.

K. P. Briullov. Moscow: "Sovetskii artist," 1964.

Kniazhnin, Iakov B. *Izbrannye proizvedeniia* (Selected works). Leningrad: "Sovetskii pisatel'," 1961.

Kornilov, Boris. *Prodolzhenie zhizni* (Continuation of life). Moscow: "Khudozhestvennaia literatura," 1972.

Kulikova, I. S. *Pol' Robson—borets za mir i demokratiiu* (Paul Robeson—fighter for peace and democracy). Moscow: "Znanie," 1952.

Kulinich, I. *Poet i tragik* (The poet and the tradegian). Kiev: "Naukova dumka," 1964.

Laserson, Max M. *The American Impact on Russia—Diplomatic and Ideological—1784–1917.* New York: Macmillan, 1950.

Lebedev, A. K. *Vasilii Vasil'evich Vereshchagin: zhizn' i tvorchestvo 1842–1904* (V. V. V.: his life and art 1842–1904). Moscow: "Iskusstvo," 1972.

Marsh, J. B. I. *The Story of the Jubilee Singers.* London: Hodder and Stoughton, 1876.

Marshall, Herbert. *Ira Aldridge the Negro Tragedian.* Carbondale, Ill.: Southern Illinois University Press, 1958.

Mayakovsky, Vladimir. *Stikhotvoreniia, poemy* (Verses, poems). Moscow: "Khudozhestvennaia literatura," 1975.

Patterson, James. *Rossiia Afrika stikhi i poema* (Russia Africa poems and verses). Moscow: "Molodaia gvardiia, 1963.

"Politika" (Politics) *Sovremennik* 1 and 2 (January/February 1863): 388.

Polivanov, L., ed. *Al'bom Moskovskoi Pushkinskoi Vystavki 1880* (Album of the Moscow Pushkin exhibition 1880). Moscow: I. I. Gagen, 1897.

Rovinskii, D. A. *Podrobnyi slovar' russkikh gravirovannykh portretov* (Unabridged dictionary of Russian engraved portraits). St. Petersburg: Imperial Academy of Sciences, 1886–1889.

Russkie khudozhniki (Russian artists). Moscow, 1964.

Russkoe iskusstvo (Russian art). Vol. 5. Pt. 1. Moscow: State Publishing House, 1962.

Starr, S. Frederick. *Red & Hot: The Fate of Jazz in the Soviet Union.* New York: Oxford University Press, 1983.

Stenograficheskii otchet VI Kongressa Kominterna (The stenographic record of the VI Comintern Congress). Moscow: Government Publishing House, 1929.

Tiutchev, Fyodor I. *Polnoe sobranie sochinenii.* St. Petersburg: A. F. Marx, 1913.

Tolstoy, Leo N. *War and Peace.* Translated by R. Edmonds. Bk. 2. Pt. 4. Baltimore: Penguin Books, 1957.

Troyat, Henri. *Pushkin.* Translated by Nancy Amphous. New York: Doubleday, 1970.

Tsevetaeva, Marina. *Moi Pushkin* (My Pushkin). Moscow: "Sovetskii pisatel'," 1967.

Uspenskii, A. I., ed. *Ikonopistsy XVII v.; Zapiski Mosk. Arkhiol. Inst.* (Icon-painters of the XVII century; notes of the Moscow Archael. Inst.). S.v. Tiutekurin. Moscow: A. I. Snegirevoi, 1910.

Yarmolinsky, Avrahm, ed. *The Poems, Prose & Plays of Alexander Pushkin.* New York: Random House, 1936.

RUSSIA AND BLACK AFRICA

Africa in Soviet Studies: Annual 1969. Moscow: Academy of Sciences Africa Institute, 1971.

Cohen, William. *The French Encounter with Africans: White Response to Blacks 1530–1880.* Bloomington, Ill.: University of Illinois Press, 1980.

Cohn, Helen D. *Soviet Policy Toward Black Africa.* New York: Praeger, 1972.

"Communism in Africa; Reds Focus on Students in Drive for Control of New Nations." *The National Observer,* 29 April 1962.

Gromyko, Anatoli. "Socialist Orientation in Africa." *International Affairs* 9 (1979): 95–104.

Hellie, Richard. *Slavery in Russia.* Chicago: University of Chicago Press, 1982.

Henriksen, Thomas H., ed. *Communist Powers and Sub-Saharan Africa.* Stanford: Hoover Institution Press, 1981.

Hooker, James R. *Black Revolutionary: George Padmore's Path from Comintern to Pan Africanism.* New York: Praeger, 1967.

Jesman, Czeslaw. "Early Russian Contacts with Ethiopia." *Proceedings of the Third International Conference of Ethiopian Studies, 1966.* Addis Ababa: Institute of Ethiopian Studies, 1969.

Kanet, Roger E. "African Youth: The Target of Soviet African Policy." *The Russian Review* (April 1968): 161–75.

Lazitch, Branko M. *L'Afrique et les Lecons de l'Experience Communiste* (Africa and the lessons of the communist experience). Paris: Edimpra editeur, 1962.

Morison, David. *The U.S.S.R. and Africa.* London: Oxford University Press, 1964.

Nkrumah, Kwame. *Consciencism: Philosophy and Ideology for Decolonization.* New York: Monthly Review Press, 1970.

Ottaway, David and Marina Ottaway. *Afrocommunism.* New York: Holmes & Meier, 1981.

Parry, Albert. "Soviets Walk Old Trails in Africa." *The American Legion Magazine,* December 1977, pp 22–23, 42–43.

Rollins, Patrick J. "Imperial Russia's African Colony." *Russian Review* 27 (1968): 432–51.

Rosen, Seymour. "The Peoples' Friendship University in the U.S.S.R.." In *Studies in Comparative Education.* U.S. Department of Health, Education and Welfare. Office of Education. Division of International Education. April 1962.

Russia Looks at Africa: A Brief Survey of Russian Writing on Africa from the Nineteenth Century to the Present Day. London: Central Asian Research Centre, 1960.

Senghor, Leopold. *On African Socialism.* New York: Praeger, 1964.

Touré, Sékou. "African Independence and Unity." An address delivered to the General Assembly of the United Nations in New York City, 5 November 1959. New York: Colby Printers, 1960.

Wilson, Edward. *Russia and Black Africa Before World War II.* New York: Holmes & Meier, 1974.

Yakobson, Sergius. "Russia and Africa." In *Russian Foreign Policy.* Edited by I. Lederer. New Haven: Yale University Press, 1962.

––––––. "The Soviet Union and Ethiopia: A Case of Traditional Behavior." *The Review of Politics* 25 (July 1963): 329–42.

Zabrodskaia, M. P. *Russkie Puteshestvenniki po Afrike.* Moscow: Geografiz, 1955.

RUSSIA AND BLACK AMERICA

Amo, A. *Negritianskie rabochie* (Negro workers). Moscow: Partiinoe izdatel'stvo," 1933.

Blakely, Allison. "Recent Soviet Interpretations on 'The Negro Problem,' " *The Black Scholar* (March/April 1979): 56–65.

Breitman, George, ed. *Leon Trotsky on Black Nationalism and Self-Determination.* New York: Pathfinder Press, 1972.

Draper, Theodore. *American Communism and Soviet Russia.* New York: Octagon Books, 1960.

Ford, James. *The Communists and the Struggle for Negro Liberation.* New York: Harlem Division of the Communist Party, 1936.

Haywood, Harry. *Black Bolshevik.* Chicago: Liberator Press, 1978.

Kornweibel, Theodore. *No Crystal Stair: Black Life and the Messenger, 1917–1928.* Westport, Conn.: Greenwood Press, 1975.

Koroleva, A. P. *20 Millionov protiv Dzhima Krou: (negritianskoe dvizhenie v SShA na sovremennom etape)* (Twenty million against Jim Crow: The present stage of the Negro movement in the USA). Moscow: "Mysl'," 1967.

Lenin, Vladimir I. *Collected Works.* Vol. 31. Moscow: International Publishers, 1966.

Likhachev, B. P. *Negritianskaia problema v. SShA* (The Negro problem in the USA). Moscow: "Znanie," 1968.

Mezhuev, Pavel G. *Istoriia velikoi amerikanskoi demokratii* (History of the great American democracy) St. Petersburg: Akts. Obshch. "Brokhaus-Efron," 1906.

———. *Sotsiologicheskie etiudy* (Sociological studies) St. Petersburg: Ts. Kraiz, 1904.

Mitrokhin, L. N. *Negritianskoe dvizhenie v SShA: ideologiia i pratika* (The Negro problem in the USA: Ideology and practice). Moscow: "Mysl'," 1974.

Naison, Mark. *Communists in Harlem During the Depression.* Urbana, Ill.: University of Illinois Press, 1983.

Nitoburg, E. L. *Chernye getto Ameriki* (America's black ghettos). Moscow: Politizdat, 1971.

Nolan, William. *Communism Versus the Negro.* Chicago: Regency, 1957.

Oostindie, Gert. "Kondreman in Bakrakondre. Surinamers in Nederland, 1667–1954" (Surinamers in The Netherlands, 1667–1954). In Gert Oostindie and Emy Maduro. *In het land van de overheerser, II. Antillianen en Surinamers in Nederland, 1634/1667–1954* (Antillians and Surinamers in The Netherlands, 1634/1667–1954). Dordrecht: Foris Publications, 1986.

Record, Wilson, *The Negro and the Communist Party.* Chapel Hill: University of North Carolina Press, 1951.

Rosengarten, Theodore. *All God's Dangers: The Life of Nate Shaw.* New York: Knopf, 1974.

Stalin, Joseph. *Marxism and the Nationalities Question.* Moscow: Foreign Languages Publishing House, 1945.

Tsimmerman, Eduard. *Soedinennye Shtaty Severnoi Ameriki (iz puteshestvii 1857–58 i 1869–70 godov)* (The United States of North America—from travels in 1857–58 and 1869–70) Moscow: Grachev and Co., 1873.

Wright, Richard. *American Hunger.* New York: Harper & Row, 1977.

INDEX